COMPUTER AND DATABASE MANAGEMENT

ENCYCLOPAEDIA OF COMPUTER MANAGEMENT SERIES

COMPUTER AND DATABASE MANAGEMENT

Edited by
S.K. Goel

ANMOL PUBLICATIONS PVT. LTD.
NEW DELHI-110 002 (INDIA)

ANMOL PUBLICATIONS PVT. LTD.
4374/4B, Ansari Road, Daryaganj
New Delhi - 110 002

Computer and Database Management

First Edition, 2000
ISBN 81-261-0347-7

PRINTED IN INDIA

Published by J.L. Kumar for Anmol Publications Pvt. Ltd., New Delhi and Printed at Mehra Offset Press, Delhi.

Contents

Preface

Management is defined as the process of achieving organizational objectives through the efforts of other people. Management is a process—i.e., management consists of a number of interrelated steps or function which, when satisfactorily performed, lead to the achievement of goals. The successful practice of management involves people working together in harmony to achieve desired results. The availability of quality information is, of course, a requirement for a smoothly functioning operation. The business manager is a practitioner of the art and science of management. It is his job to carry out the basic management functions necessary to attain company goals. Of course, the objectives pursued vary according to the manager's mission; however, the functions of *planning, organizing, staffing,* and *controlling* are performed by all managers. The planning function looks to the future; to plan is to decide in advance a future course of action. Thus, *planning* involves making decisions with regard to (1) the selection of both short-run and long-run business strategies and goals; (2) the development of policies and procedure which will help accomplish objectives or counter threats; (3) the establishment of operating standards which serve as the basis for control; and (4) the revision of earlier plans in the light of changing conditions. The organizing function involves the grouping of work teams into logical and efficient units in order to carry out plans and achieve goals. One aspect of the staffing consists of selecting people to fill the positions which exist in the organizational structure of the business. The staffing activity also includes the training of employees to meet their job requirements, the preparation of employees for promotion to positions of greater responsibility, and the reassignment or removal of employees when such action is required. Unlike planning, which looks to the future, the *control* function looks at the past and the present. It is a follow-up to planning; it is the check on past and current performance to see if planned goals are being achieved.

The process of management is a continuing one. In practice, however, managers carry out these functions simultaneously. Plans beget subordinate plans, old plans require modifications, and new plans develop while old ones are in effect. Thus, it is impractical to insist on a special time sequence for the various functions. Quality information could support good decisions; good decisions should lead to effective performance of managerial functions; and effective functional performance should lead to the attainment of organizational goals. It is not surprising, therefore, that the acquisition and use of a computer may have important managerial implications. We can consider this broad topic from at least three viewpoints. *First,* it is possible to look at the implications involved in *planning for computers. Second,* we can look at the impact of *planning with computers.* Finally, we can look at the computer-oriented *decision-making techniques* which are now gaining acceptance. In light of the importance of information in the decision-making process, it would be logical to assume that top executives have always actively participated in the planning and implementation of new systems which would influence their future decisions.

In short, many executive apparently felt that the introduction of a computer was primarily a technical problem. They were content to define the goals of the new system vaguely and then to turn the entire project over to data-processing specialists.

Top managers should realize that their serious involvement in planning for computers is perhaps the most important single factor determining the success or failure of a computer installation. They should also be aware of the magnitude of the problems which will have to be overcome. Firms which have been successful in making computers pay off have been through in the initial planning stages. Computer usage can certainly improve the effectiveness of managérial planning. But before leaving the subject of planning with computers, it should be emphasized that computers *do not* "make decisions." Rather, they follow program decisions made earlier by managers and programmers. Although experiments are being conducted by extremely able researchers attempting to improve the machines' ability to solve ill-structured problems, it is man who defines problems, selects strategies to follow, and formulates hypotheses and hunches. *Heuristic* is a word which means "serving to discover." Much of planning is judgmental or heuristic in nature, and man is far superior to machine in the heuristic area of intellectual work.

Editor

1
Computer Management: Planning and Control

What is management? For our purpose, *management* is defined as the process of achieving organizational objectives through the efforts of other people. Three important points of this definition may be emphasized. The first point is that management is a process-i.e., management consists of a number of interrelated steps or function which, when satisfactorily performed, lead to the achievement of goals. The second point is that without the establishment of specific impossible. The third point is that the successful practice of management involves people working together in harmony to achieve desired results. The availability of quality information is, of course, a requirement for a smoothly functioning operation. The business manager is a practitioner of the art and science of management. It is his job to carry out the basic management functions necessary to attain company goals. Of course, the objectives pursued vary according to the manager's mission; however, the functions of *planning, organizing, staffing,* and *controlling* are performed by all managers.

Planning

The planning function looks to the future; to plan is to decide in advance a future course of action. Thus, *planning* involves making decisions with regard to (1) the selection of both short-run and long-run business strategies and goals; (2) the development of policies and procedure which will help accomplish objectives or counter threats; (3) the establishment of operating standards which serve as the basis for control; and (4) the revision of earlier plans in the light of changing conditions. The steps followed in *planning and in arriving at rational decisions are:*

1. *Identifying the problem or opportunity.* Meaningful planning may begin when a manager understands and has correctly defined the problem or opportunity which he faces. Information is needed to bring about awareness.
2. *Gathering and analyzing relevant facts.* To plan and made decisions, managers must have information.
3. *Determining suitable alternatives.* The manager must seek out the most attractive possible course of action. The appropriateness of the options selected is determined by the manager's skill by the quality of his information.

4. *Evaluating and selecting the most appropriate alternative*. The manager must weigh the options in light of established goals and then arrive at the plan or decision which best meets the company needs. Again, the correctness of this choice depends upon managerial skill and information quality.

5. *Following up on decision*. Broad plans may require supporting supplementary plans. For example, if the result of thee above steps is a decision to acquire a computer, then additional plans must be made (a) to locate the new computer department in the organization, and (b) to staff it with operating personnel.

Organizing

The organizing function involves the grouping of work teams into logical and efficient units in order to carry out plans and achieve goals. In a manufacturing company, employees may be grouped formally into production, marketing, and finance divisions. In each of these divisions, workers may be further organized into smaller units. The marketing division, for example, might consist of advertising, direct selling, and marketing research departments. Salesmen might be further organized by territory, by products sold, and by type of customer contacted. Managers at each organizational level receive formal authority to assign goal-directed tasks; they then must motivate and coordinate employee efforts if goals are to be achieved. To sum up, *organizing* is "the grouping of activities necessary to accomplish goals and plans, the assignment of these activities to appropriate departments, and the provision for authority delegation and coordination."

Staffing

One aspect of the *staffing* consists of selecting people to fill the positions which exist in the organizational structure of the business. The staffing activity also includes (1) the training of employees to meet their job requirements, (2) the preparation of employees for promotion to positions of greater responsibility, and (3) the reassignment or removal of employees when such action is required.

Controlling

Unlike planning, which looks to the future, the *control* function looks at the past and the present. It is a follow-up to planning; it is the check on past and current performance to see if planned goals are being achieved. The *steps in the control function are:*

1. *Setting standards*. Proper control requires that predetermined goals be established by planners. These standards may be expressed in *physical terms* or in *monetary terms*. The setting of a realistic standards requires quality information.

2. *Measuring actual performance*. Timely and accurate performance information is essential to control.

3. *Comparing actual performance with standards.* Comparison is action oriented. Computer can provide this information to managers on an *exception basis only* when performance variations are outside certain specified limits.
4. *Taking appropriate control action.* If actual performance is not up to the standard, it may be because the standard is unrealistic. Therefore, replanning may be necessary to revise the standard. Unfavourable performance may have to be corrected by reorganizing work groups or by adding more employees. Thus, the control actions taken may require further planning, organizing, and staffing activities. If outstanding performance is noted, the appropriate action may be to reward the individuals or groups responsible.

The process of management is a continuing one. The *order* of the four managerial functions presented here is a logical one and we shall use this order as the basis for the presentation of the material in the next four chapters. In practice, however, managers carry out these functions simultaneously. "Plans beget subordinate plans, old plans require modifications, and new plans develop while old ones are in effect. Thus, it is impractical to insist on a special time sequence for the various functions.

Managerial implications of computers

We saw that quality information could support good decisions; good decisions should lead to effective performance of managerial functions; and effective functional performance should lead to the attainment of organizational goals. It is not surprising, therefore, that the acquisition and use of a computer may have important managerial implications.

Planning and decision-making implications

We can consider this broad topic from at least three viewpoints. *First,* it is possible to look at the implications involved in *planning for computers. Second,* we can look at the impact of *planning with computers.* Finally, we can look at the computer-oriented *decision -making techniques* which are now gaining acceptance.

Planning for computers

In light of the importance of information in the decision-making process, it would be logical to assume that top executives have always actively participated in the planning and implementation of new systems which would influence their future decisions. Alas, such leadership has often been lacking! A study conducted a few years ago by the management consulting firm of McKinsey & Company concluded that no company achieved above-average results without the active participation of top executives. The study further pointed out that 18 of 27 of the nation's *largest* computer users obtained results which, at best, could only be described as marginal. Other studies conducted in the past have arrived at similar conclusions.

In short, many executive apparently felt that the introduction of a computer was primarily a technical problem. They were content to define the goals of the new system vaguely and then to turn the entire project over to data-processing specialists. Such abdication ignored the far-reaching personnel and organizational implications of the undertaking. Without precisely defined managerial information needs and without the backing at the top echelons which is often required to secure cooperation and overcome resistance to procedural and organizational change, the specialists could be excused if their efforts resulted in marginal results.

Top managers should realize that their serious involvement in planning for computers is perhaps the most important single factor determining the success or failure of a computer installation. They should also be aware of the magnitude of the problems which will have to be overcome. Firms which have been successful in making computers pay off have been through in the initial planning stages. A careful *feasibility study* is required to answer such questions as:

1. What data-processing improvements are needed-i.e., what are the data-processing objectives of the firm?
2. Has proper attention been given to systems review and redesign?
3. Is a computer usage the best way to achieve all of the objectives? Have noncomputer alternatives been evaluated?
4. Have all computer alternatives been considered?
5. If an in-house installation is justified, have all feasible machines and vendors been considered?
6. Have different acquisition methods been studied?

If, as a result of careful study and planning, a decision is made to order a computer, then the following additional plans must be developed:

1. *Technical Preparation plans* Prior to the delivery of hardware, the computer site must be laid out and prepared; initial programs must be written and tested.
2. *Organizing plans* It is important that adequate attention be given to the composition and location of the computer department.
3. *Personnel preparation plans* Staffing plans should be made to fill the new jobs which will be created. For example, the selection and training of programmers should take place without delay so that they may begin preparing the initial programs. Plans should also be made to alleviate the hardships brought about by the elimination of jobs.
4. *Control plans* The quality of the information produced must be controlled. The accuracy of input data must be considered. And internal controls should be created to minimize error and disclose fraud when and if it occurs.

Planning with Computers. Information played an important part in he successful completion of each of the steps in the planning procedure which was presented earlier. Generally speaking, computer usage can improve planning by providing effective information which (1) leads to problem awareness, (2) supports problem analysis and selection of alternatives, (3) influences the choice of the most appropriate option, and (4) permits feedback on the implementation of decisions. More specifically, the use of computers can have an impact on the planning function by:

1. *Causing faster awareness of problems and opportunities* Computers can quickly signal out-of-control conditions requiring corrective action when actual performance deviates from what was planned. Masses of current and historical internal and external data can be analyzed by the use of statistical methods including trends analyses and correlation techniques in order to detect opportunities and challenges. Planning data stored online may permit managers to probe and query files and receive quick replies to their questions.
2. *Enabling managers to devote more time to planning* Use of the computer can free the manager of clerical data-gathering tasks and permit him to concentrate more attention on analytical and intellectual matters. The computer is an intelligence amplifier which broadens man's time dimension.
3. *Permitting managers to give timely consideration to more complex relationships* The computer gives the manager the ability to evaluate more possible alternatives. It makes it possible for managers to do a better job of identifying and assessing the probable economic and social effects of different courses of action. Awareness of such effects, of course, influences the ultimate decision. In the past, oversimplified assumptions would have to be made if resulting decisions were to be timely. More complex relationships can now be considered and scheduled. In addition to broadening man's time dimension, the computer can furnish him with planning information which could not have been produced at all a few years ago, or which could not have been produced in time to be of any value.
4. *Assisting in decision implementation* When decisions have been made, the computer can assist in the necessary development of subordinate plans which will be needed to implement these decisions. Computer-based techniques to schedule project activities have been developed and are now widely used. Through the use of such techniques, business resources can be utilized and controlled effectively.

Computer usage can certainly improve the effectiveness of managerial planning. But before leaving the subject of planning with computers, it should be emphasized that computers *do not* "make decisions." Rather, they follow program decisions made earlier by managers and programmers. Although experiments are being conducted by extremely able researchers attempting to improve the machines' ability to solve ill-structured problems, it is man who defines problems, selects strategies to follow, and formulates hypotheses and hunches. *Heuristic* is a word which means "serving to discover." Much of planning is judgmental or heuristic in nature, and man is far superior to machine in the heuristic area of intellectual work.

Decision-making techniques

A number of quantitative managerial aids have been introduced which utilize computers to provide the framework for decision-producing analyses. These techniques can be used to (1) speed up problem or opportunity awareness, (2) permit more timely considera-tion of increasingly complex relationships, and (3) assist in decision implementation. In particular, the computer-based techniques of network analyses, mathematical programming, and simulation have managerial implications.

Network analysis

Both PERT are network models which are used to plan, schedule, and control complex projects. The basic concepts of PERT and CPM are similar. The following procedure is used to set up a network model:

1. *All* the individuals *activities* to be performed in the project must be identified.
2. The sequence of each activity must be determined—i.e., it must be known what elements have to be completed prior to the start of a particular activity and what tasks cannot commence until after its completion.
3. The *time interval* required to complete each activity must be estimated.
4. The *longest sequence* of events in the project must be identified. The sum of the individual activity times in this sequence becomes the total project time, and this sequence of activities is known as the *critical path.*

Network models have gained widespread acceptance. The Department of Defense requires that they be used on all major defense contracts, and major construction projects employ them. They have proven quite effective in helping manage the transition to computer data-processing systems. The use of PERT and CPM improves the *planning* function because it forces managers to identify *all of the project activities which must be performed. Control* is also improved because attention can be focused on the sequence of activities in the critical path. Managers quickly become aware of potential problems. If a critical activity begins to slip behind schedule, steps can be quickly taken to correct the situation. By trading project cost against project time, several alternative paths can initially be computed to help in planning. By a greater commitment of resources, managers can often reduce the time required to complete certain activities in the critical path. The effect of a greater resource commitment, however, is often higher project cost. Network models can simulate the effects on time and cost of a varying resource mix. Computations for small networks can be produced manually, but a computer is needed with networks of any significant size. Most computer manufacturers have PERT and CPM packaged programs available.

Mathematical programming

The purpose of mathematical programming is to find the best strategy from among a large number of options. Most mathematical programming work involves the use of *linear programming*. Not to be confused with computer programming models are used to find the *best combination* of limited resources to achieve a specified objective. One important class of linear-programming applications is in blending operations, where the objective is often to minimize the cost involved in the production of a given amount of blended product. For example, cattle feed may be mixture of minerals, grains, and fish and meat products. The prices of these ingredients are subject to change, so the least expansive blend required to achieve specified nutritional requirements is subject to variation. Linear programming can help managers quickly determine the correct blend to use to minimize cost while meeting product specifications.

In addition to blending, linear programming is being used for such diverse purposes as scheduling manpower, selecting media for advertising purposes, determining minimum transportation costs from given supply points to specified points of delivery and determining the most profitable product mix that may be manufactured in a given plant with given equipment. Practically all linear-programming applications require the use of a computer. As a powerful *planning* tool, linear programming enables a manager to select the most appropriate alternative from a large number of options. It is also a technique which may aid the manager in carrying out his other functions. Its use in scheduling manpower, for example, has definite staffing implications.

Simulation

In the physical sciences, experiments may be performed in a laboratory using small models of a process or an operation. Many complex variations may be possible in these tests, and the results show the scientist what happens under certain controlled conditions. Simulation is similar to scientific experimentation in that managers may evaluate proposed strategies by constructing business models. They can then determine what happens to these models when certain conditions are given. Stimulation is thus a trial-and-error problem-solving *approach*; it is also a *planning* aid which may be of considerable value to executives.

Simulation models have helped managers decide, for example, whether or not to expand operations by acquiring a new plant. Among he dozens of complicating variables which would have to be incorporated into such models are facts and assumptions about (1) present and potential size of the total market, (2) present and potential company share of this total market, (3) product selling prices, and (4) investment required to achieve various production levels.

Simulation models are also used to improve inventory management. The problem of managing inventories is complicated because there are conflicting desires among organizational units, and what is best for one department may not be best for the entire firm. To illustrate, the purchasing department may prefer to buy large quantities of supplies and raw materials in order to get lower prices; the production department also likes to have large inventories on hand to eliminate shortages and to make possible long—and efficient—production runs; and the sales department prefers large finished-goods inventories so that sales will not be lost because of out-of-stock conditions. The finance department, on the other hand, views with concern large inventory levels since storage expense is increased, risk of spoilage and deterioration is increased, and funds are tied up for longer periods of time. Through the use of simulated inventory amounts and for longer periods of time. Through the use of simulated inventory amounts and simulated assumptions about such factors as reorder lead times and cost of being out of stock, managers can experiment with various approaches to arrive at more profitable inventory levels.

In short, we see from this brief summary of simulation that it can aid in planning by permitting managers to give timely consideration to complex relationships. Of course, in many respects there is nothing new about simulation.

As Franklin Lindsay points out:

> A corporate planner who sets forth half a dozen alternative investment schemes, together with the costs and expected return from each, is simulating each alternative so that his board of directors can judge their relative merits. But the new mathematical tools, together with high-speed computers, extend tremendously the capabilities of simulation processes.

Organizational implications

The organizational framework of a business is structured on the work to be done and on the human and physical resources to be committed. With the introduction of a computer, however, significant changes are likely to be made in data-processing activities and thus in those departments which are engaged in informational activities. When this happens, it is often desirable to restructure the organization in the interests of greater efficiency. Work groups may be realigned; tasks formerly assigned to a number of departments may be eliminated or consolidated in a single new computer department; and existing departments may be eliminated or the scope of their operations may be sharply curtailed. Basic changes of this nature require the attention of top executives.

We have seen earlier that broader information systems are now being designed and implemented. Related to this trend is an organizational issue of fundamental importance. The issue to be decided is to what extent the new systems should concentrate or *centralize* authority and control in the hands of the top-level managers. With a computer, a greater degree of centralized control can be supported in a business because top managers can be furnished with information from outlying divisions in time to decide on appropriate action. Without computers, such action must be determined by a a lower-level manager because of time, distance, and familiarity factors. But although greater centralized control *can be supported* with a computer, it is *not necessarily a requirement*. The defree of centralized authority and control which *should* exist in the new system is determined by managerial philosophy and judgment and not by computer usage. The impact of the path chosen on future organizational structure, basic company philosophy and policies, and managerial authority of managers below the top echelons will be great. Certainly, decisions of this magnitude require the serious consideration of top executives; they are just too fundamental to be left to data-processing specialists of lower-level managers. We shall look more closely at the questions of computer department organization and the centralization of decision-making authority.

Staffing implications

Data-processing changes often bring about organizational stress. The introduction of computer also requires employee adjustments. Staffing decisions are necessary (1) to select and train workers for new jobs and (2) to deal with employees whose jobs have been eliminated or reduced in content or appeal. REsistance may be expected from employees and managers because of significant changes occurring in the alignment of work groups, in the content of individual jobs, and in the methods of performing data-processing tasks. Proper planning and leadership can reduce this resistance.

In addition to considering the implications of filling new jobs and of coping with resistance to change top executives should also realize that it does no good to attempt to install sophisticated system if company managers at all levels are usable to (1) define their information needs, (2) develop analytical planning, decision-making, and control procedures, (3) state specifically these analytical procedures, and (4) interpret and make use of the output of the sophisticated systems. If the machines are to be effectively utilized, it will generally be necessary to undertake an educational effort to acquaint managers with computer capabilities and with the analytical tools which will make use of those capabilities.

Control implications

Several ways in which computer usage can affect the control function have already been pointed out, so we need not dwell long on the subject here. The *control implications of computer usage* include the facts that:

1. Computers can quickly signal out-of-control conditions, thus bringing about faster awareness of problems. Going a step further, programmed analyses may be carried out by the computer to present recommended courses of action to managers.

2. Triggered control reports, based on the *principle of exception*, may be prepared only when actual performance varies from planned standards. Managers are thus

relieved of much routine paper shuffling and are freed to concentrate on more important personnel and environmental matters.

3. Computer-based techniques such as PERT and CPM may permit more effective control of business resources.

4. Computer systems make it possible to centralize authority and control previously delegated to lower echelons because of time, distance, and familiarity factors.

5. Internal control and auditing techniques will generally have to be revised to accommodate computer systems.

Economic implications

From an economic standpoint, the acquisition of a computer cannot be taken lightly. An investment decision involving many thousands of dollars must be made. It is the duty of top executives to determine if a computer can be justified economically. A computer *can* improve the firm's economic position by reducing ratio of expenses to revenues in tangible and intangible ways. But there is no guarantee that profits *will* be improved merely because a computer is installed. On the contrary, many firms have invested large sums in computers and have received returns of *less* than a dollar for each dollar spent.

Computer acquisition is a difficult capital-investment decision; it must be recognized as such by the top officers in the company. They must also be aware that the level of expenditures initially required is *frequently underestimated* and that this level will probably continue to increase in the years after acquisition. Finally, they must consider the possible economic implications of *not keeping pace with competitors* in the development and use of new information systems.

Planning

Why?

1 If we cannot plan a project, we will never be able to control it.

2 We need to plan a project before we can allocate individual objectives.

Objectives

1 To fit in with our team standards

2 To fit in with our reporting.

3 To be flexible enough to allow planning for all sizes of project.

4 To permit progressive planning as more data on the project become available.

5 To permit quick recognition of any deviation from plan in actual performance.

Limitations

1 Our standard should not lead to an 'overkill' in paperwork or procedures for small projects.

2 It should fit in with a number of techniques in plan preparation, such as bar charts, networks etc.

3 Often projects are too large to be adequately planned in one step.

4 There is often insufficient information available properly to plan a project completely at the beginning.

Project estimate

This is produced during the early investigation into the feasibility of a project. There will normally be several possible solutions to the problem. In order to help decide which alternative is best, we usually need to know the comparable costs. The development cost of each possible solution must therefore be estimated. Thus, when one of the alternatives is recommended, its estimated development cost becomes the project estimate. A few points should be made about estimating.

1 It is normally done when least is known about the user's needs.

2 Nothing is known about the problems and pitfalls that will arise during the project

3 We tend to think of a straightforward solution to the problem and forget the ancillary activities of set-up, conversion, security, human inefficiency etc.

4 Subconsciously, the person making the estimate wants to please the user or their own manager and is therefore tempted to be optimistic.

5 Estimating should be based on historical data. How long has it taken us to do comparable projects in the past? What is the effective work capacity of a Team Member during a work period? Can we learn from experiences of other Project Leaders?

6 Any estimate should show a break-down of the total project into phases. A phase is a portion of the total project during which certain pre-defined tasks are carried out. This will allow us to compare each phase plan with our original estimate as the project progresses.

There are a number of surveys available on the percentage of time spent in the different phases of a project. Each company should be able to develop its own average percentages according to the type of project it undertakes and its past history of projects. For those without such averages, they could start with the following figures.

Feasibility 3%

Specification 12%

Design 20%

Programming 35%

System test 15%

Installation 15%

Phase plans

Depending upon the size of the project, we must plan it in a number of discrete phases.

For each phase, we need two types of plan; a technical plan showing the tasks, resource and time allocation, and a financial plan which translates the resources into monetary terms. The technical plan is the main document for the Project Leader. The financial plan is the communicating document between Project Leader and Project Board.

Phase plans are produced prior to the start of a phase. An exception here is the plan for the very first phase which is done as one of the first tasks of that phase.

Planning package contents

A graphic plan is inadequate alone. It needs explanation to a reader. A complete planning package should consist of:

A graphic plan

A description

Assumptions on which the plan is based

Potential problems

When our schedule slips, it will be too late to say to the contractor representative 'I thought I would have priority'. If we are making such assumptions when planning, we must make this clear to those who will approve our plan.

Resource availability plan

Before creating a technical plan for a phase, it is usually worthwhile to create a schedule showing the availability of the phase resources. This covers not only the Team Members, but also the other resources required. Such a plan will include data on when each resource becomes available, when its availability ceases, and when it is not available during the phase. The availability plan also notes holidays, training and allocation to other projects, thus providing a useful check of availability against the technical plan being created.

Deviation plan

Approval and acceptance of a phase plan means certain things. The user or customer is committed to a defined level of cost, but in turn expects the project to reach a certain point for that cost by a certain data and with a certain level of quality. If one of these factors should begin to vary beyond an agreed tolerance limit, it is the responsibility of the Project Leader to bring this to the attention of the Project Board. As described in the chapter on control, this is one at a meeting with the Project Board. At this meeting, the Project Leader will present a deviation plan.

The description part of this deviation planning package describes the problem, the reason, the impact, the possible alternatives and the Project Leader's recommendation. The graphic plan will normally cover only the problem area and will extend until either the phase end or the recovery from the deviation, if this is sooner. It is not necessary for the deviation plan to go beyond the phase end. Any recovery work to be done after that will be incorporated in the next phase plan.

Planning activities

For those who like to approach planning in a methodical fashion, here is a general sequence of actions to follow.

Complete the provisional 'duration' and 'end date' lines. This is achieved either by copying from the final estimate, or, if a project completion date is imposed by some external factor, by calculating the stage durations by working back from the end data.

Remember that this is elapsed time, not manpower.

Complete the resources section showing how much effort is available if the size of the Phase Team is already known.

Examine the task checklists and mark any which are not applicable to the particular project.

Identify any special tasks which are not in the checklists.

Identify any necessary tasks on the checklists which have already been completed. For example, a description of the current product should normally be available.

Consider the management of the project and allocate a percentage of manpower resource for this function throughout the plan.

Identify, under applicable activities, those which can only be done by a certain Team Member.

Calculate the length of time needed for each task.

Allocate the time to produce each sub-product within the project. It is usually easiest to work backwards from the completion dates of the major tasks.

Define which activities can be done on parallel and which must be serial

Define quality control points

Add to activities the time for quality control plus time for regular meetings.

Total the resources required.

Review the completed plan for individual workload balance, continuity of work for each Team Member, and re-cycle, where necessary, to smooth the workload.

Determine whether any remaining time problems are best resolved by extra resources, the purchase of external products, stretching elapsed time, or reducing the facilities to be provided by the current project.

Calculate the cost of the planned resources.

Add the tolerance percentage

Compare with the final estimate from the feasibility study.

Write the plan description to provide an explanation of the graphic plan, and how it will be implemented. This description includes information on how the plan will be monitored, and the Project Leader's proposal of a suitable tolerance level.

List the technical and business assumptions which have been made when developing the plan. It is important to document these assumptions, so that any changes to them can be quickly identified and appropriate action taken.

Identify potential problems and the likely impact on the plan should they occur.

Project definition and planning

Phase I

Staffing: The anticipated project leader and his or her manager should work closely to develop the documents required for completion of Phase I, calling on technical expertise as needed. External assistant may be required.

Problem definition: Entry into Phase I assumes that user requirements or a market study provide general project justification, or at lease Phase I justification. The first step in initiating any project must be describing the general problem to be solved. The result should be a brief but formal problem definition.

Initial project Plan: After the user (marketing manage-ment) agrees with the written problem definition, the next step is to develop an overall project plan showing critical path developments and a brief description of each research and development (R and D) problem that must be solved. Reasonably detailed cost estimates on Phase II must be prepared, possibly with minimum and maximum limits.

Review: It is necessary to conduct a formal review of the general project definition and plan as well as required changes by developer and user. Copies for reading and time for commenting should be provided before scheduled meetings. If the effort is justified, changes should be incorporated and the project should proceed to Phase II. Review should not terminate without countersignatures representing user and developer management agreement.

Phase 2: Functional analysis and specification

Staffing: Phase II requires the experience of people knowledgeable with the problem of user/costomer interface. User personnel must be dealt with carefully at all levels, and the analysis team must be groomed for marketing purposes. This is not the time to show off individual technical expertise or cleverness. The user must believe that his or her problems are in the hands of people who sincerely want to help. The use of outside expertise knowledgeable in the particular application area can be vital.

Analysis of overall system functional requirements: Unless the user constrains particular hardware specifications (for example, a particular printer, modem, and so forth), hardware should remain unspecified. At this time the user should be encouraged to be completely open as to what is desired ideally as well as realistically. Obviously, the final system must lie between the present system and the ideal system.

Development of Overall System Functional Specification

This specification, in conjunction with the initial documentation set, should completely define the user functional requirements. No reference should be made to specific hardware types unless constrained. This must be a joint development effort with user personnel who will be involved in operating and using the existing system.

Continuation plan: With the functional specifications completed, the overall project plan should be revised or refined, along with cost estimates and a detailed plan for Phase III.

Review: The last step of Phase II is to review specifications, plans, changes, and cost estimates with user/management, ensuring that total functional requirements are well defined and explained and that the plan is acceptable. If the effort is justified, changes should be incorporated, and the project should proceed to Phase III. Incremental movements from each phase to another through a formal review "gate," enable potential project problems to be adjusted.

Phase 3: Environment analysis/specification

Staffing: Emphasis during this phase must be on the enlistment of highly qualified technical personnel, particularly in the advanced systems area. At least one person should be aware of the latest technology available. Real-world experience in a similar application area is also vital.

Technology analysis: Existing hardware/software technology, applicability, and trade-offs should be analyzed to meet overall system functional specifications.

Hardware environment synthesis: The system hardware environment should be synthesized, on a building-block basis. For example, computer processors and peripherals for both the development and field environments should be selected.

Software environment synthesis: The system software environment should be synthesized, on a building-block basis. For example, operating system, language, and support software should be, selected for both the development and field environments.

Hardware/Software System Specifications: These specifications should reflect the hardware/soft ware synthesis requirements as stated above.

Preliminary documentation set: A detailed user's manual should be completed, along with the remaining detailed functional documentation, including system outline, output formats, database descriptions, and input formats.

Continuation plan: A more detailed project plan should be developed, nailing down any unresolved R and D elements along the critical path. A more detailed cost estimate should be developed, particularly for Phase IV.

Review: Specifications, documentation, changes, and estimates should be reviewed with user/management, ensuring a clear understanding of approach. If the effort is justified, changes should be incorporated and the project should proceed to Phase IV.

Phase 4: System design

Staffing: Programmers who are expected to write code for subprograms called for in the system outline should be selected to help write the corresponding detailed program documentation. In addition, particular staff members should be given specific responsibility for coordinating each of the following areas: total system documentation, detailed test procedures and full cycle test implementation plan, and quality control standards and procedures.

Detailed Program Documentation: The detailed design and corresponding documentation of each program module must include detailed narratives on each subprogram and specifications of all references, both internal and external to each module.

Detailed test plan: This must include detailed test schedules and a description of the required data sets needed to test each subprogram as part of a regression test set.

Quality control plan: Procedures should be developed for maintaining, refining, and enhancing the system, ensuring system identity and integrity of the product libraries as changes are developed and implemented.

Continuation plan: The final detailed continuation plan should include formal specifications, documentation, and cost estimates for the critical design review.

Critical design review: The critical design review evaluates the continuation plan and required changes. At this point the user must be made to understand the potential level of difficulty of incorporating changes once program development (Phase V) is under way. A reasonable amount of time should be allowed for this review/revision period because of (1) level of complexity of the decisions at this time, (2) volume of documentation and corresponding effort for changes, and (3) fermentation period to allow review of how changes propagate through the system.

Phase 5: Program development

Staffing: After the written, detailed system software documentation is reviewed, it may be desirable to shift personnel assignments. This is a critical decision step. It is most desirable that those designers who have written satisfactory documentation remain to supervise writing of the corresponding code. Poor documentation will generally indicate lack of understanding or the inability to supervise or write good code. Also, the personnel resources required to produce an adequate test set should not be underestimated.

Program development/integration: It will be necessary to coordinate emphasis on the development of critical path programs to facilitate proper test plan implementation. For example, it is necessary, to ensure construction of input edit and database update programs before accessing the database for processing and output.

Hardware facility coordination: Scheduling of required hardware facilities for compilation and testing may be crucial, depending on the environment for this phase. It is easy to accumulate day-by-day slippage owing to improper coordination of hardware test facilities, conversions, and so forth.

Test set development: As compilation gets underway, programming personnel should have gained sufficient knowledge and should have been provided sufficient time to develop detailed test procedures. In any event this time period must be planned in advance, with emphasis on input interface and database maintenance programs to ensure database integrity. It is imperative at this time to isolate personnel responsibility for the coordination of detailed test procedures and materials for a regression test set to be used in whole or part each time the system is modified.

Continuation plan: A detailed plan should be developed for operational testing (Phase VI), and plans for future phases should be refined. A detailed cost estimate should be developed for operational testing and for future phases. Sufficient resources should be included to ensure integrity of specifications and documentation for project intracommunications as well as user review. Plans for long-term system/product support and distribution should be developed at this time.

Review: Specifications, documentation, changes, plan, and estimates should be reviewed with user/ management, ensuring clear understanding of system operation and the approach to projected effectiveness of the operational testing plan.

Phase 6: Operational Testing

Staffing: Direct management responsibility for coordination of operational testing should be assigned to a specific individual. The objective is the development of a set of full system tests with effectiveness that is satisfactory to both user and developer management. The responsibility for operational testing must be kept separate from completion of final documentation and coordination of user requests for review and modification.

User personnel training: The user personnel training period provides the opportunity to "shake down" the documentation--for example, the user's manual and the operations manual--as well as the system itself. This period usually generates requests for modifications that should not be introduced without following formal procedures.

Full-Cycle acceptance testing: Final full-cycle acceptance testing must be performed with user personnel (or the equivalent) under simulated real-world conditions in order to be effective. For software products, initial versions usually can be given out at no cost to friendly users to accomplish real-life operational testing. Such user installations generally are known as alpha and beta test sites.

Quality control procedures: Formal distribution and support procedures should be implemented. Finalized procedures for processing requests for corrections, refinements, and enhancements, must ensure a thorough understanding of both user and developer management regarding the generation of new versions and releases.

Final documentation: Additions to the documentation set that depend on final program construction must be incorporated at this time. Assignment of this function to someone other than the originating programmer can be an effective method for review of internal documentation, programming practices, and skill, as well as the detailed external documentation.

Continuation plan: A detailed plan should be developed for cutover to installation and support (Phase 7), and any future plans should be outlined. Cost estimates should be included for steady-state operation as well as for the initial period. Allowances for formal modification procedures should be included as should recovery procedures to cover (1) on-site restart and (2) abort and return to operational testing phase.

Review and acceptance: This is the final review and acceptance of documentation, changes, plan, and estimates for installation and support with user and developer management. Emphasis is on recovery, maintenance, and modification procedures. Written approval and schedule to proceed should be obtained.

Phase 7: Installation and support

Staffing: Staff considerations during Phase VII include users in selecting any additional personnel required beyond those participating in operational testing, shifting present personnel where desirable, and selecting personnel for user training. The developer should assist the user in selecting user interface as well as on-site or on-call personnel for system support and in evaluating requirements for implementing and controlling product library changes. Ample time should be allowed for this step and the next before system production begins.

User personnel training/guidance: Off-site as well as on-site classroom sessions should be provided for all personnel, both user and support. Ongoing training for new and backup personnel should be considered.

Full operation implementation/product release: Timing and coordination usually are critical. Plans must include abort timing and corresponding personnel activity or nonactivity. Revovery procedures should be well documented and understood.

Quality control implementation: Formal support procedures are required to determine responsibility for system errors and the corresponding correction process. Notification for correction requests can be initiated by the system support agent as well as the user. The divergence of identity of multiple fielded systems can prove catastrophic in most applications; its avoidance depends on well-disciplined support procedures to ensure congruence. Formal procedures for processing requests for system refinements and enhancements are necessary to ensure that required resources are scoped properly and that allowance is included for preserving system identity and integrity of the product libraries. Accumulating modification requests is desirable as long as the system remains operable so that total documentation and program modification efforts can be grouped into new releases. Quality control procedures should be strictly followed for all modifications that are under direct management responsibility for process and approval. The objective is to ensure reliable operation within an effective test bed, simulating real-world conditions before each new release. Continual refinement of the regression test set and corresponding documentation will afford procedures that are easily implemented and controlled.

Continuation plan: The level of continuation planning required depends on the level of activity and scope of modification requests. Plans will fall into three basic categories: hold, implement, and major system rewrite. Major modifications should be initiated at an effective phase and developed in accordance with successive phases as applicable. Major system rewrites should start back at Phase I.

Review: The level and formality of reviews depends on continuation plan activity. In any event, formal user/management reviews should be undertaken at least once annually.

Control

Why do we need standards for the control of a project? This chapter considers the need to control various aspects of a project, and covers the control requirements of the various groups involved in a project. It is also deals with the problem of written and verbal communications in a team and project environment. The correct use of control standards enables us to answer the following questions, often asked during a project.

1. What is the quality of workmanship?
2. Are we still producing what the customer wants?
3. Are we on schedule?
4. Are we within budget?
5. Will we fail to realize that schedule or budget problems have occurred until it is too late to do anything about it?
6. How are Project Board members, not normally involved with the project on a day-to-day basis, made aware of the project status?
7. When and how often should the Project Leader meet the Project Board?
8. How do we keep control of customer requests for alterations and additional after the specification and probably the cost have been agreed? How do we prevent such requests from destroying the project schedule and budget?

Objectives

1. To pass status information upwards from Team Member to Project Board.
2. To enable the Project Leader to spot deviations from budget or schedule as soon as they occur.
3. To keep the tea informed.
4. To provide a standard procedure for meetings.
5. To identify the circumstances under which a meeting should be called.
6. To decide who should attend this meeting.

Solution

There are two major activities in control:

Collection of project information

Interpretation of that information to the correct people

The information is of two types:

Technical

Financial

In our solution, we shall consider two ways of interpreting the information and passing it on; the use of meetings and of reports. As far as our project management standards go, the collection of data will be considered from the bottom upwards. That is, gathering data from the working level and passing it upwards to Project Leader and Project Board.

The interested parties are

Project Board

Project Management Team

Project Team

Requirements

Consider the type of information each of the parties needs.

Project board

The Project Board numbers represent user and contractor management. They are not involved on a day-to-day basis. If possible, they want to manage by objectives and by exception. As management, they are mainly concerned with the status of the budget. On technical matters, they are only concerned with schedule status and knowing if the customer will get what he wants at the end of the project. They therefore do not want too much technical detail, but brief status information until things begin to go wrong. Then they need early advice of what is going wrong, together with a means of collecting all the relevant details plus technical solution proposals.

Project management team

The Project Leader needs both technical and financial information regularity. The Team Leader needs up-to-date technical progress and quality information.

Phase team

Team Members need to be able to measure their own progress against objectives, and know the status of any interfaces within the team. They need to be able to identify with the total product.

Reports

We can provide a simple recording and reporting structure to suit large and small projects. Below is a brief description of the recording and reporting activities, plus the proposed forms

Time Sheet

By: Team Members

For: Team Leader

Frequency: Daily

Team Members record efforts against tasks on time sheets.

Phase Plan

By: Team Leader

For: Project Leader

Frequency: Weekly

Effort is recorded against the phase plan from the time sheets. Completed tasks and slippages are noted.

Status report

By: Project Leader

For: Project Board

Frequency: Monthly

A brief status report is sent to the Project Board on technical status and outstanding problems.

Phase summary

By: Project Leader

For: Project Board

Frequency: Monthly

The phase summary is in graphic form to allow summarized information to be passed in a very brief document. Its main purpose is to pass financial information to the Project Board.

1 The costs of the resources consumed are recorded. A report is sent to the project Board in graphic form, comparing current phase cumulative costs and completed tasks with the plan.

2 In certain recording systems, one trap into which it is easy to fall at this time is that the team are asked to estimate 'percentage complete' for their current unfinished tasks. The danger is that this is a subjective estimate, normally optimistic, and therefore misleading. The Project Leader also has the problem of assessing all the team's estimates on different sizes of task and turning these into a single 'percentage complete' for the phase. A much better idea is the one incorporated by BP in their plan. Having produced the phase technical plan, each task in the plan is calculated as a percentage of the total phase plan. This is done by taking the total man days needed as 100% and calculating each task's effort as a percentage of that. When reporting against the plan, completed tasks are noted and their percentage totalled to give the 'percentage complete'. In reporting this figure, we ignore any tasks which have started but are not yet complete. In order for this approach to be really effective, no task in our plan should be greater than 10% of the total phase effort, or 10 man days for a small project. Any task larger than this can always be broken down.

3 The '% Work Planned Completed' is calculated by adding up the percentages of the total phase effort of those tasks which have completed so far.

Modification requests

By: Usually a user

For: Review by the Project Board

Frequency: As required

There is one other type of report which is vital if a project is to be kept under control. There must be a document produced for every major change proposed after the feasibility study, and for every major or minor change proposed after the user specification has been signed. The implementation of such changes without proper control and authority has been responsible for many project failures to meet schedule and/or budget.

Let us make this point. Having accepted the feasibility estimate, approved the user specification, and committed resources against those documents, only the Project Board has the authority to agree to any changes. Only the customer has the authority to agree to more expenditure, and this must be done at Project Board level.

The procedure should be that anyone requesting a modification should document it. The request should be assessed for its impact on the project and its likely cost. All outstanding requests should be reviewed by the Project Board at the next project review meeting. Where agreement is reached to implement certain requests, the Project Board must approve the necessary extra resources and time.

Meetings

Only two types of meeting are described here; the Phase Review Meeting and the Walkthrough. The first is the formal meeting of Project Board and Team Leader at defined times during the project. The definition of these times relates to the size of the project. The second is a quality control meeting. These are the types of meeting for which must define very clear standards. There my be other types of meeting during the projects lifetime, but normally they will not require such rigorous standards.

Phase review meeting

The purposes of this meeting are as follows.

1 For the Project Board and Project Leader to meet;

2 For the Project Board to hear a more detailed report of progress and have the opportunity to ask questions;

3 For the presentation of plan to the Project Board for their approval;

4 For the Project Board to consider changes of direction for the project;

5 For commitment of resources to the project by the Project Board;

6 To terminate the project, either at its completion, or earlier if the Project Board considers that a valid business case for the project has ceased to exist.

ost
e roles
irman,

Walkthrough

This is the second type of meeting which will be useful in project control. Its main function is not the imparting of knowledge by one person to a group, but the imparting of an evaluation by a group to one person. The definition of a Walkthrugh is:

a team method of checking product quality.

The major objectives of a Walkthrough are:

to improve quality by error identification,

to check any deviation from standards.

Walkthroughs can also help the Project and Team Leaders

to educate new Team Members.

It also imparts a greater degree of confidence in a task being completed if the end-product of that task has been the subject of a Walkthrough.

A Walkthrough has three parts:

Preparation

Review

Follow-up

Let us examine each of these parts in turn, looking at the objective of the part, the roles to be played in it, the documentation for that part, and finally the major activities during that part. It should be stressed that although there may be a number of roles to be taken, one person may often take several roles, especially in a small project. Most practical Walkthroughs will be carried out by two people, but it is still important for the to know how they have shared the various roles between them, so that they can check that they have fulfilled their obligations.

Preparation

Objective

1 To become familiar with product under review

Roles

1 Error-finding.

2 Check for completeness.

3 Check against standards.

4 Education

2

Database Management: Planning and Control

Although it is difficult to pinpoint exactly when the area of database management began, there is good reason to place its beginning with the APOLLO project of the 1960s, which was launched in response to President John F. Kennedy's stated goal of landing a man on the moon by the end of the decade. This project was certainly a vast and complex undertaking. Since, at the time, no available systems were capable of handling the coordination of the vast amounts of data required, North American Rockwell, the prime contractor for the project, asked IBM to develop one. In response, IBM developed the Generalized Update Access Method (GUAM), which went into production in 1964.

It soon became clear to IBM that this product was useful in other environments and, in 1966, the company made the product available to the general public under the name Data Language/I (DL/I). This product is really the data management component of the Information Management System (IMS), which was certainly one of the most important of the early database management systems. IMS has been enhanced over the years and is still offered by IBM.

Another development was taking place in the mid-1960s. A system called Integrated Data Store (I-D-S) was developed at General Electric by a team headed by Charles Bachman. This system led to a whole class of database management systems, the CODASYL systems, which are still popular and influential today.

In the late 1960s, the Conference on Data Systems Languages (CODASYL), the group responsible for COBOL, tackled the problem of providing a standard for database management systems. CODASYL charged a task group, the Data Base Task Group (DBTG) with the job of developing specifications for database management systems. The DBTG did this and in 1971, CODASYL presented these specifications to the American National Standards Institute (ANSI) for adoption as a national standard. Although these specifications were not accepted as a standard by ANSI, a number of systems were developed following the CODASYL guidelines. These systems are usually called CODASYL systems or DBTG systems.

In 1970, Dr. E.F. Codd presented a paper that was to have profound impact on the database community. In it, he proposed a new and, at the time, radically different approach to the management of data: the relational model. Throughout the decade of the 1970s, the relational model was the subject of intense research activity. In addition to purely theoretical research, prototype systems were developed, the most important being a system called System R, which was developed by IBM. It was not until the 1980s, however, that commercial relational DBMS's began to appear. Systems that are at least partly relational now exist in abundance on computers ranging from the smallest micro to the largest mainframe.

The 1970s and 1980s have seen the development of a number of support products to go along with DBMS's. Data dictionaries, report generators, query facilities, and non procedural languages have all been developed and, along with the DBMS, they are now a part of an entire environment, the so-called fourth generation environment. We speak of systems that contain all of these facilities as Fourth Generation Languages (4GLs) or as application generators. They represent a tremendous increase in productivity. In addition, the 1980s have seen the development of microcomputer DBMS's. As the decade has progressed, these systems have increased greatly in functionally, to the point where they rival their mainframe counterparts in a number of areas.

For an excellent account of the early history of database management, see the March 1976 issue of the *ACM Computing Surveys;* in this issue, gives the history of database management and an overview of the various models; discusses the relational model; discusses the CODASYL approach; examines the hierarchical model; and presents a comparison between the relational and CODASYL approaches.

There are a number of advantages to the database approach to processing, particularly when a powerful, full-functioned DBMS is used. The advantages are following.

1. Economy of scale
2. Getting more information from the same amount of data
3. Sharing of data
4. Balancing conflicting requirements
5. Enforcement of standards
6. Controlled redundancy
7. Consistency
8. Integrity
9. Security
10. Flexibility and responsiveness
11. Increased programmer productivity

12. Improved program maintenance

13. Data independence

1. Economy of scale

The concentration of applications in one location allows for the possibility of smaller numbers of larger and more powerful computers, which usually results in an *economy of scale*. The same economy of scale may be realized by the concentration of technical expertise. Furthermore, since many users are sharing the database, any improvement in the database will potentially benefit many different users. In general, economy of scale refers to the fact that the collective cost of several combined operations may be less than the sum of the cost of the individual operations. Database processing makes this type of combination possible.

2. Getting more information from the same amount of data

The primary goal of a computer system is to turn data into information. Even though all the data that Joan needed for a requested report was in computer files, she could not easily access it and thus could not obtain the desired information. If, however, that data were in a common database, she would be able to access it. Thus, this added *information* would now be available even though the database might not contain additional *data* not already present in the files.

3. Sharing of data

The data can be shared among authorized users, allowing users access to more of the data. Several users might have access to the same piece of data, e.g., a faculty member's address is changed, the change is immediately relayed to all users. In addition, new applications can be developed using the existing data in the database without the added burden of creating separate collections of files.

4. Balancing conflicting requirements

In order for the database approach to function adequately, there must be a person or group within the organization in charge of the database itself. This body is often called Database Administration (DBA). By keeping the overall needs of the organisation in mind, DBA can structure the database to the benefit of the entire organization, not just a single user group. While this may potentially mean that an individual user group is served less well than it might have been if it had its own isolated system, the overall organization will benefit. If the organization benefits, then, ultimately, so do the individual user groups.

5. Enforcement of standards

With the central control mentioned in the previous paragraph, DBA can ensure that standards for such things as data names, usages, and formats are followed uniformly throughout the organization.

6. Controlled redundancy

Since data that was kept separate in a file oriented system is now integrated into a single database, we no longer have multiple copies of the same data. Each of the four programmers at Marvel had his or her own FACULTY file containing, among other things, a faculty members' address. Thus the address of each faculty member appeared in at least four different places. In the database approach, since there will be only one occurrence of each faculty member, this redundancy will be eliminated. In practice, there are places where we might actually introduce some limited amount of redundancy into a database for performance reasons. But, even in these cases, we are able to keep it under tight control. This is why it is better to say that we *control* redundancy rather than *eliminate* it.

7. Consistency

Consistency follows from the control of elimination of redundancy. If a faculty member's address appears in only one place, there is no possibility that faculty member 111 will have the address 123 MAINST at one spot within our data and 466 WILLOW RD in another, for example.

8. Integrity

An integrity constraint is a rule that data in the database must follow. Here is an example of an integrity constraint: the department number given for a faculty member must be that of a department that *actually exists*. A database has integrity of data in the database satisfies all integrity constraints that have been established. In the database approach, DBA can define validation procedures that will ensure the integrity of the database.

9. Security

Security is the prevention of access to the database by unauthorized users. Since DBA has control over the operational data, it can define authorization procedures to ensure that only legitimate users access the data. DBA can further allow different users to have different types of access to the same data. The payroll department at Marvel College may be able to view and change the salary of a faculty member. The insurance department may be able to view the salary of a faculty member but not change it. The speaker's bureau may not even be able to view a salary. One way DBA achieves this security is through user views. Any data items not included in the user view for a given user will not be accessible to that user. Another means of achieving security is through the use of sophisticated password schemes.

10. Flexibility and responsiveness

Since the data that was previously kept in several different files by several different user areas is now in the same database, it is possible to respond to request for data from multiple areas in a much easier and more flexible way. Even within a single user area, the flexibility furnished by the DBMS to locate and access data in a number of different ways aids programmers in developing new programs to satisfy user requests. The use of high-level languages allows users to do some of their own programming in a very easy way. A user who employs one such language, for example, to find all the faculty members who are assigned to department 3, who are covered by insurance plan 2, and who have salary under $20,000, need only type.

```
SELECT FACULTY_NUMBER, NAME
 FROM FACULTY
 WHERE DEPT-NUMBER    = 3 AND
       PLAN-NUMBER    = 2 AND
       SALARY < 20000
```

Employing yet another language, called a natural language, a user may actually be able to type.

Give me the names and numbers of all faculty members who are in department 3, covered by plan 2 and make less than 20000.

In both cases, the user can get a response to a question concerning data in the database rapidly and easily, without having to submit a request for the creation of a special program to an already overworked data processing department.

11. Increased programmer productivity

Since programmers accessing a database do not have to worry about the mundane data manipulation activities, as they would when accessing files, they will be more productive. Studies have shown that on the average they will be two to four times more productive; i.e., a new application can be developed in one-quarter to one-half of the time it would take if it were a straight file-oriented application. In addition, with the advent of fourth-generation languages built around database management systems, the productivity increase can be much more dramatic. Ten to twentyfold increase in productivity are not uncommon.

12. Improved program maintenance

When interacting with a DBMS, programs are relatively independent of the actual data in the database. This means that many changes to the structure of the data itself may not require maintenance to existing application programs. In a straight file environment this is not true. Even simple changes to file layouts can require substantial changes in every program that access the file. In addition, since the low-level data manipulation is handled by the DBMS, details concerning this manipulation do not appear in programs. Thus, the complexity of maintaining such logic is not a concern in a DBMS environment.

13. Data independence

While improving program maintenance is one important advantage of having programs independent of the structure of the database, this independence has other advantages as well. Without such independence, changes to the database structure to improve performance and to meet changing corporate requirements become very difficult. The fact that all of the programs in the system need maintenance every time a change is made to the database structure would be strong incentive not to make any of these changes. Data independence removes this obstacle to changing the structure.

Data independence occurs when the structure of the database can change without requiring the programs that access the database to change. Data independence is achieved in the database environment through the use of external views or subschemas. Each program accesses data through an external view. The underlying structure of the database would not have to change.

The conceptual schema is the overall global organizational view of data. Finally the internal schema is the view of the database as seen by the computer. It is the responsibility of the DBMS to map one view to another.

The only requirement imposed on the external schemas is that they can be derived from what is in the conceptual schema. Certainly, if there is no *salary* field within an external schema. If there is no relationship between customers and employees in a conceptual schema, for example, there can be no relationship between them in any external schema. The important point is that the conceptual schema could change without affecting the external schemas. Obviously, an external schema would need to be changed if some field that it required were deleted from the conceptual schema.

Similarly, an internal schema can be changed without affecting the conceptual schema. Storage details or access strategies could change, for example. Where a given field was stored as zoned decimal, we may now wish to store it as packed decimal or, perhaps, in a binary format. Where direct access to a faculty member had previously been accomplished through one scheme, say hashing, we may now wish to use another scheme, perhaps some kind of index, for this purpose.

DBA could thus make changes to the internal schema to improve the performance of the database. DBA could also make changes to the conceptual schema to respond to new requirements within the organization. In both case, the external schemas could remain the same. In this way the independence described earlier is achieved.

Any decent DBMS support the external schemas of the ANSI/SPARC model. CODASYL systems call them subschemas. Many relational model systems call them views. In any case, the idea is the same: users can have their own views of what the database looks like.

Likewise, any decent DBMS support, in general the conceptual and internal schemas. In this case, however, the support is often not as complete as we would like. In the ANSI/SPARC model, logical details about the structure of the database belong in the conceptual schema, and physical details about such things as the actual storage and access methods for the database belong in the internal schema. Many DBMS products do not have this clear breakdown. Their designers may not have attempted to separate the logical from the physical at all or, if they have, the separation may not be nearly as complete as the ANSI/SPARC model requires. This is the direction in which systems are moving, however, and we have already discussed why it is a worthy goal.

Disadvantages of database processing

As you would expect, if there are advantages to doing something a certain way, there are also disadvantages. The database areas is no exception. There are several disadvantages regarding database processing, and they are follows.

1. Size
2. Complexity
3. Cost
4. Additional hardware requirements
5. Higher impact or a failure
6. Recovery more difficult

1. Size

To support all the complex functions that it must provide to users, a database management system must, by its nature, be a large program occupying megabytes of disk space as well as a substantial amount of internal memory.

2. Complexity

Again, the complexity and breadth of the functions furnished by a DBMS make it a complex product. Programmers and analysts must understand the features of the system in order to take full advantage of it. There is a great deal for them to learn. In addition, with many choices to make when designing and implementing a new system using a DBMS, it is possible to make these choices incorrectly, especially if the understanding of the system is not thorough enough. Unfortunately, a few incorrect choices can spell disaster for the whole project.

3. Cost

A good DBMS is an expensive product. By the time all the appropriate components related to the DBMS are purchased for a major mainframe system, the total price can easily into the $ 100,000 to $ 400,000 range.

4. Additional hardware requirements

Because of the size and complexity of a DBMS, greater hardware resources are required tan would be necessary without the DBMS. This means that if the hardware resources are not increased when a DBMS is purchased, users of the system may very well notice a severe degradation in performance. Purchasing additional hardware resources represents yet another added cost.

5. Higher impact of a failure

Since many of the data processing resources are now concentrated in the database, a failure of any component has much more far-reaching effect than in a non database environment.

6. Recovery more difficult

Because of the added complexity, the process of recovering the database in the event of a catastrophe is a more complicated one, particularly if the database is being updated by a large number of users concurrently.

In the early 1800's Charles Babbage, a man ahead of his time, designed the first mechanical calculating machine which had all of the components of a modern computer, including data storage areas, an output mechanism, a control unit for directing the machine's operations, and an arithmetic logic unit for performing additions at the "lightning" rate of one per second. Babbage did not call the components of his difference and analytical engines by these names of course, but his design paved the way for later development of these concepts. Babbage's *Reflections on the Decline of Science in England and on Some of its Causes* led to the foundation of the British Association for the Advancement of Science. His concern was that science not be pursued only by the aristocracy but that it really should be a profession of those who could apply it in business and manufacturing.

After 1842, Babbage's collaborator in computer design was Ada Byron, Countess of Lovelace, the daughter of the poet, Lord Byron. Ada developed the concept of programming loop and earned the reputation of the first computer programmer. Unfortunately, Ada and Babbage were frustrated in their designs because the technology was not capable of building a full-scale difference engine. Babbage's son after the turn of the 20th century, did have the machine built, and proved that it really worked unfortunately, long after cancer had claimed Ada's life at age 36.

Virtually all computers before 1950 were calculating machines. When the Electronic Numerical Integrator and Calculator was built in the early 1940's by John Mauchley and J. Presper Eckert, it could perform 3000 multiplications per second. The ENIAC contained several thousand vacuum tubes. Since the mean lifetime before failure of a vacuum tube was about 300 hours, one could expect to run the ENIAC for approximately 14 minutes before a breakdown. In those days, backup of data was already very important. The computer would be run for 10 minutes; then the contents of memory would be dumped onto a secondary storage medium, so that a relatively smooth startup could be achieved when the computer did go down. Often, hours were spent diagnosing the source of the failure before the defective tube was found and replaced.

In those early days programming a computer was a very different task from now. Rather than having the program stored in memory, the computer had to be rewired or instructions entered by switches for each program change. Though slow and ponderous, the machines still represented a tremendous breakthrough; even with hours of downtime and hours of programming, calculations were performed much more rapidly and accurately than could be done by hand.

John von Neumann is given credit for developing the concept of storing programs in the computer, along with the data, in the late 1940's. Thereafter, changing a program simply meant changing the contents of the memory locations where the program was stored. The development of codes for storing instructions and distinguishing them from data was major accomplishment of this period.

By the mid 1950's most programmers began to tire of writing their own routines for driving auxiliary memory and input/output devices each time a new program was written. For each other, they were borrowing stacks of cards which contained prewritten program to handle I/O operations. Ultimately, a number of general purpose I/O subroutines were written which could be loaded with appropriate interpreters each time a program was run. By the late 1950's FORTRAN compile-and-go routines had been composed. The programmer needed only to load program and data into the computer; the routines for compilation and I/O were already within the computer memory or readily accessible to the computer from magnetic tape or another card reader. By the early 1960's Input/Output Management Programs and routines to control the flow of jobs through the machine were built into most computers. These programs were stored as *operating Systems* on tape, drum, or disk auxiliary storage known as the "system residence" devices.

Operating systems

Operating Systems are a set of programs stored more or less permanently within the computer memory for handling tasks that have to be done for most jobs. They made it easier for programmers and began to open entirely new possibilities for using computers. Until the 1960's most computers had been run in an "open shop"; when programmers wanted to run their jobs, they signed up on the schedule for a block of time when they could use the computer. It was their responsibility to lean how to operate the computer, much as personal microcomputer owners now do. The programmers would load whatever decks of cards they needed, including compilers and I/O handlers if necessary, into the card reader, punch the button, and wait to see what happened. Much of their time was spent looking at lights on the console and flipping switches to correct errors. The computer was idle much of the time while the programmer/operators were trying to figure out why their programmers were not working. Often they performed a core dump, listing out the contents of primary memory, and took the listings home to study before their next turn at the machine.

It was apparent that the "open shop" was a tremendous waste of programmer talent, computer time, and money. Computers were so expensive that only the elite in science and engineering could afford them, and time was scarce. It was too expensive to buy more machines. What was to be done? Why not put programs into the Operating System to allow several jobs to be run in sequence? If one job bombs, dump the core automatically, provide the output for the programmer, and proceed to load and process the next job. This was the concept of Batching Processing. It shortened turnaround time considerably and relieved the programmer of the burden of learning how to run the computer. A new job description, that of computer operator, was created.

The next obvious step was to overlap operations. Why couldn't the Operating System handle Input/Output operations on the peripheral devices while the central processing unit was processing another program or another segment of the same program? This could further reduce equipment time, improve turnaround, and make more efficient use of the machines.

By the early 1970's operating systems had been developed which would even allow concurrent processing, two or more users on the same machine, sharing the facilities at small intervals of time. Jobs could be swapped on an *event-driven* basis; when on job ended a particular task, the status of the job could be saved, and another task could be performed. By allowing more than one job at a time on the computer, greater interchangeability of data between programs was possible, and the process of turning raw data into useful information was speeded up even more.

The next obvious step was the time sharing. Without sophisticated operating systems, stored permanently within each computer, this process was impossible. Now many users can sit at remote terminals, all believing they have complete control of the machine. Their jobs are switched in and out of the CPU at such rates, that by the time they get control after each break, only a few milliseconds have elapsed, often in time periods shorter than the persistence of vision. Time-sharing is *time-driven*; that is, each user gets a fixed block of time, usually a millisecond or two, in order.

Another major benefit of Operating Systems is that errors are reduced when the machines is under program control rather than operator control. The user's program is separated from the computer system. Either can be modified without changing the other.

Tasks and problems which must be handled by an operating system

The tasks performed by an operating system must include:

Job scheduling. Of all the jobs entered into the computer, whether in an event-driven environment or in a time-sharing situation, whose job gets run when? Ideally, a good operating would be able to distinguish between high and low priority jobs and also schedule tasks for the most efficient use of the CPU and peripherals. The scheduler part of a control program is responsible for these tasks.

Supervision. How is the core memory allocated to the jobs which need it? Are entire programs loaded into core at one time, or are they divided into segments or pages and an alogrithm applied to determine which pages or segments swapped out when new ones are needed? The operating system keeps track of what locations in memory are used for which tasks. The user need to be concerned about memory allocation. What if the program page swapped out happens to be the next one needed? Such a situation results in program segments being swapped in and out vigorously with no processing being done, the computer is said to be *"thrashing."* A good operating system will be capable of recognizing this situation and correcting it by choosing another swapping alogrithm, at least temporarily.

Resource allocation. If two users need the same tape drive at the same time, the operating system must be capable of allocating and deallocating, temporarily suspending operation of one program until the other releases the device. If program 1 is using Drive A and program 2 is using Drive B, what happens when program 1 requests drive B and program 2 requests drive A? Both programs would normally stop and wait for the other to release the requested drive. Such situation is called *deadlock* or "deadly embrace." The operating system must be aware of such problems and be written to avoid situations when the computer is doing nothing.

Communication with the operator and recovery from failures. An operating system must communicate with the operator, providing messages about I/O devices, machine status, which jobs are running, which tapes or disks need to be loaded or unloaded, etc. Also, should there be a failure—whether it be with the building power, a problem in memory, or of any other type—a good operating system should be able to store and then find and restart on the status at some time before failure. The operator must be given the status information and instructions by the operating system on how restart is to proceed. Ideally, data and status will be stored automatically by the operating system at short intervals so that it can be easily retrieved and updated, not just during failure but also on demand from the user.

Accounting. Most computer system require detailed statistics on who uses the machine and its peripherals for what periods of time so that appropriate billing can be done. It is a fact of life that someone must pay for the computers and their operations. Unless a machine is entirely dedicated to one department or operation, the costs must be divided. For the computer to stop each time a new user signs on or off, so that the operator can be record the time from the clock on the wall, would not only be wasteful of computer and operator time, but also would not give a true picture of how much CPU time was used, how much peripheral time of what type was used, etc. Operator error would be inevitably lead to arguments and problems regarding who gets charged how much. Therefore, these functions are now usually written into the operating system. If you have used a large computer you are aware that at log off you are usually told how much time you have used.

I/O Handling. Historically, the I/O handler part of operating systems is the justification for their development. Now I/O handlers are just one part of a comprehensive system on most machines. I/O handler programs tell the computer exactly how to write or read data to or from specific peripheral devices. Generally, each device is different, they use different data formats and have different data transfer rates, different buffer size and different methods of data transfer. Programs are stored within the operating system to handle these differences. Even if you are using a microcomputer, you will have some I/O handling operations built into the system, such as how to print onto your printer, how to write on the CRT, how to read information from the keyboard, and how to store information on and read from a disk or cassette.

The I/O handler allocates devices and auxiliary storage space to your programs and data. It control how the devices operate, organize, and close data files; maintain catalogs, and store and retrieve data. It should be noted that I/O handlers are *machine dependent.* They must be written for a specific computer and a specific peripheral attached to a machine. Also, they are not entirely self-sufficient; the user must tell the computer the parameters to be used by the data handler when information is to be transferred.

Efficiency. A perfect operating system should operate as efficiently as possible. It should be apparent that instructions for moving data from one point to another in the system are probably by far the most heavily used instructions in an operating system. These must be quickly accessed and executed. Providing status in an easily stored and retrievable form to recover from *interrupts,* whether anticipated in the form of time-driven swapping in a time sharing environment or unexpected error conditions, is critical.

Testing a newly written operating system is a difficult task at best. It is impossible to predict the uses to which the programmers will put it. Inevitably, someone wants to do something that the system was not designed to do or performs a procedure in an unexpected fashion that causes the system to fail. Normally, because of the myriad of situations encountered that could not be anticipated by the system designer, it takes months of operation on a large machine to get the bugs out of an operating system. Also, until a system is installed at its permanent location, the designer does not know what devices the operating system should be designed to support. Everybody wants something different, and operating systems must be written as generally as possible with the realization that changes and additions will be inevitable.

Units of data

Before beginning a discussion of types of data storages and modes of computer operation, it is important to understand the basic concepts of how data is organized.

All information in a digital computer is written in binary form. That is, in terms of binary digits, 0 or 1, called *bits.* A binary sequence of 8 bits is called a *byte:* e.g., 10110011 would be a byte. Normally, one byte is required to represent an alphabetic or numeric character, using one of the common codes to be discussed in the next chapter. A computer *word* consists of a small number of bytes. For example, a small microcomputer may have an 8-bit word, whereas a large scientific mainframe may have as many as 8 bytes per word. The computer word is a physical concept, having reference to the computer itself and how it stores information. The word is usually the smallest amount of information that can be stored or retrieved at one time.

Logically, the way we like to see our data, a character is generally the smallest unit of data. Remember, usually a character is physically one byte long. Characters are grouped logically into fields. A *field* would be a string of characters representing an employee identification number, a name, etc. Fields are collected in *records.* A record might contain, for example, all of the information for a given student, such as student number, year in schools, age, address, courses enrolled in, etc. A collection of records, such as all of the records for the students in a given course, would be called a *data file,* or simply a *file.*

Types of storage

Data and programs are stored in two main locations in a computer. Ideally everything would be stored in high-speed main memory within the Central Processor. This memory is called *primary memory* or core storage. Before 1970 most primary memory was made of magnetic beads or "cores" approximately one millimeter in diameter, threaded on wires. Each core was capable of holding a binary bit, 0 or 1, depending upon the direction in which it was magnetized. Core memory was bulky as well as difficult and expensive to build. Now primary memory is almost always "semiconductor" memory, integrated circuits in which, roughly speaking, a current flowing past a point represents a binary 1 and no current is a binary 0. Semiconductor memory has advantages over core; it is much easier to build, thousands of binary bits can be packed into one small integrated circuit ship, and it is relatively cheap. Its major disadvantage is that it is "volatile"; that is, when the power goes off, no more current flows, and the memory has been lost. Core memory was permanent; a loss of current did not affect its contents. Primary memory is often still called "core" memory, even though it may not consist of magnetic cores at all.

The other location for storing data is in *auxiliary memory* Secondary memory is always a peripheral medium such as cards, magnetic tape, disks, drums, etc. Two things make auxiliary memory more attractive than primary memory for large storage capacity. First, for keeping large amounts of data, auxiliary storage media are cheaper than main memory. More information can be stored per unit cost. Second, and perhaps more important, on machines with a small number of bits per computer word, if only one or two words are reserved for addressing, the amount of primary memory which can be directly addressed is quite small. For example, if an address is limited to 16 binary bits, then the maximum number of directly addressable memory cells is 2 = 65,536. This is the situation in many small microcomputers where the address registers are indeed two bytes long.

The properties of auxiliary storage media and devices will be discussed in considerable detail through this text

Operating modes

The methods of storing and processing data can be categorized in many different ways. It is especially informative to consider the operating modes of the computer which is handling the data.

Batch

In *batch* processing mode, jobs are entered into the computer and processed one at a time sequentially. Indeed, there may be at any one time a number of different tasks waiting at the gate, for the computer to process. However, each job is completed before the next job is started. In batch mode, data is collected and sorted before being entered into the computer memory. When the data is recorded in auxiliary memory a *master* file is created; that is, the permanent file of data is recorded in sequential order. The order of the information in the file is determined by one field, called a *key,* in each record.

Updating a master file, inserting new information or deleting some records, generally requires a complete rewrite of the file. New information is collected and sorted into order by keys in a *transaction* or *detail* file. Updating is performed by a merge sort. The first records are read from the master file and from the transaction file and compared. The one which comes first is written to a new master file. Then the next records are compared, and so forth until the entire file has been rewritten. By this time a new master file has been created which contains all of the changes. The old master and transaction files are kept as *backup* at least until the next update of the file, so that information can be retrieved in case something happens to the new master file.

Assume that a master file contains record with information about types of small computers: their cost, memory size, peripherals, dealers, etc. The key by which each record is identified is the name of the company which makes the computer. The master file contains records for

1. Apre
2. Ather
3. Crab
5. Olson
6. Tarpen
7. Tinbox

Remote job entry

Closely related to the concepts of time sharing and virtual memory is the *remote job entry* operating mode. In this case, many users are connected to the machine, just as in time-sharing. However, instead of providing a response as soon as a RETURN or ENTER key is pushed at the end of each line or record, the computer generally waits until the entire job has been transmitted before it begins any program execution or data processing operations.

Direct processing

With the exception of batch sequential processing, all the modes of operation discussed above require some kind of direct processing. In direct processing mode, the data and programs can be used and stored as they are needed. It is most necessary to collect data and sort it before placing it into memory. Access to the required data or programs is "instantaneous," or at least much more rapid than having to look at all the contents of auxiliary memory in order to retrieve the particular records desired. Direct processing has been made possible by *Direct Access Storage Devices* represented by disk and drum type auxiliary memory. You can see that direct access to data would be very difficult to achieve if that data were stored on cards or magnetic tape.

In general, direct processing mode allows more effective management of data and better controls on its security than batch mode; however, this may be at the expense of wasted space in secondary memory. As time progress, and DASD's become larger and faster, batch mode processing is being replaced more and more by direct modes of operation. Time-sharing is the accepted way of handling users on mainframe computers and on many intermediate-sized minicomputers. Even some larger microcomputers, especially those used in educational institutions, are capable of handling time-sharing, direct access mode processing.

What direct access methods have made possible

Here are more specific examples of programming which are possible only with direct mode devices and operating systems.

1. Data files which require large amounts of storage and fast access are now feasible. For example, assume you have an inventory requirement for an automobile parts store. There are more than 8000 items in your inventory, and you need to be able not only to print out the inventory periodically but also to keep a running total of parts on hands, so that when supplies are low you can order more immediately. Thus, you can avoid having overstocks of items which tie up your capital. With direct access storage, when a part is sold or a shipment arrives, the inventory of that part can be updated immediately, without rewriting the entire inventory file. You can demand reports of items which are low in number, you can have the computer automatically warn you when an items is in short supply, and you can get your complete inventory reports when they are due.

2. We would all be very upset if we had to wait for hours for a response to a request. How many of us would visit the office of a travel agent more than once if we were told to come back tomorrow or next week to find out if our airline reservations had been made? Virtually all airline reservations are now made on-line. A computer terminal shows flights available, a punch of a button confirms your reservation or puts you on a waiting list. Access to flight times and bookings is immediate. There is no waiting for long distance telephone calls or for a clerk to go through a file of thousands of cards or to read a magnetic tape.
3. In a bank it is impossible to predict which accounts will be active on any given day. Customer accounts must be retrievable rapidly and randomly. If there are 30,000 accounts at the bank, and the average rate of activity is 400 accounts per day, it would be absurd to have to read all accounts sequentially to find the balance for each customer who asks. In such a *low activity* situation direct access processing ideal and could not be done efficiently at all without direct access devices.
4. Suppose the management of a company wishes to expand the plant and change the way billings and payroll are handled. If that happens rarely, the files can be searched sequentially and updated by rewriting the master file. The programs can be rewritten, and the entire processing procedure can be changed. Suppose, however, you are building computers or some other high technology product, and daily changes are necessary in your programs or accounting methods. Then you want to be able to get at the exact data and the exact program segments which you wish to change, without having to change the entire package.
5. Each evening all salespersons on your force report their daily sales, what items were sold, how many, and to whom. Your records must store this information for each salesperson, temporarily, in the order in which it is reported. Then, at the end of the pay period, the computer takes the information stored temporarily on the DASD's sorts it, updates the master payroll records, and calculates the commissions. This *intermediate storage* of information saves untold hours of processing time, which would be necessary if the information had to be sorted and processed piece by piece as it was collected.
6. Suppose you have 40 terminals in a student computer lab, and only one high-speed printer, if each student wrote directly to the printer from the computer, the system would become deadly slow, since most printers print information at a maximum rate of only a few hundred characters per second. Instead, your direct access storage device handles *spooling*. When printer output of a file is requested, the computer instead sends the data to a spool area on the DASD. The printer constantly polls the spool area to see what is there. When information is to be printed, it is read from the spool area of the DASD, not directly from the computer. Hence the computer does not have to slow down for the printer. If the spool area

becomes full faster than the printer can empty it, the operating system may not allow you to write into the spool area until there is room.

The computer system

Let's look briefly at the computer system needed to perform the operations we have discussed above. Every computer must have at least one *central processor,* where control operations and processing is actually done. Every central processor will have a *control unit,* whose job is to fetch and decode instructions and to keep track of where the next instruction is located. Also within the processor will be an *arithmetic logic* unit where calculations are performed and which directs the computer where to store results. Main or *primary memory* is also directly attached to or part of the central processing unit.

In addition, on large systems there will be *I/O channels* which run the programs necessary to drive the peripheral units. Also, one *controller* is required for each type of input or output device attached to the machine. *Auxiliary memory* storage devices, whether sequential or direct, are simply specialized input/output peripherals. A typical computer configuration is shown in the following figure.

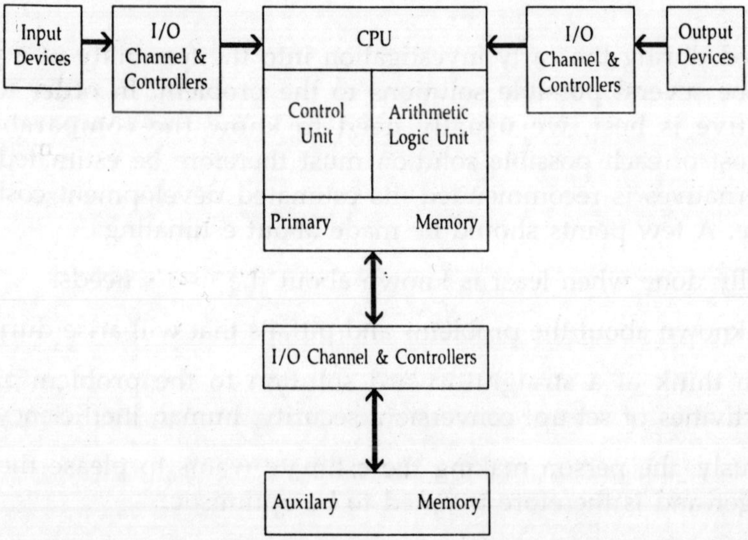

Fig.: Block diagram of a computer system

Planning

Why?

1 If we cannot plan a project, we will never be able to control it.

2 We need to plan a project before we can allocate individual objectives.

Objectives

1 To fit in with our team standards

2 To fit in with our reporting.

3 To be flexible enough to allow planning for all sizes of project.

4 To permit progressive planning as more data on the project become available.

5 To permit quick recognition of any deviation from plan in actual performance.

Limitations

1 Our standard should not lead to an 'overkill' in paperwork or procedures for small projects.

2 It should fit in with a number of techniques in plan preparation, such as bar charts, networks etc.

3 Often projects are too large to be adequately planned in one step.

4 There is often insufficient information available properly to plan a project completely at the beginning.

Project estimate

This is produced during the early investigation into the feasibility of a project. There will normally be several possible solutions to the problem. In order to help decide which alternative is best, we usually need to know the comparable costs. The development cost of each possible solution must therefore be estimated. Thus, when one of the alternatives is recommended, its estimated development cost becomes the project estimate. A few points should be made about estimating.

1 It is normally done when least is known about the user's needs.

2 Nothing is known about the problems and pitfalls that will arise during the project

3 We tend to think of a straightforward solution to the problem and forget the ancillary activities of set-up, conversion, security, human inefficiency etc.

4 Subconsciously, the person making the estimate wants to please the user or their own manager and is therefore tempted to be optimistic.

5 Estimating should be based on historical data. How long has it taken us to do comparable projects in the past? What is the effective work capacity of a Team Member during a work period? Can we learn from experiences of other Project Leaders?

6 Any estimate should show a break-down of the total project into phases. A phase is a portion of the total project during which certain pre-defined tasks are carried out. This will allow us to compare each phase plan with our original estimate as the project progresses.

There are a number of surveys available on the percentage of time spent in the different phases of a project. Each company should be able to develop its own average percentages according to the type of project it undertakes and its past history of projects. For those without such averages, they could start with the following figures.

Feasibility 3%

Specification 12%

Design 20%

Programming 35%

System test 15%

Installation 15%

Phase plans

Depending upon the size of the project, we must plan it in a number of discrete phases.

For each phase, we need two types of plan; a technical plan showing the tasks, resource and time allocation, and a financial plan which translates the resources into monetary terms. The technical plan is the main document for the Project Leader. The financial plan is the communicating document between Project Leader and Project Board.

Phase plans are produced prior to the start of a phase. An exception here is the plan for the very first phase which is done as one of the first tasks of that phase.

Planning package contents

A graphic plan is inadequate alone. It needs explanation to a reader. A complete planning package should consist of:

A graphic plan

A description

Assumptions on which the plan is based

Potential problems

When our schedule slips, it will be too late to say to the contractor representative 'I thought I would have priority'. If we are making such assumptions when planning, we must make this clear to those who will approve our plan.

Resource availability plan

Before creating a technical plan for a phase, it is usually worthwhile to create a schedule showing the availability of the phase resources. This covers not only the Team Members, but also the other resources required. Such a plan will include data on when each resource becomes available, when its availability ceases, and when it is not available during the phase. The availability plan also notes holidays, training and allocation to other projects, thus providing a useful check of availability against the technical plan being created.

Deviation plan

Approval and acceptance of a phase plan means certain things. The user or customer is committed to a defined level of cost, but in turn expects the project to reach a certain point for that cost by a certain data and with a certain level of quality. If one of these factors should begin to vary beyond an agreed tolerance limit, it is the responsibility of the Project Leader to bring this to the attention of the Project Board. As described in the chapter on control, this is one at a meeting with the Project Board. At this meeting, the Project Leader will present a deviation plan.

The description part of this deviation planning package describes the problem, the reason, the impact, the possible alternatives and the Project Leader's recommendation. The graphic plan will normally cover only the problem area and will extend until either the phase end or the recovery from the deviation, if this is sooner. It is not necessary for the deviation plan to go beyond the phase end. Any recovery work to be done after that will be incorporated in the next phase plan.

Planning activities

For those who like to approach planning in a methodical fashion, here is a general sequence of actions to follow.

Complete the provisional 'duration' and 'end date' lines. This is achieved either by copying from the final estimate, or, if a project completion date is imposed by some external factor, by calculating the stage durations by working back from the end data.

Remember that this is elapsed time, not manpower.

Complete the resources section showing how much effort is available if the size of the Phase Team is already known.

Examine the task checklists and mark any which are not applicable to the particular project.

Identify any special tasks which are not in the checklists.

Identify any necessary tasks on the checklists which have already been completed. For example, a description of the current product should normally be available.

Consider the management of the project and allocate a percentage of manpower resource for this function throughout the plan.

Identify, under applicable activities, those which can only be done by a certain Team Member.

Calculate the length of time needed for each task.

Allocate the time to produce each sub-product within the project. It is usually easiest to work backwards from the completion dates of the major tasks.

Define which activities can be done on parallel and which must be serial

Define quality control points

Add to activities the time for quality control plus time for regular meetings.

Total the resources required.

Review the completed plan for individual workload balance, continuity of work for each Team Member, and re-cycle, where necessary, to smooth the workload.

Determine whether any remaining time problems are best resolved by extra resources, the purchase of external products, stretching elapsed time, or reducing the facilities to be provided by the current project.

Calculate the cost of the planned resources.

Add the tolerance percentage

Compare with the final estimate from the feasibility study.

Write the plan description to provide an explanation of the graphic plan, and how it will be implemented. This description includes information on how the plan will be monitored, and the Project Leader's proposal of a suitable tolerance level.

List the technical and business assumptions which have been made when developing the plan. It is important to document these assumptions, so that any changes to them can be quickly identified and appropriate action taken.

Identify potential problems and the likely impact on the plan should they occur.

Control

Why do we need standards for the control of a project? This chapter considers the need to control various aspects of a project, and covers the control requirements of the various groups involved in a project. It is also deals with the problem of written and verbal communications in a team and project environment. The correct use of control standards enables us to answer the following questions, often asked during a project.

1. What is the quality of workmanship?
2. Are we still producing what the customer wants?
3. Are we on schedule?
4. Are we within budget?
5. Will we fail to realize that schedule or budget problems have occurred until it is too late to do anything about it?

6. How are Project Board members, not normally involved with the project on a day-to-day basis, made aware of the project status?
7. When and how often should the Project Leader meet the Project Board?
8. How do we keep control of customer requests for alterations and additional after the specification and probably the cost have been agreed? How do we prevent such requests from destroying the project schedule and budget?

Objectives

1. To pass status information upwards from Team Member to Project Board.
2. To enable the Project Leader to spot deviations from budget or schedule as soon as they occur.
3. To keep the tea informed.
4. To provide a standard procedure for meetings.
5. To identify the circumstances under which a meeting should be called.
6. To decide who should attend this meeting.

Solution

There are two major activities in control:

Collection of project information

Interpretation of that information to the correct people

The information is of two types:

Technical

Financial

In our solution, we shall consider two ways of interpreting the information and passing it on; the use of meetings and of reports. As far as our project management standards go, the collection of data will be considered from the bottom upwards. That is, gathering data from the working level and passing it upwards to Project Leader and Project Board.

The interested parties are

Project Board

Project Management Team

Project Team

Requirements

Consider the type of information each of the parties needs.

Project board

The Project Board numbers represent user and contractor management. They are not involved on a day-to-day basis. If possible, they want to manage by objectives and by exception. As management, they are mainly concerned with the status of the budget. On technical matters, they are only concerned with schedule status and knowing if the customer will get what he wants at the end of the project. They therefore do not want too much technical detail, but brief status information until things begin to go wrong. Then they need early advice of what is going wrong, together with a means of collecting all the relevant details plus technical solution proposals.

Project management team

The Project Leader needs both technical and financial information regularity. The Team Leader needs up-to-date technical progress and quality information.

Phase team

Team Members need to be able to measure their own progress against objectives, and know the status of any interfaces within the team. They need to be able to identify with the total product.

Reports

We can provide a simple recording and reporting structure to suit large and small projects. Below is a brief description of the recording and reporting activities, plus the proposed forms

Time Sheet

By: Team Members

For: Team Leader

Frequency: Daily

Team Members record efforts against tasks on time sheets.

Phase Plan

By: Team Leader

For: Project Leader

Frequency: Weekly

Effort is recorded against the phase plan from the time sheets. Completed tasks and slippages are noted.

Status report

By: Project Leader

For: Project Board

Frequency: Monthly

A brief status report is sent to the Project Board on technical status and outstanding problems.

Phase summary

By: Project Leader

For: Project Board

Frequency: Monthly

The phase summary is in graphic form to allow summarized information to be passed in a very brief document. Its main purpose is to pass financial information to the Project Board.

1 The costs of the resources consumed are recorded. A report is sent to the project Board in graphic form, comparing current phase cumulative costs and completed tasks with the plan.

2 In certain recording systems, one trap into which it is easy to fall at this time is that the team are asked to estimate 'percentage complete' for their current unfinished tasks. The danger is that this is a subjective estimate, normally optimistic, and therefore misleading. The Project Leader also has the problem of assessing all the team's estimates on different sizes of task and turning these into a single 'percentage complete' for the phase. A much better idea is the one incorporated by BP in their plan. Having produced the phase technical plan, each task in the plan is calculated as a percentage of the total phase plan. This is done by taking the total man days needed as 100% and calculating each task's effort as a percentage of that. When reporting against the plan, completed tasks are noted and their percentage totalled to give the 'percentage complete'. In reporting this figure, we ignore any tasks which have started but are not yet complete. In order for this approach to be really effective, no task in our plan should be greater than 10% of the total phase effort, or 10 man days for a small project. Any task larger than this can always be broken down.

3 The '% Work Planned Completed' is calculated by adding up the percentages of the total phase effort of those tasks which have completed so far.

Modification requests

By: Usually a user

For: Review by the Project Board

Frequency: As required

There is one other type of report which is vital if a project is to be kept under control. There must be a document produced for every major change proposed after the feasibility study, and for every major or minor change proposed after the user specification has been signed. The implementation of such changes without proper control and authority has been responsible for many project failures to meet schedule and/or budget.

Let us make this point. Having accepted the feasibility estimate, approved the user specification, and committed resources against those documents, only the Project Board has the authority to agree to any changes. Only the customer has the authority to agree to more expenditure, and this must be done at Project Board level.

The procedure should be that anyone requesting a modification should document it. The request should be assessed for its impact on the project and its likely cost. All outstanding requests should be reviewed by the Project Board at the next project review meeting. Where agreement is reached to implement certain requests, the Project Board must approve the necessary extra resources and time.

Meetings

Only two types of meeting are described here; the Phase Review Meeting and the Walkthrough. The first is the formal meeting of Project Board and Team Leader at defined times during the project. The definition of these times relates to the size of the project. The second is a quality control meeting. These are the types of meeting for which must define very clear standards. There my be other types of meeting during the projects lifetime, but normally they will not require such rigorous standards.

Phase review meeting

The purposes of this meeting are as follows.

1 For the Project Board and Project Leader to meet;

2 For the Project Board to hear a more detailed report of progress and have the opportunity to ask questions;

3 For the presentation of plan to the Project Board for their approval;

4 For the Project Board to consider changes of direction for the project;

5 For commitment of resources to the project by the Project Board;

6 To terminate the project, either at its completion, or earlier if the Project Board considers that a valid business case for the project has ceased to exist.

Walkthrough

This is the second type of meeting which will be useful in project control. Its main function is not the imparting of knowledge by one person to a group, but the imparting of an evaluation by a group to one person. The definition of a Walkthrugh is:

a team method of checking product quality.

The major objectives of a Walkthrough are:

to improve quality by error identification,

to check any deviation from standards.

Walkthroughs can also help the Project and Team Leaders

to educate new Team Members.

It also imparts a greater degree of confidence in a task being completed if the end-product of that task has been the subject of a Walkthrough.

A Walkthrough has three parts:

Preparation

Review

Follow-up

Let us examine each of these parts in turn, looking at the objective of the part, the roles to be played in it, the documentation for that part, and finally the major activities during that part. It should be stressed that although there may be a number of roles to be taken, one person may often take several roles, especially in a small project. Most practical Walkthroughs will be carried out by two people, but it is still important for the to know how they have shared the various roles between them, so that they can check that they have fulfilled their obligations.

Preparation

Objective

1 To become familiar with product under review

Roles

1 Error-finding.

2 Check for completeness.

3 Check against standards.

4 Education

Documentation

1 Request to attend a Walkthrough

2 Checklist of questions to ask for this type of product

3 The piece of work to be reviewed

4 Minor errors list.

Activities

1 Distribution of the work to be reviewed.

2 Review of the product.

3 Compilation of list of minor errors

4 Noting points for discussion

Review

Objective

1 To review the product and produce a list of any corrections needed.

Roles

1 Chairman.

2 Secretary.

3 Review.

4 Reviewer(s).

Documentation

1 Product.

2 Lists of minor errors.

3 Action list.

Activities

1 Collection of minor errors.

2 Chairman's introduction.

3 Listing of problems.

4 Step-by-step review. It is up to the Chairman to:

sense consensus,

stop repetition,

take a problem off-line if no agreement can be reached,

maintain impetus.

5 Secretary notes actions.

6 Action list read-back.

7 Who will take action to correct the identified errors?

8 Who will check the corrective actions?

9 Go to follow-up or re-schedule?

Objectives

1 To ensure that all errors notified during the review are corrected.

Role

1 Actioner

2 Checker

Documentation

1 Completed action list.

2 Revised product.

3 Notification to management.

Activities

1 Resolution of errors.

2 Sign-off by nominated reviewers of the individual action items.

3 Sign-off by the Chairman at the foot of the action list, confirming that all items have been corrected and approved.

4 Notification to Project Leader.

We have now described the formal procedure for a Walkthrough. Not all Walkthroughs in a project will be formal meetings with four or more attendees. Were this the case, we should be spending far too much time and resource in Walkthroughs. To avoid this, there are a number of options open to the Project Leader and Team Leader when making their decisions on how many Walkthroughs to hold.

1 What are the key points in the project? Where are critical decisions made from where a lot of work will stem? Where is it most important to check that we are right?

2 What is known about the quality of work of individual Team Members? Can some members be allocated just a few Walkthroughs, with more for trainees?

3 Which Walkthrough can be handled by only two people? In practice, most Walkthroughs will be of this informal type, with two people sharing the roles between them. For example, in the reviewer might also take the role of chairman, leaving the reviewee to be also the secretary.

3
Computer Networking Systems

Data processing (DP) users are becoming more and more confused about the different approaches to producing and maintaining their software systems. Some talk of expensive methods within the framework of a strict phase concept, others of simple, friendly user languages which will satisfy users' requirements simply and cheaply. What is the case of this apparent contradiction? The answer is readily at hand.

The field of data processing has become ever larger and, as with everything which grows, has split into subfields. Contradictory tendencies develop for the different application areas, and the user, depending on which area he is currently concerned with, things that the approach used there is the only correct one. One firm quite often has three different application areas, namely:

- technical and scientific processing
- process data processing
- commercial data processing.

Technical and scientific processing
Here great emphasis is placed on creating a prototype of the product. The developer and the user are often the same. There should be as few formalisms as possible, and a strict phase concept is not adopted. Most programming is done in FORTRAN. The most important factor is the static and dynamic analysis of programs. Osterwell's TOOLPACK" toolkit package is characteristic of developmental approaches in this area.

Process data processing
Here the emphasis is on a valid processing concept with accompanying quality control of the project. Here the specification and verification of programs should be as formal as possible, and so specification languages and test techniques are very important, as critical control processes must be correct and reliable. This need not be overly expensive, as such process control usually has only limited amounts of data and functionality. Programs are written in languages such as PASCAL, PEARL and ADA.

Lauber's 'EPOS' system and Alford's 'REVS' system are characteristic of the developmental approaches in this area.

Commercial data processing

There are two different approaches to commercial data processing. On the one hand, increasingly high-level languages are becoming available which allow the user or the developer to program, test and get applications running quickly and easily without too many formalities. This tendency goes alongside decentralization of corporate data processing. It is supported by PC systems such as DBase-III and Open Access as well as by 4th generation languages such as NATURAL, RAMIS, FOCUS, IDEAL and MANTIS. What all these systems have in common is that they offer users a relatively simple interface for defining their ideas. The developer can therefore be a layman. These widely varying approaches come within the framework of individual data processing. On the other hand, there is much discussion of software engineering and the software life cycle. Here expensive methods such as HIPO, MJSD, SADT and Structured Analysis are used and programming is done in languages such as COBOL or PL/1. The development process is divided into phases and is subject to strict control. Developers are professional programmers and analysts.

The nature of software engineering work is subject to numerous conditions. Almost half the cost goes on documentation. The other half is taken up mainly by systematic testing. The actual programming is the smallest part. The basic difference between these two subfields of commercial data processing consists in their opposing objectives. In individual data processing the system is simply a willing and more-or-less intelligent 'slave' of the individual person. The user can do with it what he wants. He can input data in various forms, store it, and view it on demand. The user is self-sufficient, that is, he can solve his problems quickly and cheaply, independently of anyone else.

There are, however, complex applications which cannot be implemented in terms of a short dialogue between the user and the computer. These are mainly applications involving a number of people, primarily automated processes such as stock control, job processing and payrole management, which have to be planned and specified just as carefully as process data processing and programming, which must maximise their use of available resources.

Individual data processing programs are thrown away once they are obsolete. They are designed to be disposable from the start. Automated processes are different. They are maintained and developed over many years., Maintenance represents more than two-thirds of their costs. This leads to the emphasis on the systems' maintainability and extensibility, highlighting such characteristics as modularity, flexibility and ease of maintenance. It should not, therefore, be surprising that the development costs of such a system are many times higher than those of individual programs. It is in the nature of the beast. Management of corporate software development must therefore include, as a prime requisite, a typology of software systems in the company. On the one hand we have the classical division into:

- technical and scientific systems
- production control systems
- commercial systems.

We should note that these systems may overlap considerably. On the other hand we have the newer division into:

- individual, short-lived programs
- complex, long-lived systems.

Different methods and tools are necessary for each of these types of system. The dream of a uniform procedural model for all software development in a company is just as unattainable as the dream of a single model of society. This is the first lesson that a software manager must learn. He must also, like a good politician, be in a position to make compromises between, and even coordinate, conflicting interests and working practices. That is the true art of software management.

Software system types

The typology of software systems gives us three types of software system in all application areas:

- throw-away systems
- static systems
- evolutionary systems.

Throw-away systems

Throwaway systems are the result of individual data processing. In general, they are implemented by one person at the site of their application for one quite specific purpose. They are of only local importance and can be written inside six months are minimal costs. According to Gumaraes, their average lifetime is less than two years. They are neither maintained nor developed further. When they are obsolete, they are thrown away. Such systems can be likened to daily newspapers, which are of only transitory value.

Static systems

Static systems are integrated operational applications in a well-defined area of application. While they are of universal importance, they can be written within two years. After that they are maintained and developed to only a limited extent. Their annual rate of change is less than 10%; in other words, they are relatively static. Once developed, they remain in use until they become obsolete on technical grounds.

Evolutionary systems

Evolutionary systems are systems which come into being step by step through iterative repetitions of the software life cycle. Each passage through the life cycle expands the available system and makes it more complete, so that the development of such a system can last many years. The system will pass through several intermediate states or versions during its development. Applications for such systems are not sufficiently precisely defined and/or they are constantly changing, so that the development process is never completely finished. Maintenance and further development can hardly be distinguished from one another. The cost of the first version is of course only a fraction of the total cost of the system. It is therefore very important to plan and document these systems carefully.

The software life cycle

The 'software life cycle' is a central concept in software engineering. This encompasses the view of the software development as an iterative process or as a loop, in which each iteration builds on the results of the previous iteration. There is no final result, as the applications that the software represents are themselves always in a state of flux and the technical environment in which the software exists is also changing. A software system is therefore maintained as long as it is needed and is not obsolete. Software becomes obsolete to the extent that it can no longer be adapted to the changes in the application. Software systems are similar to biological systems in this respect. They arise out of a painful birth, require intensive care at the beginning, slowly mature, reach their state of maximum benefit after several years, become increasingly inflexible and difficult to suport, die, and leave behind experience from which grows a new generation of systems. This birds-eye view of software development is one of the most important prerequisites for successful software management. The project manager must always be aware that his project is only one iteration in a series and that his results are the starting point for the next project. Each software element should therefore be constructed such that it can be changed or extended at any time with minimal effects on other elements. For the purposes of project management it is worthwhile dividing the development of complex systems into three stages:

- primary development
- further development
- maintenance.

Initial development

Initial development is the first iteration of the software life cycle. It derive from a limited system, perhaps a prototype developed beforehand to serve as a model of the production system. On the other hand, the system might, first be formally specified by modelling the application which is to be automated. In any case, the system passes through several phases in which the operational requirement is translated into an executable and reliable product. Finally the product is introduced into the company according to the agreed delivery criteria.

Further development

Further development represents those iterations of the software life cycle which follow the operational introduction of the first version and where the system is extended and made more comprehensive. Static systems undergo no further development, only maintenance.

Evolutionary systems may however pass through numerous cycles of further development until the system is fully mature. Each passage through the phases of the life cycle gives rise to a new version of the software. Each version enhances and completes the previous version. The rate of change can be as high as 5% to 25% from one version to the next. This change entails the simultaneous updating of all the software elements, the specification and documentation as well as the programs and test suites. A software system quickly becomes obsolete if all its components are not compatible with each other. This step-by-step further development of a complex software system makes considerable demands on both the software developer and the software manager. Discipline and systematic ways of working are essential here.

Maintenance

Maintenance denotes keeping a system in a functioning form. This includes correcting faults and, in addition, adapting the software to changes in the technical environment. Changes in component systems, such as database systems, graphics terminals and operating systems must be catered for immediately. Critical errors must be corrected or avoided. Functional changes are only undertaken where previous performance has to be maintained. For this reason, the cost of maintenance is sporadic and so difficult to plan. It is therefore ad hoc in nature and should not be confused with the planned phases of further development.

Software development phases

A project is a passage through the software development cycle. In consequence, a software product is a version of a system, one stage in the automation of an area of application. As projects can take up to two years, they last too long to allow effective project control. Management, however, needs to be able to measure the progress of a project. In addition, many individual activities in a project must be structured, and to this end projects are divided into phases.

There are many different phase concepts, typified by those of the DoD, ACM, IEEE and IBM-FSD. Almost every company that produces software has its own phase concept with its own terminology for the phases. One of the best-known phase concepts in Germany is ADV-Orga's ORGWARE concept.

What almost all phase concepts have in common is that they differentiate between implementation and planning. Implementation involves producing the kernel of the software the programs themselves. Planning involves designing the system as a whole. A distinction is also usually drawn between application-oriented and technical planning. Application-oriented planning leads to an application concept, whereas technical planning leads to the technical DP concept. There is often a difference, too, between programming and testing in the implementation stages. Finally, there is a phase at the end of the project to allow for delivery and introduction of the new product. Hence we have the following five project phases:

- application specification
- system design
- programming
- testing
- delivery.

Application specification

In the application specification phase, the requirements of automating an application are established, analysed and assigned priorities. They then serve as a starting point for the rough specification using a function model and a data model. The external users' view and the internal data structures are drawn up from the data model, and program structure and decision logic are drawn up on the basis of the function model. Finally, all the data and function elements relevant to the application are catalogued. This phase should result in a comprehensive, formal, consistent and plausible concept for the application.

System design

During the design phase the application concept is translated into a technical DP concept for the particular target environment. This involves converting the logical data model into a physical database schema, the logical function model into a program outline and the user views into physical masks, reports and so on. A test environment is designed at the same time. In this phase developers use data description languages for the relevant database systems and use program specification languages to design the programs. The aim is to standardize the data structures and to ensure that the programs are modular and structured. This phase should result in a system design that is ready to be implemented.

Programming

In the programming phase the design elements are coded into a particular compiled programming language and/or a database language. This should bee the least problematical phase of all, as program coding has recently become highly automated. This phase should result in executable programs and accessible databases.

Testing

The first part of the test phase is to run the individual program modules in a test framework, checking their logical correctness. This involves testing each branch of a module, validating all results and confirming that all the parts of the module work together as they should. Here the programs are being checked against their specification. Next the databases are fed test data, terminal interfaces are simulated with test masks and the programs are tested in combination with one another and with the databases. Here the interfaces are being checked. Finally the programs are tested in this latter environment with actual users and under real production conditions. Here the system's interaction with the user and with the technical environment are being validated. This phase should result in a fully tested program system.

Delivery

In the last phase, the fully tested system, complete with the application's documentation, is handed over to the end user or installed at the end user's site. At this point the programs may be checked again to ensure that they conform to their guidelines and to the application documentation. This phase results in an automated or semi-automated application.

Aims of Software management

In a narrow definition, software management has two main aims:

- to increase software productivity
- to improve software quality.

In addition to these purely technical aims, the software should serve the following corporate financial aims:

- the automation of all corporate application
- machine storage of all corporate data.

These four aims are of course interconnected, and so it is not possible to pursue one aim without affecting the others. In the final analysis, everything is related to everything else.

Increasing software productivity

Software productivity is measured in units produced, be they statements, function points, components, data elements, decisions or a combination of these elements. What is important is quantifiability of productivity. Without being able to quantify productivity, we cannot measure it. Without being able to measure productivity, we cannot measure the extent to which we have achieved our aim. Software is, of course, a multidimensional product. Individual phase results — the application concept, the system design, the programs, the test environment, the user documentation are in one dimension. In the other dimension we have the measures of the phase results, such as the number of:

- objects, procedures, functions, data, decisions and relationships in the application concept
- databases, DC-interfaces, data records, data fields, processes, programs, modules and pseudo-code statements in the system design
- database descriptions (DBDs), maps, modules, branches, paths, arguments, results, predicates and statements in the programs
- test cases, test data, test procedures, test drivers and test stubs in the test environments
- pages of text and diagrams in the user documentation.

Improving software quality

Software quality is measured by a variety of characteristics, such as:

- reliability
- security
- efficiency
- user friendliness
- maintainability
- adaptability
- portability.

Here, too, we must quantify quality. For example, reliability can be measured by the relationship between the number of errors and the number of test cases, or maintainability by the relationship between the cost of maintenance and the cost of development. Quality is of course relative to the user's expectations. For some users, security is everything, while for others it is efficiency, and for yet others user friendliness is the most important factor. Quality characteristics must therefore be weighted according to the user's criteria.

Automating corporate applications

The degree to which corpoarte applications are automated is measured by the extent to which the firm's functions are supported by machines. I measure this of course implies that we need to know the firm's function Only then can we determine which of these function are automated.

Functions requireing physical energy should be carried out by robots and functions requiring mental energy should be carried out by programs. This means that the application is completely automated once no-one working in the pure application area.

Automating corporate data

Automation of corporate data is measured by the percentage of the firm' data which is stored on a machine and can be processed by machine. Her too we must of course know what data the firm needs. We can determine this from an analysis of corporate data, and at the same time we can establish which of these data items are stored on machines. Stored on machines mean that the data exists in a codified, machine readable form which programs can access without human interaction.

Software management tasks

With regard to the aims stated above, software management is responsible for a series of related tasks ranging from analysis of the firm's operation through to management of existing software systems. In particular, this includes:

- establishing and documenting corporate applications (both actual an target)
- establishing and documenting corporate information requirement (both actual and target)
- defining and costing DP projects to meet requirements
- planning and managing DP projects
- managing DP systems in operation
- advising users on the use of the DP systems on offer.

It should of course be borne in mind that, alongside these mainstream activities, software management has numerous peripheral activities such as looking after corporate users, advising corporate managers and extending the actual production environment. The introduction of modern software technology is in itself a far-reaching project which demands many resources without, bringing immediate benefits. Benefits are only gained in the medium term from the firm's own software production and improved quality. Nevertheless such support tasks are indispensable for the achievement of the main aims.

Establishing and documenting corporate applications

To achieve the aims of automating corporate applications, the software manager must know to what extent current applications are automated and to what extent they should be automated in the immediate future. He must therefore examine the firm's procedures and data flows, identify individual processes and determine the level of automation. This actual situation must be documented and at the same time a projected target situation must be modelled incorporating a higher degree of automation of existing applications. This should be done by using procedural analysis methods.

We should mention at this point that on-line data processing is only a temporary state of automation, a state of semi-automation. What many proclaim as progress, namely tying the user to a terminal screen, is for others a new form of salvery. The user is forced to react to the machine and to serve it as part of the on-line access to a system, be it a PC or a host.

Establishing and documenting corporate information requirements

An analysis of information requirements goes hand in hand with the analysis of corporate applications. here we have to establish which data is used from existing applications, how it is used and in what form it is stored. Once this is done, the next task is to establish future information requirements on the basis of the applications planned, i.e. how the corporate data is to be structured, stored and used. Here information analysis methods should be used. It ought to be obvious that total automation of a firm's operations presupposes machine capture of all corporate data.

Analysing corporate requirements

The demands made on data processing arise out of the difference between the actual and the target state of affairs, both in automating functions an storing data on machines. It is incumbent on the software manage measure this difference and to define various levels of automation. E level should be achievable within two years. In addition, the demands should be categorized by subject area. The demands can then be divided their respective subject areas and time units.

Evolutionary software implies hauling oneself up from subject are subject area and from level to level. Automation is therefore implemented in many small steps instead of in one large jump. The demands are dealt one after another.

This of course presupposes that all the data processing demands can precisely formulated, identified and recorded. That is the task of demand analysis.

Defining and costing DP projects

A DP project is a bundle of tasks having a time limit. The aim of the tasks to achieve a higher level of automation. A project may encompass on more demands. Defining a software project involves determining the scope of the target software system which is to be produced or altered. Software systems defined in terms of their quantity and quality. The quantity of a system i sum of all the affected elements in the system plus the sum of their relationships. The quality of a system is the product of its quality characteristics. Costing a software project involves calculating the expense and duration of a project. The quantity and quality factors are accompanied by productivity factor. To be able to cost the project, the software man must be able to establish the productivity of his software developers and to compare quantitative and qualitative demands with the time and cost constraints. The result is what is feasible for the project.

Planning and managing DP projects

Once a project has been evaluated and authorized, the software man has to plan and manage the implementation of the project. Planning a software project involves dividing it into phases and phases into tasks. At the same time the product is divided into p products and the partial products into individual resuls. Then a time-scale for the tasks must be drawn up and their interdependencies must be explicit. Finally, corporate resources must be allocated to the tasks.

Managing a software project involves monitoring deadlines and cost as well as progress and quality and, if necessary, making corrections or altering plans. Deadlines and costs can be derived from an acounting system. The project's progress can be measured form the number of tasks completed. Product quality can be determined with appropriate machine aids as well as from reviews and inspections. Planned deadlines, tasks, progress and quality are regularly compared with their actual counterparts to establish any variances from the plan.

Introducing and managing finished systems

Developing a complex DP system is one thing, introducing and managing it is another. Introducing the system entails allocation of necessary corporate resources, training users and often reorganizing the areas affected. It is obvious that this is not a painless operation. It is not only staff that have to be systematically prepared from a new system; the corporate organization must also be adapted, particularly as far as communication with neighbouring systems is concerned. This is a difficult corporate economic, sociological and technical task.

Once a new system is in use, the software manager has to maintain the software components of the system. To do this, he must use the techniques of configuration management. ALl the software components and documentation in use must be identified and recorded. The state and location of the software must be tracked and responsibility must be regulated. In addition, error reporting and changes must be kept up to date. The software manager is responsible for recording all reported errors and changes and for ensuring that they are included as new demands. This requires a certain software 'bureaucracy'.

Looking after software users

A final, but no less important, task of the software manager is to look after software users. As long as there are people who have to interact with systems, there will be problems with man-machine communication. It is therefore incumbent on the software manager to make staff available in a user support centre —who can advise and help users in carrying out their daily tasks. This is just as true for systems developed in house as for systems acquired from outside.

The support staff must, of course, themselves have been trained in the use of the new systems as well as in dealing with users. This support task is becoming more and more important as automation increases.

Software maintenance

System management entails planning, controlling and monitoring software maintenance. The question is, though, what is software maintenance, and what happens in the maintenance phase? The maintenance of software is fundamentally different from that of hardware. Hardware components wear out and thus no longer deliver their original level of performance. Defective hardware components have to be identified and replaced by new ones. It is therefore important to build hardware in a modular fashion so that worn-out components can easily be replaced. With software the situation is different. Software does not wear out. Many components do have defects built in from the beginning, but that is another story. Software does, however, age to the extent that it can no longer meet the demands of its environment. To understand that, we must first understand the nature of software. Software is a representation of a model of reality. Data records are representations of data objects, which in turn represent real-world entities. Programs are representations of processes, themselves representing actual events or business operations. If the operations or information requirements change in real life, the model must change too and software with it.

Obsolete software is therefore software that has not kept up with the physical environment.

This physical environment can be viewed in two ways. On the one hand, there is the technical or business application that the software is supposed to support. This may be a manufacturing process, stock control or a corporate information system. Changes in the application necessitate changes in the software, which may involve simply redesigning the VDU screen layout, bringing a new file on-line, or changing the decision logic. On the other hand, there is the software's DP environment. Every application is part of a particular DB-DC environment, running under a particular operating system, on a particular computer. There are usually numerous interfaces between the application and this environment. If the environment changes, e.g. the database system is enlarged or the method of data communications changes, the application software must be adapted to suit the new conditions. The software systems that the users develop are therefore sandwiched between two moving layers, the application above and the technical environment below. It has to be updated continuously to remain current.

Apart from the necessity of keeping software up-to-date, software differs from hardware in two other respects:

- defectiveness
- time and space efficiency.

Software defectiveness

In general, hardware is tested much better than software. The amount of testing carried out on normal applications programs is shockingly low. It has been shown that programs have around 1.5 errors per 100 lines; the programmer will recognize around 50% of them. That leaves approximately 0.75 errors per 100 lines still in the program. A 10 000 line program would therefore have 75 errors in it. Only some of these errors are discovered before the software goes into use. Many are spotted only once the software is in production, and the resulting costs are considerable. The localization and correction of such errors is termed maintenance.

Time and space efficiency

Newly installed software systems are not only unreliable, but in general they also gobble up resources, i.e. they use more time or space in carrying out their tasks than is actually necessary. Programs are seldom optimized before they are first released. This led Michael Jackson to formulate the motto, 'First structure, then optimize'. Optimization therefore comes under maintenance as well.

Looking at a software system that has been released clarifies the nature of software maintenance; it entails:

- corrective measures
- progressive measures.

Corrective software maintenance

- stabilizing (removing errors)
- optimizing (improving performance).

Progressive software maintenance

- making alterations
- expanding the system.

We can turn to much of the literature to support this definition:

- *Ogdin* describes maintenance as keeping the system up-to-date and modifying it: 'Maintenance is the continuing process of keeping the program running or improving its characteristics. Program modification has as its objective the adaptation to a changing environment.

Riggs defines maintenance as 'the activity associated with keeping operational computer systems continuously in tune with the requirements of users, data processing operations, associated clerical functions and external demands from governmental and other agencies'.

Mooney sees maintenance as the interdependence between the three activities 'repair, revisions and enhancements'.

Swanson divides maintenance into three categories:

(1) corrective — dealing with processing, performance or implementation

(2) adaptive responding to anticipated change

(3) perspective enhancing processing efficiency, performance or system maintainability.

Boehm distinguishes only between 'software update' and 'software repair'. In the first case, the demands change, in the second, they do not. Gilb defines the notion of' evolutionary software development'. The represents a software development strategy in which complex applications systems are developed step by step.

The first release of a system is seen simply as a prototype or test version which is designed to stimulate a dialogue with the user the so-called zero version. The first production system is released afterwards, this being the first version that the user can actually work with. This does not however mean that the user's requirements have all been met, for new requirements appear as the system is used more and more. The system is constantly expanded from version to version, from level to level, in an iterative and incremental way. Weaknesses are removed and new functions are added. The system slowly becomes more mature. This sort of evolutionary software development sees no difference between development and maintenance. We can however make the distinction between:

- stabilization
- optimization
- changing functions
- extending functions.

The term 'maintenance' is misleading.

The importance of maintenance depends greatly on the nature of the application. End-user programs written in a language such as SQL, APL, BASIC or NATURAL do not create any maintenance problems, as there is no maintenance they are throwaway programs. They are written quickly and cheaply to meet a momentary need. When the need changes, a new throwaway program is written. Throwaway programs have a maximum life expectancy of two years. The situation is different with integrated systems designed to automate organizational procedures. These systems have to be planned and developed in an engineering manner. If the application is well defined and relatively stable, there will be a development cycle and a maintenance cycle. During the development cycle the system is specified, programmed and tested. During the maintenance cycle, the original version is corrected and improved slightly.

Applications that are difficult to define or are very dynamic obey the laws of evolutionary software development, where the system is simultaneously maintained and developed. In this context, maintenance is equivalent to further development.

The attention that has been paid to maintainability therefore depends greatly upon the type of application:

- End-user systems are hardly maintained at all; they are replaced instead. Their maintainability is therefore irrelevant.
- Integrated applications developed over a period of up to two years and expected to last up to seven years will almost certainly have to be maintained, as they will change by up to 10% a year during their lifetime. These systems must be designed to be maintainable and extensible from the outset. This means that the programs must be as modular, as standardized, as structured and as parameterized as possible. It falls to software quality assurance to guarantee that this is the case. What is skimped in development will be paid for many times over in maintenance.

Evolutionary applications which take from two to five years to mature and last over seven years require a high level of maintainability, portability and extensibility. Quality assurance plays an even greater part here. If the system is not modular, flexible, portable and well-structured, it will never mature properly. We therefore need constant configuration management to keep an eye on any permanent changes. To a very large extent it is a picture of reality and so is subject to changes in reality. It is quite different from simple static systems and requires central control and ongoing quality assurance.

Categorizing software systems properly and then planning them accordingly is a management task with far-reaching consequences for life cycle costs. Anyone who tries to develop an evolutionary system with the methods and tools of throwaway systems will have to pay dearly later on.

Software configuration management

The term 'software configuration management' describes all the activities relating to the checking and maintenance of existing software systems. Until now, 'software development management' has been at the forefront of research, but increasing maintenance costs have meant that configuration management is becoming more and more important. Lientz and Swanson's latest surveys show that 53% of costs are devoted to maintenance, as against 47% to development; the maintenance of existing systems has become the largest factor in software costs. It has also become obvious that the management of software maintenance obeys laws different from those of software development. It therefore requires a different management technique, a method concentrating on maintenance. Configuration management has arisen in response to this need. We need to answer the following five key questions:

(1) Why configuration management?

(2) What is being managed?

(3) How is it being managed?

(4) With what is it being managed?

(5) Who should manage it?

The first question addresses the purpose of configuration management. Why has it become an indispensable part of software engineering?

The second question deals with the definition of software configuration. What is it that is being managed, what is the subject of configuration management? The third question relates to the method of system management. What activities does the new discipline entail?

The fourth question is devoted to the tools of configuration management. Which tools are needed, to manage software systems efficiently and cost-effectively? Finally, the last question is one of organization. What form of organization is best suited to managing existing software systems?

Purpose of configuration management

Configuration management is part of software engineering and, like much in that discipline, stems from the field of hardware production where it is used to identify and describe individual parts, as well as to monitor their assembly and maintenance.

In a conventional production process, project managment encompasses:

- planning
- organization
- management

- control.

Configuration management makes the control function operational. As such, its purpose is to make the production and maintenance of complex systems more transparent so that these systems do not get out of control. Configuration management plays a similar role in the field of software production. A software system, like a hardware system, consists of a large number of individual parts whose quality and quantity are critical to the functioning of the whole. The whole is only as good as its weakest part.

The number of elements is particularly high in software production. This is not only because software systems contain a large number of parts, but also because each element appears at least twice and sometimes three times:

- as executable code
- as a formal development document
- as an informal user document.

Configuration management has to ensure that all three incarnations are current and agree with each other. Every change in the code must filter through to the development and user documents.

This strict control is necessary to avoid the software becoming obsolete or breaking down prematurely. A software system can be compared to a biological system. It grows slowly, reaches a stage where it more or less works, increases its functionality and, sooner or later, reaches a point where it is no longer adaptable and starts to die. Any defect in its development causes it to age more quickly. The consistency of its parts can be guaranteed, and its functionality prolonged, only by disciplined and systematic working. This is extremely important in view of the enormous costs of software development. The purpose of configuration management is therefore to bestow the longest possible life on the software system. In contrast to system development, it is a discipline of preservation.

Subject of configuration management

The subject of configuration management is the software system. Until now, software has been understood to mean, more or less, the programs which contain the executable code. The software configuration, however, comprises two component types:

- non-executable
- executable.

What is executable and what is non-executable code has not yet been defined.

Pseudo-code that the processor can work with is also quasi-executable, and the same is true of test data assertions. The non-executable components must therefore be subdivided as follows:

- formal
- informal.

A function description written in English is an informal document. The same function in a design language is a formal document. 'Formal' denotes everything that can be processed by another program.

We should remember that software configuration deals with three component types:

- executable code
- formal documents
- informal documents.

These individual components can be grouped according to their level of abstraction, their usage, or their common objects.

As far as abstraction and usage are concerned, we have:

- a specification or technical concept
- a design or technological concept
- the programs themselves
- a test concept
- an integration concept.

The *specification* or *technical concept* includes all the formal and informal documents describing the system from the application view point, i.e. the data and function requirements.

The *design* or *technological concept* consists of all the formal and informal documents describing the implementation from the view point of the virtual machine, i.e. the data organization, program structures and interface designs. The *programs* are made up from the descriptive and executable code pieces, i.e. the data description and procedures.

The *test concept* includes all the documents formal and informal describing the test environment, the test data and the test procedures, along with the test data and results themselves. The *integration concept* contains all the documents necessary for the system's integration and introduction, including the user documentation and instructions for use.

This is the horizontal or phase-oriented view of software. There is also a vertical or function oriented view. For example, all the documents, program pieces and test data relating to a particular process can be brought together in one software group. The same is true of data objects.

Software components can be grouped in different ways, depending on the point of view. As far as configuration management is concerned, it is only important to identify clearly each component, each document, each section of code and each test data procedure and to be able to put them in order. This is the prerequisite for configuration management.

Methodology of configuration management

Any method of software configuration managment must take the software system life cycle concept as its starting point. This concept envisages the system passing through particular phases before it matures complctely. The system thus develops slowly in different stages of functionality. Each passage through the life cycle results in an executable, but incomplete system with additional functions and data objects. In principle, then, the system is never finished; it simply reaches higher levels of functionality. The system is only finished when it is not worth investing any more time or money in it. This process is also called evolutionary software development.

At each stage of development the development passes through the same phases. The phases themselves are still debated, but in general they are as follows:

- *definition phase,* where new requirements are evaluated and the scope of the next stage of expansion is laid down (planning)
- *specification phase,* where the new, extended, technical concept is worked out in detail (technical conceptualization)
- *design phase,* where the implementation concept, the database design and program designs are drawn up (DP conceptualization)
- *programming phase,* where the data descriptions and modules are coded(implementation)
- *testphase,* where the programs' static form and dynamic behaviour are examined (verification and validation)
- *integration phase,* where the components of the system are brought together and installed in their target environment (introduction)
- *maintenance phase,* where the latest stage of the system is stablized and optimized.

These or similar phases are a vital prerequisite for manageable software development. Configuration management *per se* cannot be used without them. Configuration management has the following four major functions:

- configuration identification
- configuration control
- configuration tracking
- configuration checking.

Configuration identification is the clear recognition and description of each software element. Every process and function including their associated modules and test procedures along with every data object and data element including their related data descriptions and test data— has to be identified and described. This requires a naming convention and a central catalogue, a project library in which to record these elements.

Configuration control is the process of accepting, recording, checking and authorizing all error reports and changes desired. This is where all software system requirements are dealt with. No changes may be made to the system without passing through this control process. This of course means that the necessary organizational and technical measures must be taken, such as setting up a change request committee and designing a suitable request form. To categorize requirements better, we can subdivide them into: corrections; changes; extensions.

Configuration tracking means that the effect of every correction, improvement, change, or extension to the existing system is measured to see what its impact on the software components is. Here we want to establish which software elements are affected, and by how much, and which new software elements are added. We must be able to trace all the ramifications of any change from the technical concept, via the DP concept, through to the actual code and to the user documentation. Every change leaves a long trail through the software configuration. Configuration tracking aims to find this trail and to follow it.

Configuration checking consists in checking whether the corrections, changes etc. carried out are reflected in all the parts of the system, i.e. in all the documents and code sections affected. A module must not be changed without the corresponding design, specification and test procedures being changed as well. The different software components must agree with each other at all times, otherwise the configuration becomes inconsistent. Configuration checking should ensure that code and design are maintained at the same time, for failure to do so can lead to the system's downfall.

Tools for configuration management

Appropriate tools are an important prerequisite for configuration management. These tools must be rather more powerful than traditional programmers' aids, for not only are programs being managed, but specification and design documents and test data and procedures are too. In addition, error reports and change requests should be automated as much as possible. A configuration management toolkit must therefore provide a whole series of different tools.

Configuration management is based on the project database or project library, where both formal and informal documents and programs are stored. Here we need rapid and accurate access to programs and documents, a friendly editor and some way of recording any changes made. At least six tools are necessary:

- a text editor for managing informal documents and user documentation
- a data dictionary system for managing programs
- a program library management system
- a test system for managing test data and test procedures
- a project management system for managing requests and error reports
- a revision system for comparing partial databases.

The *text editor* stores textual documents and allows them to be changed. It is important that the system records any changes so that they can be understood later.

The *data dictionary system* stores the elements and relationships in the specification and design. This system is different from the text editor in that the designs are stored as discrete elements with pre-defined attributes and relationships. The actual design documents are generated on demand. This system must also allow the user to change designs easily and to recognize what changes have been made.

The *program library system* stores macros,, source segments and object modules. Here too an editor is important for editing source code. Different program versions must be listed here to aid configuration management, and the differences between versions are marked and recorded. The *test system* stores the test data, test procedures, drivers and stubs. It must also provide a means of bringing the test environment up-to-date and recording any changes made to it.

The *project management system* stores error reports and tracks their status. This system must allow regular reporting, must enable the user to find out the status of requests, and allow the developer to change their status.

The *revision system* compares partial databases with each other so as to report any differences. This tool exists to ensure that the software configuration is consistent.

Organization of configuration management

The key to success in configuration management is finding the right form of organization even more so than in development. Responsibility for configuration manage-ment must be clearly distributed on the basis of expertise, and everyone must know what they should do when.

Configuration management demands an *authorization department for configuration control.* This may be a working group, a standing committee or one individual, but in any case the department must be able to decide whether, and in what order, to carry out:

- error corrections
- improvements
- changes desired.

This department therefore needs secretarial assistance to collect, record and store requests.

Next there should be a department which *checks the implementation of requests,* such as a quality control department. On no account should this be the project leader or the developer, however, as the point of the checking would then be lost.

Finally, the developers who maintain the software configuration, i.e. make corrections, changes and improvements, should be organized along the same lines as the configuration. Each subsystem should be allocated to a particular developer, and there should be a chief developer responsible for the system as a whole who coordinates the subsystems. It is important to adapt the maintenance organization to suit the software configuration, as this makes it easy to determine who is responsible for which errors, changes or extensions.

Configuration management is not fundamentally new. Similar procedures have existed for a long time in other fields. It is only new in the field of software because we could not define what software configuration was before now. Once we have done that, the other steps the procedures, the tools and the organization follow automatically. One thing is certain: the more software is developed, the more will have to be maintained. Too little attention has been paid to software maintenance for some time now. The task of configuration management is to rectify the situation.

Smart systems

The protocols used in a computer network are the mechanisms by which the hosts exchange information over physical distances. In the OSI model, the network layer is the primary layer for host-to-host communication. The network layer makes use of services from the link and physical layers; it also provides an end-to-end service to the transport layer. The network layer can utilise a number of physical networks to provide its services. The two services provided by the network layer are the connectionless services, and the connection-orientated service. This chapter begins by looking at the connection orientated service provided by the X.25 protocol. This protocol is important as it is being used on all public packet-switched networks operated by the PTTs. The X.25 protocol defines the necessary operation of layers one, two and three. Within any layer, a connection orientated protocol has two common tasks: error control and flow control. Error control is concerned with detecting, and correcting, errors that may have occurred in the information being transferred. Flow control is concerned with managing the resources of bandwidth and storage so that no single user can monopolise these resources, and the two endpoints are kept in step with each other. This is usually achieved by keeping the sending and receiving rates of information transfer approximately in step. The X.25 protocol covers the three lower layers of the protocol hierarchy. X.25 is defined as an access protocol, which means that it is used between a host and a node (in most X.25 networks the nodes are called 'exchanges') for the host to access the network so that communication between remote hosts is possible. The X.25 protocol has been adopted by the CCITT as a standard, which means that nearly all future networks will use it. The latest version of X.25 will be adopted by ISO as an international standard.

As well as describing the particulars of X.25, the principles of error and flow control will be shown and the mechanisms used to implement them in each layer explained. The description of level 2 is very detailed, as this is the first consequential level to be met in the bottom-up approach. The discussion of level 2 examines a number of problems which occur at many other protocol layers. For instance, the mechanisms used at level 3 for flow control and protocol synchronisation are very similar to those of level 2, so less detail is given in the level 3 explanation and references are made to the level 2 mechanisms.

In the X.25 parlance a host is called a DTE (Data Terminating Equipment) and a node is called a DCE (Data Communications Equipment). X.25 provides a standard mechanism for a DTE to access and use a DCE to transport data across a network to a remote DTE via its remote DCE.

X.25 level 1--the physical circuit level provides the physical communication by specifying the electrical signals, voltages, plug shape and pin assignment that the DTE needs to connect physically to the DCE. The DTE/DCE boundary is shown on the host side of the MODEM at the host site. This would be the normal arrangement, as the supplier of the network (usually the PTT) will provide the MODEM link to the node (DCE) from the user's premises. The actual specification of level I is contained in the CCITT X.21 recommendation. For practical purposes the user will order a computer interface to this standard which plugs straight into the computer at one end and into the MODEM at the other. The user will normally also be able to buy the software necessary to handle the interface.

As the level 1 hardware is bought as a ready-made unit, no further discussion of it is necessary. The important information needed about level 1 is the type of interface it presents to level 2, and the functions it must perform. The level 1 will provide transport for a bit stream from the DTE to a (remote) DCE. The level 2 will present the level 1 with the bits which are then delivered to a level 2 at the DCE. The hardware of level 1 will also indicate if the physical circuit is working correctly, that is whether the

MODEMs are switched on and able to exchange synchronised data. So the interface has two parts

1. the sending and receiving of a serial bit stream
2. the control signals indicating the status of the physical circuit.

X.25 level 2 -- link level

The purpose of level 2 is to control the physical link between the two ends of the level 1 circuit to provide a reliable transfer of information for level 3 between the DTE and DCE. X.25 level 2 uses a link control protocol based on the ISO HDLC (Higher Data Link Control) protocol. The advantages of using an existing protocol are greater than those to be gained from designing a new one. For instance, a new protocol would have to be adopted by a large number of people wishing to communicate; adoption of the protocol would then require a lot of effort. Other link protocols have been designed: IBM use one called SDLC (Synchronous Data Link Control) on their SNA network, which is not dissimilar to HDLC; DEC have their own as well.

Information is passed from level 2 to level 1 in blocks called 'frames'. The use of frames enables easier management of storage and error control. Each frame consists of some protocol information added by level 2, and possibly an information packet from level 3. 1 will use the convention of calling level 2 blocks frames and level 3 blocks *packets. The* functions performed by level 2 are

1. To establish the link connection to a level 2 at a remote site.
2. To transfer packets for level 3 securely, and in sequence.
3. To disconnect the link without loss of level 3 information.

To carry out these functions, the X. 25 level 2 uses three types of frame format. The uses of each format are shown in the next section, but first the fields in the frames are detailed

Flag field

This is a unique 8 bit pattern (01111110) which marks the beginning and end of each frame. The use of the flag as a delimiter presents a problem: to ensure that the end of the frame is correctly interpreted by the receiver, the flag pattern must not appear anywhere within the data in the frame. This means that the frame must be transparent to the hardware looking for a flag to mark the beginning or ending of a frame. The problem of transparency occurs in all link level protocols as they all use special bit patterns for synchronisation and for marking various parts of the frame. In X. 25 level 2 the flag is used as the level 1 synchronisation character. To ensure that the flag pattern does not occur within the frame, X.25 uses a technique called 'bit stuffing'. The bit stuffing technique involves the sender in inspecting the frame contents prior to transfer to level 1. Whenever a sequence of five Is occurs a 0 is inserted.

Notice that the 0 is inserted regardless of the value of the sixth bit. Bit stuffing in this way is easily implemented by hardware and only increases the length of the frame by 1 bit for every sequence of five Is. As the receiving hardware scans the incoming frame, a 0 following a sequence of five Is is removed. If the sequence of five Is is followed by a further 1, then the flag may have been found. The seventh bit is then inspected: if it is a 0 the flag has been found (01111110), whereas if the seventh bit is another 1 (01111111) then the frame is in error. Thus a sequence of seven Is is used to abort the frame.

There are other ways of providing transparency, such as using escape characters, or bit counts, but none is quite so efficient and flexible as bit stuffing.

Address field

This is really redundant in a point-to-point link. The intention in the HDLC protocol was to use this as an address for multipoint lincs, but the present X. 25 recommendation does not include multipoint lines. However, X.25 uses the field as an additional check in the protocol, as well as having the field ready should multipoint lines be considered in the future. The addresses used in this field allow commands and responses to be separated. The level 2 link can be thought of as two separate channels.

Channel A for transferring data from the network (DCE) to the host (DTE) and

Channel B for transferring data from the host (DTE) to the network (DCE).

Any frames relating to information flow from the DCE to the DTE carry the address A (11000000) including any frames from the DTE to the DCE relating to information transfer from the network to the host; similarly for channel B (10000000). To help separate the channels, frames are divided into two classes: *commands* and *responses,* Commands always flow in the direction of information on a channel; responses flow in the opposite direction. Responses are obviously the receiver's replies to various commands.

Command field

This 8 bit pattern determines the type of the frame, as well as being used for sequence numbering and acknowledgement. The command field has a different meaning for the three types of frame (information, supervisory, unnumbered). A 0 in bit 1 indicates that this is an information frame. An information frame is the only type that carries a level 3 packet in the information field. Bits 2, 3 and 4 contain the sequence number of this frame, bits 6, 7 and 8 contain the acknowledgement number. The sequence number and acknowledgement number are used in the ARQ techniques explained in chapter 6 for error correction and flow control. Level 2 uses a stop-go flow control. Bit 5 is the poll/final (P/F) bit. This is set in a command frame as a poll bit and the receiver will set the final bit in any response frame that is a reply to a command frame with the poll bit set. The use of the poll/final bit enables the sender of a command to recognise the corresponding response frame.

Bits 1 and 2 set to 10 indicate a supervisory frame. Bits 3 and 4 indicate which type of supervisory frame, Supervisory frames are not given sequence numbers as they do not contain any level 3 information, but they may be used to acknowledge information frames and so bits 6, 7 and 8 contain an acknowledgement number. Bit 5 is the poll/final bit which is the same as before. The command field format for the *unnumbered frame,* so called because it contains neither sequence number nor acknowledgement number. Bits 1 and 2 set to 11 indicate an unnumbered frame and bit 5 is the poll/final bit. The remainder of the bits are used to indicate the type of unnumbered frame.

Information field

This field only occurs in information frames; it is the position in the frame where the whole level 3 packet is placed. The other level 2 fields provide an envelope for the level 3 packet during the level 2 transfer.

Frame check sequence

The FCS field is found by counting 16 bits back from the terminating flag. This is a 16 bit field to contain the CRC remainder used in error checking. The remainder is calculated using the CCITT recommended generating polynomial of $X^{16} + X^{12} + X^5 + 1$.

It is interesting to note that all the fields of the X.25 level 2 header and the CRC are multiples of 8 bits. This makes transmission easier, because the 8 bit byte is the lowest common multiple of most modern computer word sizes, as well as being the character frame size for synchronous transfer. However the information field and the CRC may be increased by bit stuffing for level 1 transmission.

Operation of X.25 level 2

This section describes the semantics of level 2, with the various commands and responses being explained in context. The level 2 at the DTE (host) end of the connection performs the protocol functions with the level 2 at the DCE, using the HDLC protocol over the level 1 physical connection.

Establishing the link connection

An earlier specification of the X.25 protocol included a lever 2 initialisation procedure called LAP (Link Access Protocol) This procedure has been superseded by a simpler *balanced* procedure called LAPB. The LAPB method of initialisation sets up both channels simultaneously.

Data transfer

Level 2 should provide a sequenced, error-free transport of lever 3 packers from the

DTE to the DCE and vice versa. As only 3 bits are allowed for the sequence number and acknowledgement number in the C field, the maximum window size is 7. In X. 25 the link level window size is fixed when the subscriber first applies to use the network. The operation of the data transfer allows the use of limited buffers at the sender (no more than 7) and no requirement for extra buffers to handle out-of-sequence frames at the receiver. The cost of the small buffer requirement is extra channel capacity taken up with retransmission. The use of X.25 to connect hosts to networks would normally involve a fairly high-speed circuit between the DTE and DCE The limiting factor in performance is more likely to be the network and level 3, so a superefficient level 2 is not necessary; thus simpler techniques, such as Go-Back-N, can be used.

The transfer of sequenced frames of information is straightforward but what makes the operation complex (and this applies to every protocol) is the handling of exceptions and errors. There are two basic errors that can occur during data transfer.

1. The frame check sequence indicates an error in the packet.
2. The packet appears to contain no transmission errors but the contents of the A and C fields are not those expected.

In case 1 above the frame is thrown away and no further action is taken by the receiver. Obviously when a frame is discarded the next frame received is not the one expected. In case 2 there are a number of inconsistencies that can be classed as errors. The most common would be a sequence error where a previous packet had been lost or discarded. To ensure that the frame sequence is maintained at the receiver, any frame that does not contain a sequence number matching that of the next expected frame variable, V(R), is an error. If the sequence number of the error frame is within the window, the receiver returns an REJ response to indicate, in the N(R) field, the frame from which the sender should retransmit. If the frame sequence number is not within the window then the sequence numbers of the two ends have become unsynchronised. The only way to recover from a synchronisation problem is to reset the sender and receiver to a known state. The CMDR (command reject) frame initiates a reset which is completed by going through the link establishment exchange. After a reset, the two end-stations will be in a known, initial state. The reset procedure is used to recover from all errors other than the loss of an information frame. A reset may be caused by the receipt of a command or response that is not expected; for instance, a UA if the data transfer is in progress, or the setting of the P/F bit in a response when no command has been sent with that bit set.

The RNR (receiver not ready) frame tells the data sender that the receiver will ignore any further information frames (flow control stop). Once the receiver has returned an RNR response to an information frame, no more information frames are accepted, but the *N(R)* field in the header of any further information frames is inspected so that information frames in the opposite direction are properly acknowledged. The RNR response only stops information on one channel; the other channel is unaffected. When the receiver has more buffer space, an RR (receiver ready) frame is sent to inform the information sender on that channel that more information frames may be transmitted (flow control go), starting at *N(R)*. Note that both RNR and RR have acknowledgement numbers, *N(R)*. The RR frame has another use: if the receiving station does not have any information frames to be sent on the opposite channel, the acknowledgements cannot be piggybacked, and the RR frame is then used to acknowledge the information frames.

A receiver, especially a DCE (node), may not have enough buffers to take a full window for every level 2 link to which it is connected. Instead a statistical allocation could be used which assumes that not all links will be fully active at the same time and that the data is forwarded within a given time. When the network becomes busy this allocation means that a receiver may run out of buffers and need to use some technique to stop the flow of data from one or more links. Every frame, whether it is data or control, needs some buffer space for its receipt. If all the buffers are used up by one link then none of the other links will be able to continue transferring information. Also, if every buffer is allocated, there may be no more buffers to receive a control frame acknowledging a data frame and releasing buffer space! To avoid these problems, complex buffer allocation methods may be used. Normally, enough free buffers are always kept to receive at least one frame on each link so that control information can be exchanged even if data cannot. An information frame would be received, the control information used (for example *N(R)*), and then the frame discarded so that the buffer may be used again.

The loss of information frames as a result of buffer starvation means that information is lost not only because of errors in transmission, but also because of the internal operation of the nodes of a network, especially when the network becomes heavily loaded.

Link disconnection

The LAPB procedure for closing a link requires an exchange of a DISC command and a UA response. The poll/final bit is used to obtain synchronisation between the DCE and DTE.

X.25 level 3 -- the network level

The function of level 2 is to carry a level 3 packet across a link. The function of the network level is to carry a piece of information from one host (DTE) to another via intermediate network nodes. The transfer of the level 3 information will involve a number of level 2 links. The X. 25 specification only covers the link between the DTE and DCE, but we will assume a similar protocol is used between each node of the network as well. Each level 3 packet contains a certain amount of level 3 protocol information in a header, and possibly some user data (from the transport level). The major differences between levels 2 and 3 are the use of addresses and logical channel numbers. Most hosts will be connected to the network by one level 2 link. This link then has to be used to enable the host to communicate with several other hosts by multiplexing logical channels on to the one physical link. Level 3 is used to achieve this multiple connection via a single link. Using level 3 a host establishes a logical channel to another host by making a connection request using the full address of the remote host. When the connection is established it becomes a logical channel with a unique number, the logical channel number. The logical channel number is unique only for each link. Using the logical channel concept, packets for several calls may pass across the same level 2 link as they are all identified by the unique channel number. At the DCE the channel number is used to decide which route the packet will take. The logical channel is in fact a virtual circuit.

The network level has the same basic functions to perform as the link level.

1. Connection establishment.
2. Data transfer.
3. Connection disconnection.

The difference for the network level is that these functions are now carried out (apparently) between two hosts.

Packet format

The X.25 level 3 headers are used to contain a variety of information, so they are not of uniform size like the level 2 frame headers. The level 3 headers are different for every type of packet, which makes the format quite complex. The general format identifier (GFI) field indicates which format of level 3 header follows. The logical channel group number and logical channel number provide a 12 bit channel-numbering field. Splitting the field may allow subdivisions to be used for, say, different services. Call request and incoming call packets contain the address of the remote host (DTE). The addresses may contain fields indicating a particular process on a host as well as identifying a host. The address fields are of variable length, preceded by a byte count.

Connection establishment

To begin a call, a host uses the full address of the remote host in a call request packet sent from the DTE to the DCE. The DCE will respond with either a call accepted packet if the request was successful, or a clear indication packet if the call was refused.

At the remote host the DCE will send an incoming call packet to the host to indicate that a remote call has been requested. The DTE receiving an incoming call packet will inspect the header to decide if the call is to be established or not. If the call is accepted a call accept packet is sent to the DCE; if the call is rejected a clear request is sent to the DCE. The channel number chosen for a new outgoing call by the DTE is the lowest available number. The channel number for an incoming call is chosen by the DCE as the highest available number. If the DTE and DCE agree on the channel numbers, and the DCE will accept the call, all subsequent packets on that call will only use that channel number, not the full address. A call has been established to a remote DTE when a host receives a call accepted packet having the same channel number as the call request packet. The call is established at the remote DTE when the call accepted packet is sent to the remote DCE.

Information transfer

Level 3 transfers data to the network in a sequenced stream using Go-Back-N ARQ. The techniques of sequence numbers, piggybacked acknowledgements, RNR, RR and REJ responses are the same as for level 2, but they control the data flow across the network and into the remote host for each, independent logical channel. The use of windows and sequence numbers was for error control in level 2 as the level 1 link was prone to errors. At level 3 the level 2 link is assumed to be error free so. the emphasis is different. The windows and sequence numbers are now used primarily for end-to-end flow control. The receipt of acknowledgements allows more information into the network, while the window limits the number of data packets in flight at any one time. Complete suspension of the data flow can be achieved by using a level 3 RNR, but the flow can be partially adjusted by the rate of acknowledgement.

Interrupt

An extra mechanism is used at level 3 to handle what is known as *out-of-band* transmission. Normal user data on an X.25 virtual call is kept in strict sequence; this is called *in band* transmission. However, a user application often requires a special signal which is not subject to the normal flow control. Such a signal is the abort character which a terminal user would type to stop a runaway program. X.25 level 3 uses an interrupt packet to carry this out-of-band signal. The interrupt is not subject to the normal information flow control, the idea being that the interrupt could overtake information packets already in the network. The interrupt packet contains a field to indicate the cause of the interrupt; it is up to the application to decide what to do both with the interrupt and any subsequent data. When the DTE sends an interrupt packet the DCE responds with an interrupt confirmation.

Resets and restarts

In level 2 the reset was introduced as a mechanism for recovering from a protocol error where the two ends in the link became unsynchronised. The same thing can happen between the DTE and DCE at level 3, except that there are two areas where problems may occur.

The first problem is due to the information frames and sequence numbers becoming out of synchronisation on a single call. This may be detected by receiving a sequence number outside the window or an acknowledgement for a packet that was not sent. An error may also have been detected by a higher-level protocol, perhaps because of a network failure. In these cases only the one logical channel is affected so a *reset* is used. This sets the level 3 sequence numbers to 0 at the DTE and DCE. The reset will also be propagated to the remote DTE-DCE pair. The reset can be initiated from either the DTE or DCE and requires the usual request-confirmation exchange. A reset may cause the loss of any information packets within the network so a higher-level protocol will need to recover any lost data.

More drastic action is needed if the DTE and DCE become unsynchronised over global level 3 operation. An example is the choice of a channel number for a call request. If the DCE does not agree with the DTE over the chosen channel number (it should be the lowest free number) it means one of them thinks it has more logical calls opened than the other! The freeing of logical channel numbers correctly is the reason for the clear-request and clear-confirmation pair. When the whole level 3 needs resynchronisation a restart is initiated. This affects all the logical channels on the DTE-DCE link. A reset on the level 2 link is propagated as a restart at level 3.

Call disconnection

A DTE wishing to terminate a call issues a clear request packet, to which the DCE will respond with a clear confirmation packet when the call has been cleared in the DCE. This may involve waiting for the forwarding of any information packets still held there. When the clear confirmation is received the channel number is freed for further use. At the remote end the DCE wit send a clear indication packet indicating that the remote host has closed, and no more information packets will follow. The remote DTE will respond with a clear confirmation packet when all outstanding information packets have been acknowledged.

Data flow

The level 3 transport mechanism requires the data from the higher-level protocols to be broken into packets for transfer across the DTE-DCE interface. The X.25 recommendation specifies possible data lengths of 128 256, 512 and 1024 bytes, where 128 is the preferred maximum. It is probable that the PTT networks will guarantee 128 byte data packets. This means a user message must be broken into 128 byte sequences, the last one being perhaps less than 128 bytes. To enable the receiver to reassemble a message from multiple packets, level 3 uses a *more data bit* (M) in the information packet header to indicate that the current packet is not the last one of a message.

Just as the level 2 and level 3 need to include control information in the frames and packets as well as information from the next higher level, it is likely that a higher-level protocol would like to send control and data over level 3. The higher-level protocol may decide to add the control bits to the front of messages it passes to level 3. However, level 3 provides a mechanism that allows a higher-level protocol to multiplex data and control information on to the level 3 packet stream, thus maintaining the sequence of data and control across the network. This mechanism is the Q *bit.* The Q bit is set when the packet contains control information, and is clear when the packet contains data. Thus the higher-level protocol can quickly separate control and data information when receiving level 3 packets.

X.25 implementation

An advantage claimed for X.25 is that it only describes the host-to-node (DTE-to-DCE) interface. The network itself (internode) can use any convenient protocols, even completely different protocols, and the user would be unaware of them. In fact the proposed PTT networks are all planning to use X.25, or variations, within the networks for node-to-node transfer. The problem considered here is the implications of two methods of implementing an X.25 interface in a DCE that produce quite different results for the user. The discussion will show that even standards have complex problems of *meaning* (or semantics).

The two methods of implementation involve the mechanism for generating responses to various DTE packets at level 3. From the above description it can be seen that a command response sequence is used throughout level 3. The X.25 specification indicates quite clearly what responses are required, but leaves it up to the implementer to decide when, and under what criteria, the responses are made.

Consider the implementation that produces the DCE response as soon as the DTE's packet has been processed at the (local) DCE. This means the DCE's answer is sent to the DTE at the same time as the original request is forwarded across the network and well in advance of its arrival at the remote DTE. Such an implementation would give a very quick response to the user host. For instance, as data is passed to the DCE it is acknowledged immediately, even before it has crossed the network. The DCE-DTE flow control would ensure the DCE was not flooded with data, but large amounts could be in transit within the network before the call has been established at the remote end. This implementation would give the host the appearance of high throughput, as the DCE-DTE flow control would be the only restraint. If the DTE receives a level 3 acknowledgement for a data packet, does this mean that the remote DTE has received it, or only that the local DCE has? To be consistent in this implementation it would have to be the latter, so the DCE has taken on the responsibility for delivery of that data. A higher-level protocol would be needed, with its own flow control, to handle the host-to-host transfer.

This implementation has the effect, mentioned above, of apparently providing a fast throughput. A host may be able to open a call (to the local DCE), send data, and close the call, before the remote DTE has received any data. The network, however, will contain a large amount of unacknowledged packets as the DTE-DCE flow control will accept packets as fast as the DCE can forward them into the network. This makes end-to-end flow control in the network difficult and can quickly lead to congestion.

In the second implementation we only allow the DCE to respond to the DTE when the response from the remote DTE has been received by the local DCE. Data sent from the DTE is not acknowledged until the remote DTE has accepted the packet. This gives the host an impression of a long delay. In fact the delay is the round trip to the remote host, plus processing. This end-to-end use of the level 3 protocol reduces the amount of processing required from higher-level protocols. The sending DTE will only be able to have a window of packets outstanding which will represent the maximum number of data buffers which the whole network will need for the call. This makes the resource management within the network easier and is less likely to produce congestion. The cost is the lower performance seen by the user. Each packet takes longer to be acknowledged, thus reducing the throughput. There is also the problem of gaps which occurs when a window full of packets is sent rapidly, which is followed by a delay until the first acknowledgement comes back. This *bursty* mode of operation gives the network an uneven response and is difficult for both the host and DCE to manage.

The current X.25 recommendation allows a subscriber (DTE) to set a D bit in a data packet at level 3. This bit requires the acknowledgement to have end-to-end significance, as in the second example above. The D bit is an option, which means a network does not have to implement it.

The communications techniques covered so far have been concerned with centralised systems. Terminal networks are all built around a central computer; similarly remote job entry stations are usually connected to a single computer. In the remaining chapters some of the problems and techniques of a network of intercommunicating devices are discussed. The devices at present connected to networks are usually generalpurpose computers, with their own terminal networks. One reason for networking multiaccess computers, rather than terminals or smaller devices, is that these computer systems already existed when networking was proposed. A second reason is that the protocols used in computer networks are very complex so that only a large computer system would have sufficient spare computing power to implement them. However, terminals can be directly attached to a network, by using a dedicated computer. In the near future computer networks will become as widespread as the telephone network, and large scale integration will enable cheap processors to handle the protocols. The result will be the networking of every sort of computing device. The current trends indicate that powerful, single user, workstations will replace terminals for network use. The workstations will be directly connected to a local area network and use the resources of larger computers via the network.

This chapter is primarily concerned with the technology used to connect the computers and devices that make up a computer network. For the purposes of description the range of technology has been divided into three areas

1. wide area networks
2. Radio and satellite broadcast networks
3. Local networks

The network technology includes the techniques used to interconnect the computing devices and physically transfer information from one computing device to another.

Wide area networks

The term 'wide area network' is applied to a network that covers a large physical area, say a whole country or large area under one administration. Such an area may be worldwide where a multinational organisation owns the network. The basic communication media used are dedicated circuits, usually of about 50 kHz bandwidth. Where digital circuits are available the bandwidth would be 64K bps. The recent introduction of fibre optics in longdistance trunks has make link bandwidth of 2-3M bps available. Wide area networks will be using these links over the next few years. Examples of such networks are PSS, ARPANET, Tymnet, Telenet, etc.; details of some of these networks are given at the end of this section. The physical circuits are usually provided by a PTT, although in the case of PSS the whole network is also run by the PTT.

Although 50 kHz bandwidth seems to be a lot compared with the 3 kHz nominal bandwidth of the voice telephone line, it is not very much when highspeed or large-volume transfers of information are required. Even at these high speeds the channel capacity is a resource that needs to be used efficiently.

It is now necessary to see how information can be transferred from one computer to any other on the network. The problem falls into two parts. The first is that of transferring information via a medium, such as a wire. The second part is concerned with addressing and routing. If there were only two computers on a network, then they could be connected by two channels, one for each direction, and whatever one computer transmitted the other would be bound to receive. When more computers are added, the bidirectional connection solution can be extended by having each computer connected to every other computer by a full duplex connection. To send a message to a particular computer the appropriate connection is selected; thus the routing of a message is carried out by the sender. Using a dedicated connection between every computer on the network is very expensive. If there are n computers on the network then $n(n-1)/2$ lines are needed, and have to be paid for! As a single computer would not normally be communicating with every other computer on the network at the same time, most of the lines would be unused in a fully connected network. Therefore to increase the utilisation of the connection circuits, their number is reduced, and switching is introduced within the network.

There are three forms of switching that can be used in communications: circuit switching, message switching, and packet switching.

Circuit switching

Circuit switching is used on the PSTN to connect telephone subscribers. To use it for a computer network each computer would have a private circuit to a local exchange, and the exchanges would be connected to form a network.

Whenever two computers wish to exchange information, a physical path is established between them via the exchanges. The path is then disconnected when the connection is closed. The circuit has been switched by the exchanges. This method of connection is not used on established computer networks. The major disadvantages of circuit switching are

1. The cost of the equipment is very high, whereas the resulting circuit is not necessarily of high enough quality for computer communications.
2. The resulting circuit can only be used by the two computers on the call, thus the equipment is dedicated to the circuit. In particular the connection from the computer to the exchange is dedicated. To enable a single computer to communicate with more than one other computer at the same time, extra equipment is needed for each simultaneous call. If there are no connections all the equipment is idle but being paid for.
3. The time taken to set up the physical path can be very long in computer terms.

As high-speed connection using good-quality circuits is important for efficient computer networks, circuit switching is discounted in favour of the other methods. Circuit switching is used for some networks connecting computers-for instance, the Nordic Data Network.

Circuit switching has two advantages

1. Charges are made only for the time that a call is connected. If infrequent and short connections are all that is required, then circuit switching may be advantageous to the customer. It is expected that many slower devices, such as terminals, will be connected to national computer networks via the PSTN to gain this advantage.
2. Where a single device is used for long periods, such as a facsimile machine, circuit switching is economically advantageous. This is particularly true where digital facilities, such as X.21, are available.

The above discussion is based on the existing PSTN services offered by the PTTs. When the ISDN service is widely available, then it will be an attractive mechanism for some computer networks. Each host will be able to set up calls, use the 64K bps bandwidth, and quickly close the call, as required. The circuits will still carry packets for the end-to-end data transfer; but circuit switching will be the main link-switching mechanism. In the UK it is intended to bring all the PTT communications together into Integrated Digital Access (IDA). This will combine ISDN, X.25 networking and special digital services into a common access interface.

Message switching

To overcome problems in setting up and taking down physical circuits via exchanges, computer networks use permanent circuits and switch the data, A partially connected network is used in which each computer has a permanent circuit to a number of its neighbours, but not to all computers on the network. An example will illustrate the basic operation of *information switching* where the unit of information is a message.

If the computer at A wishes to send a message to B, the message must pass through either D or C. The points on the network are called *nodes. A will* address the message to B by placing the address of B in the message header. The message and address are then sent on the circuit to D. At D the node inspects the address; if the address is 'D' the message is given to the computer; if the address is not D the message is forwarded on a circuit that the node believes will enable the message to be delivered, In this case D will forward the message to B. Thus the node at D has switched the message on to the appropriate output circuit. In this example two major characteristics of a computer network can be seen.

Addressing

The message is addressed to a remote destination and sent on the next stage of its route.

Store and Forward

Each message is received into the node storage so that it can be processed as a whole unit. Usually an error check is carried out and the whole message has to be received before this can be completed. The message is then inspected for routing information so that the node can decide which output circuit to use to forward the message.

The nodes have been introduced in the network to carry out the functions of routing and store and forward, so the host computer is separated from the network operation as much as possible. The 'hosts' are the user computers which wish to use the network. Often a number of hosts will be attached to a single node.

The node computers are usually minicomputers chosen for their ability to respond in real time to the communications devices. Each node receives incoming messages and stores them. When a complete message has been received the destination address is inspected so that the message can be placed on the output queue of a circuit to forward the message. If the message is for a host attached to the node, the output circuit will be the one connected to the host. If the message is for a distant host the node must forward the message to another node on the route to the distant host. While the message is in the node store, waiting to be processed or waiting for output, it is, of course, being delayed.

The link into any one node may be used to carry messages from several different computers, as may the connection between the node and host. The physical equipment involved is used more efficiently than in circuit switching as a result of this multiplexing. Message multiplexing is the most important advantage of message and packet switching computer networks.

To distinguish between message and packet switching it is necessary to understand what a message is. This has already been introduced in earlier chapters, but a more detailed discussion is given here. The easiest way of defining a message is to say that it is a unit of information which is exchanged by users of a network. This means the characteristics of a message are only dependent on the user or the application. A message could be a few bits or a file, or even a whole database. In a message-switching network the whole message is passed from one node to another as a complete entity. Compared with circuit switching, a message-switching network has the following characteristics.

1. Any computer can communicate with any other computer without having a direct physical connection.
2. Any computer can communicate with several others using the same equipment by multiplexing messages.
3. There is no delay arising from circuit set up, but messages are delayed when they pass through a node *enroute*.

The messages can be transferred between nodes, and nodes and hosts, using an *ARQ* protocol.

Characteristic 3 implies that there is no delay arising from the use of a network other than the store and forward operation of the nodes. This is true in some networks using pure datagram techniques. However, in most networks the internode protocol used within the network introduces some delays. Any network using a virtual circuit protocol, at any level, will introduce a delay when the message or packet is given to the network. In many networks the local node negotiates for resources within the network before actually forwarding a message. This is true of an X.25 network when the call is first set up, and is true of every message on the ARPA network. A user of a message-switching network will pass the network a message, together with a destination address, and the user will receive messages as single units.

Advantages and disadvantages

The advantages of message switching, over circuit switching are

- The sender may dispatch the message when convenient, even if the receiver is not ready, as the network will store the message for delivery, However, if network resources run out, an undelivered message may be deleted and thus lost; this depends on the network protocols.
- Computers can exchange information at different speeds, as the network will buffer the message.
- Broadcasting of a message may be possible.
- Equipment is used more efficiently.
- Messages may be handled by priority.

Each message is treated as a single unit. However, there are also some disadvantages.

- A very long message will hold up other, perhaps more urgent, messages as it monopolises a circuit for the duration of its transmission.
- As a message may be very large, the node computer may not have enough memory to store it before forwarding it; in this case the message is lost. Further, this message will never be delivered as the network does not have the required resources.
- A very large message may monopolise the storage of a node, because it cannot be delivered, so that other messages cannot be received by this node.

Packet switching

The disadvantages of message switching relate to the possible occurrence of *large* messages, where the exact value of 'large' will depend on the network. If a network could be certain of only handling small messages, the disadvantages would disappear. The transfer of messages is a user requirement, so a network that meets user needs must be able to handle very large messages as well as small messages. The solution to these two conflicting requirements is to break the user's message into small *packets* for transfer through the network and have the packets reassembled into the message by the receiver. Note that the message header is included as the data in the first packet and that each packet has its own header. This refinement produces packet switching, which is the most widely used switching technique for computer networks.

The physical organisation of a packet-switching network is the same as for message switching. The network is a partially connected mesh of nodes. For practical reasons most wide area networks use special node computers to perform the switching, with the user computers being attached to the nodes. The term 'host' is now widely used to mean a user computer system attached to a network. The nodes are part of the network, so the hosts use a well-defined interface for accessing the node to enable data transfer across the network. By using a node separated from the host, all of the packet-switching functions, such as storage and routing, are removed from the host. However, the host still needs considerable software to handle the protocols used to access the node and to transfer data to other computers on the network.

The advantages that packet switching has over message switching are

- The small maximum packet size makes storage allocation and management easier in the switching nodes, sufficiently so for minicomputers to be used.
- The multiplexing of packets enables several messages to be interleaved on one circuit, reducing the delay seen by the user.
- The total transmission time through the network is reduced. It shows a message passing from A to B which would normally require 6k + d seconds to reach B, where 3k is the transmission time of the whole message on one link and d is the node delay. If the message is broken into three packets, each taking k seconds to transmit, the whole message arrives at B in 4k + d seconds. The difference increases with the number of links traversed and the size of the message.

It would appear that packet switching solves all the problems of wide area network organisation: it uses fixed highspeed lines and minicomputers for nodes; it is also more efficient and responsive than message switching. However, although packet switching is a better technique with which to implement a computer network, users still want to transfer messages. Packet switching introduces another layer of complexity and translation between the user and the physical network transporting the bits. Fortunately, the cost of processing is falling so the extra cost is outweighed by the practical advantages. A second cost, not so easily overcome, is that each packet will have its own overheads as well as those used by each message; this will reduce the efficiency of the physical circuits.

The conclusion drawn from consideration of these three switching techniques is that packet switching, especially used in a partially connected mesh of nodes with wideband circuits, is currently the best technique for wide area computer networks. Packet switching is also used in other network technologies, rather than message switching, for the same reasons.

Wide area networks have been in existence since the early 1970s. The best known example is the ARPA network in the United States. This network was established by a government research agency to link together computer centres that had contracts for government research so that research workers could share the available computing resources. The network itself also forms part of a research project to evaluate the feasibility of a large computer network, and to investigate techniques that could be used in such a network. The ARPA network has been very successful in showing that the concept of resource sharing by use of a network is feasible. One of the most noticeable advantages that the network has introduced is a mail facility. This allows each user with access to a computer on the network to exchange mail with all the other network users. The mail facility is probably one of the main sources of traffic on the ARPA network and has certainly improved the amount of communication between researchers at different sites.

The basic techniques used within the ARPA network have been influenced by the defence aspects of the research, particularly the need for a fast response and resilience to the failure of any part. The network consists of a mesh of partially connected nodes called Interface Message Processors (IMPs). Each IMP can have up to eight hosts connected to it and may be connected to up to eight other IMPs. Each IMP accepts messages from the hosts of up to 8K bits in length. The IMP breaks the message into IK bit packets which are then forwarded through the network of IMPs to the IMP attached to the destination host. This destination IMP reassembles the message before delivering it to the destination host. If a host wishes to send a message of more than 8K bits it must break the message up itself, into 8K packets, and the destination host must reassemble the message from the 8K packets. Thus the translation between messages and packets takes place at two levels. Within the network of IMPs, packets (1K) are sent individually along whichever route is best at the time, so that packets in a single message may use different routes and may arrive at the destination IMP out of sequence. The destination IMP has to reassemble the message from the packets as they arrive. However, messages passed from the host to the IMP are delivered in the same sequence to the destination host. The technology developed for the ARPANET is now used in a number of commercial wide area networks all over the world.

The British Telecom network PSS (Packet Switching Stream) is an example of a network provided by a PTT as a public service. The design requirements for such a network are different from those of the ARPA network so they have resulted in a network with different characteristics. The network topology consists of a number of *exchanges* which are also partially connected. Each exchange is connected to a number of host computers in its area. The exchanges contain the node computers, the number of node computers in each exchange depending on the number of hosts attached to the exchange. The hosts use an access protocol called X.25 to enable them to make virtual calls to other hosts. A host will give the local exchange the destination address of the host with which it wishes to communicate. The network will route the call to the destination exchange which will then complete the call to the destination host. The call is represented by information kept at all the exchanges on the route. The information is then used to forward the packets transferred on the call. Once the call has been established the hosts may exchange their own information. This is very similar to circuit switching on the PSTN although it is provided using packet-switching techniques. The PSS network techniques are different from those on the ARPA network, where each message is addressed and transferred separately. The hosts can use a single link to the PSS exchange to carry a number of virtual calls to other hosts, thus the link is used to multiplex the calls.

Radio and satellite broadcast networks

These networks differ from wide area networks in the way in which the channel is used for communication between users. Broadcast networks use a channel to which all the users are connected, so all the users receive any transmission made on the channel. At present the two types of channel in use are local radio, covering up to a few hundred kilometres, and satellite channels which are used to span very large distances.

Networks using radio and satellite channels have special problems because noise in the channel can cause errors. There is also the problem of allocating the channel for transmission. The first operational broadcast computer network was built at the University of Hawaii using local radio transmission; many of the techniques and much of the terminology derive from this first network.

Every node receives all packets transmitted on the broadcast channel. When the received packet is complete, the node checks the packet for errors and then checks the destination address. If the address of the receiver matches the packet destination address, it is accepted; otherwise it is discarded. The problems particular to a broadcast network occur in the allocation of the channel to a node for transmitting a packet. Different solutions are used for radio and satellite links. Each node is only able to communicate with each other node via the common channel, so some scheme is needed to coordinate transmission. The schemes that have been proposed and used are discussed here in increasing complexity and are compared for channel efficiency.

The simplest transmission technique is called *pure aloha;* when a node has a packet to transmit it does so immediately. Having transmitted the packet, the node waits for an acknowledgement. This is therefore a positive acknowledgement protocol. If an acknowled-gement is not received within a time out period, the packet is assumed lost. Transmission collisions, which occur when two nodes transmit at the same time and thus interfere with each other's transmission, are detected by the time out mechanism. When a collision is detected, each node waits a period of time of random length before retransmitting the packet to of traffic increases, the rate of collision will increase and more re-transmissions will be needed. As the older packets are re-transmitted, more stations will have newer packets to transmit, causing more collisions, etc. Analysis has shown that a pure aloha scheme can only use a maximum of about 18% of the channel bandwidth. A node may transmit at any time, thus the maximum length of time the channel is wasted as a result of a collision is 2t, where t is the transmission time for one packet. The 2t period is the worst case, where one node begins transmitting just before the previous transmission is complete.

An improvement on pure aloha is *slotted aloha* in which the transmission channel time is divided into time slots of *t*. Each node is then only allowed to begin transmitting a packet at the start of a time slot. The nodes are kept in synchronisation by a time signal on the channel. Now if a collision occurs only one slot *is* wasted, so the maximum efficiency rises to about 34% of the channel capacity. When a collision is detected, a transmitter must wait for a random number of time slots before retransmitting. When the traffic is light the wait can be quite short, but as the traffic load increases the waiting period should be increased.

From the aloha schemes it can be seen that it is collisions that cause problems, so a collision avoidance mechanism should improve efficiency. In packet radio networks a scheme known as Carrier Sense Multiple Access (CSMA) is used. When a node is transmitting all other nodes can receive the transmission, so they can avoid a collision by not transmitting themselves until the channel is free. A transmission is detected by the presence of the carrier signal in the medium. When a node has a packet to transmit it looks for the carrier; if there is no carrier the packet is transmitted. If the carrier is detected the node waits for a random length delay and tries again.

Even in a radio broadcast the signal from a transmitter takes a finite amount of time to reach all the receivers in the network. When two nodes find the channel free, they may both begin transmission because neither has heard the other one. This case is most likely to happen when two stations are waiting for the channel to become free. The length of time it takes to propagate the signal to all receivers is the time band in which collisions may occur, but it is less than the total packet transmission time. As with the aloha technique, the CSMA technique can be improved by dividing the channel time into slots and only allowing the transmission of packets to begin at the start of a time slot. The slot length is set to the propagation delay, not the packet transmission time.

The CSMA technique has been further refined by modifying the action of the node when the channel is busy. When the node samples the channel again and finds it free, it transmits its packet with a probability p, or waits for a further delay of random length, with a probability (1-p). This is called persistent CSMA or p-persistent transmission. If p is high then the delay before transmission occurs is lower, but the possibility of collision increases if two stations are waiting for another station to finish. In persistent CSMA a trade off is made between channel efficiency and delay with the value of p. Channel efficiencies of about 80% may be achieved using these techniques.

Packet radio networks have a small delay between the start of a transmission and the detection of the transmission by all stations on the network. On a satellite broadcast network there is a very long delay between transmission and receiving, of the order of a quarter of a second. A satellite network operates by each transmitter sending its signal to the satellite. The satellite then broadcasts the signal to all of the Earth stations, which may be spread over a very large area. One satellite system currently used for packet switching connects nodes in England, Norway and North America using a satellite in stationary orbit over the North Atlantic. A different channel allocation technique is used on satellite broadcast networks because of the long propagation delay.

This satellite channel allocation technique involves making reservations for the future use of slots in the channel. The channel is divided into frames consisting of a number of reservation slots and a number of packet slots. Each reservation slot represents a packet slot in the second part of the frame. All ground stations are synchronised to the frame timing by the satellite transmission. During the first part of the frame the ground stations reserve slots for the packets they have ready by transmitting a marker during the reservation slot time. When the reservation slot is heard on the satellite down channel, the ground station inspects the slot to see if it contains its own marker. If so it can transmit a packet in the corresponding packet slot in the second part of the frame. This scheme uses some of the channel capacity to avoid the collisions which could reduce the network to a pure aloha scheme.

Obviously more than one ground station may attempt to reserve a particular packet slot by transmitting during the reservation slot time. There are a number of algorithms to overcome this, including allocating some slots to busy stations. Thus if a station successfully obtained a packet slot in the last frame, the same slot is allocated to that station in the next frame without competition. If an allocated slot is not used then the slot is open for competition in the following frame. Usually there are some slots that all stations can compete for in every frame. Another mechanism involves using a central allocation station to which each station sends its requirements and the central station allocates the slots. This has two disadvantages: firstly, the central station becomes a weakness in the network reliability, and secondly, the delay between requesting an allocation and receiving the allocation may be of the order of 1 or 2 seconds before the packet can be transmitted. A chapter in the book by Kuo is dedicated to broadcast satellite protocols.

Local area networks

A local, or private, network is a communication system connecting computers in a small geographical area, say less than a few kilometres between the furthest points. The network is wholly owned and run by one administration. There are currently two basic types of technology used on such a network: these are cable, or bus, technology and ring technology.

Whereas wide area networks and satellite networks use nodes to separate the internal network switching from the user hosts, local networks are meant to be as cheap as possible and so the separate node computer is omitted. In both local network technologies all the computers are directly attached to the transmission medium by a special interface, and all the interfaces receive all the packets. The difference between a ring and a bus system is the way in which the channel is allocated. Local networks are designed for use in local computing by allowing the interconnection of very small computers, such as microprocessors, personal workstations and peripheral devices. If the local network is to be useful, the cost of the computer interfaces into the network channel has to be low compared with the cost of the computer or peripheral, and microprocessors are very cheap in computer terms. A widely forecast use of local networks is connecting word processors within a set of offices for the exchange of information and electronic mail. The cost constraints, the limited processing power of the small computers and the protocols used on a local network are different from those used in wide area networks. A local network usually has a very high bandwidth channel of between I and 10 MHz and a very low error rate say one bit in several million might be corrupted. These characteristics permit the use of simple protocols. The lowest level protocol for using the transmission medium is built into the computer interface.

Cable or bus networks

These networks usually use a length of coaxial cable, or an existing cable such as that used for closed circuit television (CCTV). The medium is used in a broadcast fashion, exactly as described in the previous section on broadcast networks. The channel allocation techniques vary slightly on the theme of the CSMA techniques, or on a centralised slot allocation. The most popular broadcast local network is the Ethernet system developed by Xerox. The Ethernet principles can be used on any broadcast medium: radio, telephone lines, coaxial cable and optical fibres have all been used successfully. The Ethernet uses a base band signal, rather than a modulated signal, to simplify the broadcast transmitter and receiver, with a modified CSMA channel access technique. To obtain the maximum efficiency from the broadcast medium an Ethernet transmitter can listen to its own broadcast to detect a collision and abort the transmission. This extra complexity is known as CSMACD (CD = collision detection) or listen-while-talk. As with the other CSMA techniques a station does not begin transmitting until the broadcast medium is free. Two stations waiting for another station to finish a transmission will begin transmitting together, and thus interfere with each other. The collision is detected by the stations and they both abort the transmission immediately. To enforce the protocol a station that aborts a transfer then jams the ether. After a collision each station waits for a random time before trying again.

The CSMA-CD technique enables the Ethernet system to obtain up to 95% of the broadcast channel bandwidth. The improvement in performance over ordinary CSMA is due to the stopping of transmission as soon as a collision is detected. Note that no slots are used so a network-wide timing signal is not required. The transceiver handles all of the CSMACD access, including the retries and delay calculation which is varied with the traffic load. Thus only complete, and checked, packets are passed up to the station interface and only one request is made for a packet to be sent. The checksum generation and checking are carried out within the hardware: bad packets are discarded. A time out mechanism is used to retransmit packets that may have been lost as a result of errors.

Ring networks

The ring technique originated in the USA. The idea was then developed in parallel at Cambridge University in the UK and at two research centres in the USA. The version developed at Cambridge is known as the Cambridge ring in the UK. The computer interface is divided into two parts: the repeater and the interface proper. A ring uses a twisted pair of wires as the transmission medium. However, to improve reliability, the repeater is powered from the ring and electrically isolated from the computer interface, so four wires are used to connect the repeaters. The four wires are used as two pairs for signalling and carry sufficient power for the repeaters. In this way the computer can be switched off and removed from the ring without switching off the repeater. With the ring the medium is terminated at each station, whereas in the cable network it is not. Each station is represented by a repeater, several of which are then connected together into a ring. The repeater is a simple device containing a shift register and some logic to detect certain conditions in the information being passed around the ring. The repeater normally passes any information received on to the next repeater, so transmission only occurs in one direction. When a station transmits data, the repeater transmits the information from the station instead of the information received from the previous repeater.

Slotted ring

There are slight differences in the channel allocation mechanism used in the Cambridge ring and in those rings developed in the USA. In the Cambridge ring a fixed size mini-packet is used which constantly circulates in the ring, and a special station called a monitor is used to generate and maintain the mini-packet and provide the power for the repeaters. In the American versions a variable-size packet is used which may be lost and regenerated as required by each repeater. The current format of the Cambridge mini-packet. Note that only 16 bits of information are carried in a ring mini-packet whereas the broadcast network packet may contain several hundred bytes. The assembly of information into a block has to be done by the computer. The monitor station also provides a buffer if the ring is not physically long enough to hold a complete mini-packet. The monitor performs a check on the mini-packet each time it passes to ensure that it is intact, and to replace it if not. The monitor is an obvious weakness in the Cambridge ring design so far as reliability is concerned; however, experience so far has shown that monitor failures are rare. The advantage of the monitor is that the repeaters can be very simple as well as cheap, which is the purpose of a local network.

To use the ring to send a packet of information, the station will wait until an empty mini-packet is detected by the repeater. When the full/empty bit in the mini-packet passes the repeater it is set to one. If the packet was already full no change has been made to the bit; if the packet was empty (full/empty bit = 0) the mini-packet is now reserved by this station, The repeater will use this mini-packet if the full/empty bit was received as 0. The addresses of the source and destination stations are placed in the address fields followed by the next 16 bits of the information that the station wishes to send; these are placed in the data field from the station buffer. The reserved mini-packet then travels round to all the other stations on the ring. Each station has a source select register in which an address is placed. If the source address in a mini-packet matches the contents of the source select register, and the destination address matches the station address, the data field is copied into the station receive buffer and the accept status is set at the end of the packet. If the packet is refused, or the destination station is busy, the destination repeater will set the appropriate value in the status bits at the end of the mini-packet. No other change is made by the receiving repeater, and all other repeaters will pass on the mini-packet unchanged. Special values which can be used in the source select register are: all ones, which means accept any source station address, and all zeros, which means do not accept the data from any mini-packets.

When the mini-packet returns to the sending station the full/empty bit is reset to 0 and the status bits are checked to see if the information was accepted. As an error check, the station also reads back the 16 data bits and checks them against the data in its buffer. Having reset the full/empty bit, the station must now wait for another empty mini-packet before it can send the next 16 bits of information. In this way the now empty packet becomes available to successive stations around the ring and the packet slot is allocated in a round robin fashion.

The variable nature of packet traffic in a local network makes it difficult to design a system that will provide a very fast response, especially when there is little traffic, and yet not become overloaded or unfair when the traffic becomes heavy. The broadcast techniques provide a low delay, especially in low-volume traffic, as the transmitter can usually send a packet as soon as one is available. However, as the volume of traffic increases, the broadcast system suffers from collisions and longer delays which can eventually lead to an unstable situation. In the slotted ring the channel is allocated by means of a round robin mechanism so collisions never occur, and during a burst of traffic each station is able to continue transmitting with only a larger delay. During periods of low traffic volume the ring does introduce a delay while a station waits for the empty packet to come round.

Proponents of both systems argue that because of the very high bandwidth available on the channel, and the low processing power of the computers attached to the local network, the volume of traffic is nearly always low in a broadcast network and the delay is negligible in a ring.

Token Ring

The token ring attempts to provide the advantages of broadcast access in low-volume traffic periods, with the inherent sharing of the slotted ring during high-volume traffic periods. The physical topology of the ring is the same, but instead of a circulating mini-packet there is a circulating token. Any host requiring access to the ring waits for the token to arrive; it then changes the token to indicate that a packet is following. The modified token is then followed immediately by the data packet, which can be of any size up to some system maximum. All hosts detect the modified token and examine the packet to see if it is addressed to them; if it is the packet is copied off the ring. The receiving host still sends the packet on though, so the data packet goes all the way round the ring to the sender. The sender takes the packet off the ring. Normally the sender receives the front of the data packet before it has finished transmitting the rest of the packet, owing to the short length of the ring. When the receiver detects the end of the data packet it marks its status by changing the last few bits, as in the Cambridge ring mini-packet; thus the sender knows if the packet was accepted or not. Immediately the sender has finished the packet it puts a token on the ring so another host may have a go.

The token ring is a simple idea, but it is more complex than the Cambridge ring and the interfaces are more expensive. The initialise sequence which is required to start the ring is quite complex as the token has to be put on the ring to start data transfer; of course there can only be one token. The mechanisms for detecting duplicate tokens and lost tokens, without the use of a monitor station, add to the cost of the computer interfaces. IBM carried out extensive tests and simulations of all the local area network technologies, and decided that the token ring was the best available. The company now intends to use the token ring as the basis of its local area network products.

The computer network

The protocols used in a computer network are the mechanisms by which the hosts exchange information over physical distances. In the OSI model, the network layer is the primary layer for host-to-host communication. The network layer makes use of services from the link and physical layers; it also provides an end-to-end service to the transport layer. The network layer can utilise a number of physical networks to provide its services. The two services provided by the network layer are the connectionless services, and the connection-orientated service. This chapter begins by looking at the connection orientated service provided by the X.25 protocol. This protocol is important as it is being used on all public packet-switched networks operated by the PTTs. The X.25 protocol defines the necessary operation of layers one, two and three. Within any layer, a connection orientated protocol has two common tasks: error control and flow control. Error control is concerned with detecting, and correcting, errors that may have occurred in the information being transferred. Flow control is concerned with managing the resources of bandwidth and storage so that no single user can monopolise these resources, and the two endpoints are kept in step with each other. This is usually achieved by keeping the sending and receiving rates of information transfer approximately in step. The X.25 protocol covers the three lower layers of the protocol hierarchy. X.25 is defined as an access protocol, which means that it is used between a host and a node (in most X.25 networks the nodes are called 'exchanges') for the host to access the network so that communication between remote hosts is possible. The X.25 protocol has been adopted by the CCITT as a standard, which means that nearly all future networks will use it. The latest version of X.25 will be adopted by ISO as an international standard.

As well as describing the particulars of X.25, the principles of error and flow control will be shown and the mechanisms used to implement them in each layer explained. The description of level 2 is very detailed, as this is the first consequential level to be met in the bottom-up approach. The discussion of level 2 examines a number of problems which occur at many other protocol layers. For instance, the mechanisms used at level 3 for flow control and protocol synchronisation are very similar to those of level 2, so less detail is given in the level 3 explanation and references are made to the level 2 mechanisms.

In the X.25 parlance a host is called a DTE (Data Terminating Equipment) and a node is called a DCE (Data Communications Equipment). X.25 provides a standard mechanism for a DTE to access and use a DCE to transport data across a network to a remote DTE via its remote DCE.

X.25 level 1--the physical circuit level provides the physical communication by specifying the electrical signals, voltages, plug shape and pin assignment that the DTE needs to connect physically to the DCE. The DTE/DCE boundary is shown on the host side of the MODEM at the host site. This would be the normal arrangement, as the supplier of the network (usually the PTT) will provide the MODEM link to the node (DCE) from the user's premises. The actual specification of level I is contained in the CCITT X.21 recommendation. For practical purposes the user will order a computer interface to this standard which plugs straight into the computer at one end and into the MODEM at the other. The user will normally also be able to buy the software necessary to handle the interface.

As the level 1 hardware is bought as a ready-made unit, no further discussion of it is necessary. The important information needed about level 1 is the type of interface it presents to level 2, and the functions it must perform. The level 1 will provide transport for a bit stream from the DTE to a (remote) DCE. The level 2 will present the level 1 with the bits which are then delivered to a level 2 at the DCE. The hardware of level 1 will also indicate if the physical circuit is working correctly, that is whether the MODEMs are switched on and able to exchange synchronised data. So the interface has two parts

1. the sending and receiving of a serial bit stream
2. the control signals indicating the status of the physical circuit.

X.25 level 2 -- link level

The purpose of level 2 is to control the physical link between the two ends of the level 1 circuit to provide a reliable transfer of information for level 3 between the DTE and DCE. X.25 level 2 uses a link control protocol based on the ISO HDLC (Higher Data Link Control) protocol. The advantages of using an existing protocol are greater than those to be gained from designing a new one. For instance, a new protocol would have to be adopted by a large number of people wishing to communicate; adoption of the protocol would then require a lot of effort. Other link protocols have been designed: IBM use one called SDLC (Synchronous Data Link Control) on their SNA network, which is not dissimilar to HDLC; DEC have their own as well.

Information is passed from level 2 to level 1 in blocks called 'frames'. The use of frames enables easier management of storage and error control. Each frame consists of some protocol information added by level 2, and possibly an information packet from level 3. 1 will use the convention of calling level 2 blocks frames and level 3 blocks *packets. The* functions performed by level 2 are

1. To establish the link connection to a level 2 at a remote site.
2. To transfer packets for level 3 securely, and in sequence.
3. To disconnect the link without loss of level 3 information.

To carry out these functions, the X. 25 level 2 uses three types of frame format. The uses of each format are shown in the next section, but first the fields in the frames are detailed

Flag field

This is a unique 8 bit pattern (01111110) which marks the beginning and end of each frame. The use of the flag as a delimiter presents a problem: to ensure that the end of the frame is correctly interpreted by the receiver, the flag pattern must not appear anywhere within the data in the frame. This means that the frame must be transparent to the hardware looking for a flag to mark the beginning or ending of a frame. The problem of transparency occurs in all link level protocols as they all use special bit patterns for synchronisation and for marking various parts of the frame. In X. 25 level 2 the flag is used as the level 1 synchronisation character. To ensure that the flag pattern does not occur within the frame, X.25 uses a technique called 'bit stuffing'. The bit stuffing technique involves the sender in inspecting the frame contents prior to transfer to level 1. Whenever a sequence of five Is occurs a 0 is inserted.

Notice that the 0 is inserted regardless of the value of the sixth bit. Bit stuffing in this way is easily implemented by hardware and only increases the length of the frame by 1 bit for every sequence of five Is. As the receiving hardware scans the incoming frame, a 0 following a sequence of five Is is removed. If the sequence of five Is is followed by a further 1, then the flag may have been found. The seventh bit is then inspected: if it is a 0 the flag has been found (01111110), whereas if the seventh bit is another 1 (01111111) then the frame is in error. Thus a sequence of seven Is is used to abort the frame.

There are other ways of providing transparency, such as using escape characters, or bit counts, but none is quite so efficient and flexible as bit stuffing.

Address field

This is really redundant in a point-to-point link. The intention in the HDLC protocol was to use this as an address for multipoint lines, but the present X. 25 recommendation does not include multipoint lines. However, X.25 uses the field as an additional check in the protocol, as well as having the field ready should multipoint lines be considered in the future. The addresses used in this field allow commands and responses to be separated. The level 2 link can be thought of as two separate channels.

Channel A for transferring data from the network (DCE) to the host (DTE) and

Channel B for transferring data from the host (DTE) to the network (DCE).

Any frames relating to information flow from the DCE to the DTE carry the address A (11000000) including any frames from the DTE to the DCE relating to information transfer from the network to the host; similarly for channel B (10000000). To help separate the channels, frames are divided into two classes: *commands* and *responses,* Commands always flow in the direction of information on a channel; responses flow in the opposite direction. Responses are obviously the receiver's replies to various commands.

Command field

This 8 bit pattern determines the type of the frame, as well as being used for sequence numbering and acknowledgement. The command field has a different meaning for the three types of frame (information, supervisory, unnumbered). A 0 in bit 1 indicates that this is an information frame. An information frame is the only type that carries a level 3 packet in the information field. Bits 2, 3 and 4 contain the sequence number of this frame, bits 6, 7 and 8 contain the acknowledgement number. The sequence number and acknowledgement number are used in the ARQ techniques explained in chapter 6 for error correction and flow control. Level 2 uses a stop-go flow control. Bit 5 is the poll/final (P/F) bit. This is set in a command frame as a poll bit and the receiver will set the final bit in any response frame that is a reply to a command frame with the poll bit set. The use of the poll/final bit enables the sender of a command to recognise the corresponding response frame.

Bits 1 and 2 set to 10 indicate a supervisory frame. Bits 3 and 4 indicate which type of supervisory frame, Supervisory frames are not given sequence numbers as they do not contain any level 3 information, but they may be used to acknowledge information frames and so bits 6, 7 and 8 contain an acknowledgement number. Bit 5 is the poll/final bit which is the same as before.

The command field format for the *unnumbered frame,* so called because it contains neither sequence number nor acknowledgement number. Bits 1 and 2 set to 11 indicate an unnumbered frame and bit 5 is the poll/final bit. The remainder of the bits are used to indicate the type of unnumbered frame.

Information field

This field only occurs in information frames; it is the position in the frame where the whole level 3 packet is placed. The other level 2 fields provide an envelope for the level 3 packet during the level 2 transfer.

Frame check sequence

The FCS field is found by counting 16 bits back from the terminating flag. This is a 16 bit field to contain the CRC remainder used in error checking. The remainder is calculated using the CCITT recommended generating polynomial of $X^{16} + X^{12} + X^5 + 1$.

It is interesting to note that all the fields of the X.25 level 2 header and the CRC are multiples of 8 bits. This makes transmission easier, because the 8 bit byte is the lowest common multiple of most modern computer word sizes, as well as being the character frame size for synchronous transfer. However the information field and the CRC may be increased by bit stuffing for level 1 transmission.

Operation of X.25 level 2

This section describes the semantics of level 2, with the various commands and responses being explained in context. The level 2 at the DTE (host) end of the connection performs the protocol functions with the level 2 at the DCE, using the HDLC protocol over the level 1 physical connection.

Establishing the link connection

An earlier specification of the X.25 protocol included a lever 2 initialisation procedure called LAP (Link Access Protocol) This procedure has been superseded by a simpler *balanced* procedure called LAPB. The LAPB method of initialisation sets up both channels simultaneously.

Data transfer

Level 2 should provide a sequenced, error-free transport of lever 3 packers from the DTE to the DCE and vice versa. As only 3 bits are allowed for the sequence number and acknowledgement number in the C field, the maximum window size is 7. In X. 25 the link level window size is fixed when the subscriber first applies to use the network. The operation of the data transfer allows the use of limited buffers at the sender (no more than 7) and no requirement for extra buffers to handle out-of-sequence frames at the receiver. The cost of the small buffer requirement is extra channel capacity taken up with retransmission. The use of X.25 to connect hosts to networks would normally involve a fairly high-speed circuit between the DTE and DCE The limiting factor in performance is more likely to be the network and level 3, so a superefficient level 2 is not necessary; thus simpler techniques, such as Go-Back-N, can be used.

The transfer of sequenced frames of information is straightforward but what makes the operation complex (and this applies to every protocol) is the handling of exceptions and errors. There are two basic errors that can occur during data transfer.

1. The frame check sequence indicates an error in the packet.
2. The packet appears to contain no transmission errors but the contents of the A and C fields are not those expected.

In case 1 above the frame is thrown away and no further action is taken by the receiver. Obviously when a frame is discarded the next frame received is not the one expected. In case 2 there are a number of inconsistencies that can be classed as errors. The most common would be a sequence error where a previous packet had been lost or discarded. To ensure that the frame sequence is maintained at the receiver, any frame that does not contain a sequence number matching that of the next expected frame variable, V(R), is an error. If the sequence number of the error frame is within the window, the receiver returns an REJ response to indicate, in the N(R) field, the frame from which the sender should retransmit. If the frame sequence number is not within the window then the sequence numbers of the two ends have become unsynchronised. The only way to recover from a synchronisation problem is to reset the sender and receiver to a known state. The CMDR (command reject) frame initiates a reset which is completed by going through the link establishment exchange. After a reset, the two end-stations will be in a known, initial state. The reset procedure is used to recover from all errors other than the loss of an information frame. A reset may be caused by the receipt of a command or response that is not expected; for instance, a UA if the data transfer is in progress, or the setting of the P/F bit in a response when no command has been sent with that bit set.

The RNR (receiver not ready) frame tells the data sender that the receiver will ignore any further information frames (flow control stop). Once the receiver has returned an RNR response to an information frame, no more information frames are accepted, but the *N(R)* field in the header of any further information frames is inspected so that information frames in the opposite direction are properly acknowledged. The RNR response only stops information on one channel; the other channel is unaffected. When the receiver has more buffer space, an RR (receiver ready) frame is sent to inform the information sender on that channel that more information frames may be transmitted (flow control go), starting at *N(R)*. Note that both RNR and RR have acknowledgement numbers, *N(R)*. The RR frame has another use: if the receiving station does not have any information frames to be sent on the opposite channel, the acknowledgements cannot be piggybacked, and the RR frame is then used to acknowledge the information frames.

A receiver, especially a DCE (node), may not have enough buffers to take a full window for every level 2 link to which it is connected. Instead a statistical allocation could be used which assumes that not all links will be fully active at the same time and that the data is forwarded within a given time. When the network becomes busy this allocation means that a receiver may run out of buffers and need to use some technique to stop the flow of data from one or more links. Every frame, whether it is data or control, needs some buffer space for its receipt. If all the buffers are used up by one link then none of the other links will be able to continue transferring information. Also, if every buffer is allocated, there may be no more buffers to receive a control frame acknowledging a data frame and releasing buffer space! To avoid these problems, complex buffer allocation methods may be used. Normally, enough free buffers are always kept to receive at least one frame on each link so that control information can be exchanged even if data cannot. An information frame would be received, the control information used (for example *N(R)*), and then the frame discarded so that the buffer may be used again.

The loss of information frames as a result of buffer starvation means that information is lost not only because of errors in transmission, but also because of the internal operation of the nodes of a network, especially when the network becomes heavily loaded.

Link disconnection

The LAPB procedure for closing a link requires an exchange of a DISC command and a UA response. The poll/final bit is used to obtain synchronisation between the DCE and DTE.

X.25 level 3 -- the network level

The function of level 2 is to carry a level 3 packet across a link. The function of the network level is to carry a piece of information from one host (DTE) to another via intermediate network nodes. The transfer of the level 3 information will involve a number of level 2 links. The X. 25 specification only covers the link between the DTE and DCE, but we will assume a similar protocol is used between each node of the network as well. Each level 3 packet contains a certain amount of level 3 protocol information in a header, and possibly some user data (from the transport level). The major differences between levels 2 and 3 are the use of addresses and logical channel numbers. Most hosts will be connected to the network by one level 2 link. This link then has to be used to enable the host to communicate with several other hosts by multiplexing logical channels on to the one physical link. Level 3 is used to achieve this multiple connection via a single link. Using level 3 a host establishes a logical channel to another host by making a connection request using the full address of the remote host. When the connection is established it becomes a logical channel with a unique number, the logical channel number. The logical channel number is unique only for each link. Using the logical channel concept, packets for several calls may pass across the same level 2 link as they are all identified by the unique channel number. At the DCE the channel number is used to decide which route the packet will take. The logical channel is in fact a virtual circuit.

The network level has the same basic functions to perform as the link level.

1. Connection establishment.
2. Data transfer.
3. Connection disconnection.

The difference for the network level is that these functions are now carried out (apparently) between two hosts.

Packet format

The X.25 level 3 headers are used to contain a variety of information, so they are not of uniform size like the level 2 frame headers. The level 3 headers are different for every type of packet, which makes the format quite complex. The general format identifier (GFI) field indicates which format of level 3 header follows. The logical channel group number and logical channel number provide a 12 bit channel-numbering field. Splitting the field may allow subdivisions to be used for, say, different services. Call request and incoming call packets contain the address of the remote host (DTE). The addresses may contain fields indicating a particular process on a host as well as identifying a host. The address fields are of variable length, preceded by a byte count.

Connection establishment

To begin a call, a host uses the full address of the remote host in a call request packet sent from the DTE to the DCE. The DCE will respond with either a call accepted packet if the request was successful, or a clear indication packet if the call was refused.

At the remote host the DCE will send an incoming call packet to the host to indicate that a remote call has been requested. The DTE receiving an incoming call packet will inspect the header to decide if the call is to be established or not. If the call is accepted a call accept packet is sent to the DCE; if the call is rejected a clear request is sent to the DCE. The channel number chosen for a new outgoing call by the DTE is the lowest available number. The channel number for an incoming call is chosen by the DCE as the highest available number. If the DTE and DCE agree on the channel numbers, and the DCE will accept the call, all subsequent packets on that call will only use that channel number, not the full address. A call has been established to a remote DTE when a host receives a call accepted packet having the same channel number as the call request packet. The call is established at the remote DTE when the call accepted packet is sent to the remote DCE.

Information transfer

Level 3 transfers data to the network in a sequenced stream using Go-Back-N ARQ. The techniques of sequence numbers, piggybacked acknowledgements, RNR, RR and REJ responses are the same as for level 2, but they control the data flow across the network and into the remote host for each, independent logical channel. The use of windows and sequence numbers was for error control in level 2 as the level 1 link was prone to errors. At level 3 the level 2 link is assumed to be error free so. the emphasis is different. The windows and sequence numbers are now used primarily for end-to-end flow control. The receipt of acknowledgements allows more information into the network, while the window limits the number of data packets in flight at any one time. Complete suspension of the data flow can be achieved by using a level 3 RNR, but the flow can be partially adjusted by the rate of acknowledgement.

Interrupt

An extra mechanism is used at level 3 to handle what is known as *out-of-band* transmission. Normal user data on an X.25 virtual call is kept in strict sequence; this is called *in band* transmission. However, a user application often requires a special signal which is not subject to the normal flow control. Such a signal is the abort character which a terminal user would type to stop a runaway program. X.25 level 3 uses an interrupt packet to carry this out-of-band signal. The interrupt is not subject to the normal information flow control, the idea being that the interrupt could overtake information packets already in the network. The interrupt packet contains a field to indicate the cause of the interrupt; it is up to the application to decide what to do both with the interrupt and any subsequent data. When the DTE sends an interrupt packet the DCE responds with an interrupt confirmation.

Resets and restarts

In level 2 the reset was introduced as a mechanism for recovering from a protocol error where the two ends in the link became unsynchronised. The same thing can happen between the DTE and DCE at level 3, except that there are two areas where problems may occur.

The first problem is due to the information frames and sequence numbers becoming out of synchronisation on a single call. This may be detected by receiving a sequence number outside the window or an acknowledgement for a packet that was not sent. An error may also have been detected by a higher-level protocol, perhaps because of a network failure. In these cases only the one logical channel is affected so a *reset* is used. This sets the level 3 sequence numbers to 0 at the DTE and DCE. The reset will also be propagated to the remote DTE-DCE pair. The reset can be initiated from either the DTE or DCE and requires the usual request-confirmation exchange. A reset may cause the loss of any information packets within the network so a higher-level protocol will need to recover any lost data.

More drastic action is needed if the DTE and DCE become unsynchronised over global level 3 operation. An example is the choice of a channel number for a call request. If the DCE does not agree with the DTE over the chosen channel number (it should be the lowest free number) it means one of them thinks it has more logical calls opened than the other! The freeing of logical channel numbers correctly is the reason for the clear-request and clear-confirmation pair. When the whole level 3 needs resynchronisation a restart is initiated. This affects all the logical channels on the DTE-DCE link. A reset on the level 2 link is propagated as a restart at level 3.

Call disconnection

A DTE wishing to terminate a call issues a clear request packet, to which the DCE will respond with a clear confirmation packet when the call has been cleared in the DCE. This may involve waiting for the forwarding of any information packets still held there. When the clear confirmation is received the channel number is freed for further use. At the remote end the DCE wit send a clear indication packet indicating that the remote host has closed, and no more information packets will follow. The remote DTE will respond with a clear confirmation packet when all outstanding information packets have been acknowledged.

Data flow

The level 3 transport mechanism requires the data from the higher-level protocols to be broken into packets for transfer across the DTE-DCE interface. The X.25 recommendation specifies possible data lengths of 128 256, 512 and 1024 bytes, where 128 is the preferred maximum. It is probable that the PTT networks will guarantee 128 byte data packets. This means a user message must be broken into 128 byte sequences, the last one being perhaps less than 128 bytes. To enable the receiver to reassemble a message from multiple packets, level 3 uses a *more data bit* (M) in the information packet header to indicate that the current packet is not the last one of a message.

Just as the level 2 and level 3 need to include control information in the frames and packets as well as information from the next higher level, it is likely that a higher-level protocol would like to send control and data over level 3. The higher-level protocol may decide to add the control bits to the front of messages it passes to level 3. However, level 3 provides a mechanism that allows a higher-level protocol to multiplex data and control information on to the level 3 packet stream, thus maintaining the sequence of data and control across the network. This mechanism is the Q *bit.* The Q bit is set when the packet contains control information, and is clear when the packet contains data. Thus the higher-level protocol can quickly separate control and data information when receiving level 3 packets.

X.25 implementation

An advantage claimed for X.25 is that it only describes the host-to-node (DTE-to-DCE) interface. The network itself (internode) can use any convenient protocols, even completely different protocols, and the user would be unaware of them. In fact the proposed PTT networks are all planning to use X.25, or variations, within the networks for node-to-node transfer. The problem considered here is the implications of two methods of implementing an X.25 interface in a DCE that produce quite different results for the user. The discussion will show that even standards have complex problems of *meaning* (or semantics).

The two methods of implementation involve the mechanism for generating responses to various DTE packets at level 3. From the above description it can be seen that a command response sequence is used throughout level 3. The X.25 specification indicates quite clearly what responses are required, but leaves it up to the implementer to decide when, and under what criteria, the responses are made.

Consider the implementation that produces the DCE response as soon as the DTE's packet has been processed at the (local) DCE. This means the DCE's answer is sent to the DTE at the same time as the original request is forwarded across the network and well in advance of its arrival at the remote DTE. Such an implementation would give a very quick response to the user host. For instance, as data is passed to the DCE it is acknowledged immediately, even before it has crossed the network. The DCE-DTE flow control would ensure the DCE was not flooded with data, but large amounts could be in transit within the network before the call has been established at the remote end. This implementation would give the host the appearance of high throughput, as the DCE-DTE flow control would be the only restraint. If the DTE receives a level 3 acknowledgement for a data packet, does this mean that the remote DTE has received it, or only that the local DCE has? To be consistent in this implementation it would have to be the latter, so the DCE has taken on the responsibility for delivery of that data. A higher-level protocol would be needed, with its own flow control, to handle the host-to-host transfer.

This implementation has the effect, mentioned above, of apparently providing a fast throughput. A host may be able to open a call (to the local DCE), send data, and close the call, before the remote DTE has received any data. The network, however, will contain a large amount of unacknowledged packets as the DTE-DCE flow control will accept packets as fast as the DCE can forward them into the network. This makes end-to-end flow control in the network difficult and can quickly lead to congestion.

In the second implementation we only allow the DCE to respond to the DTE when the response from the remote DTE has been received by the local DCE. Data sent from the DTE is not acknowledged until the remote DTE has accepted the packet. This gives the host an impression of a long delay. In fact the delay is the round trip to the remote host, plus processing. This end-to-end use of the level 3 protocol reduces the amount of processing required from higher-level protocols. The sending DTE will only be able to have a window of packets outstanding which will represent the maximum number of data buffers which the whole network will need for the call. This makes the resource management within the network easier and is less likely to produce congestion. The cost is the lower performance seen by the user. Each packet takes longer to be acknowledged, thus reducing the throughput. There is also the problem of gaps which occurs when a window full of packets is sent rapidly, which is followed by a delay until the first acknowledgement comes back. This *bursty* mode of operation gives the network an uneven response and is difficult for both the host and DCE to manage.

The current X.25 recommendation allows a subscriber (DTE) to set a D bit in a data packet at level 3. This bit requires the acknowledgement to have end-to-end significance, as in the second example above. The D bit is an option, which means a network does not have to implement it.

The communications techniques covered so far have been concerned with centralised systems. Terminal networks are all built around a central computer; similarly remote job entry stations are usually connected to a single computer. In the remaining chapters some of the problems and techniques of a network of intercommunicating devices are discussed. The devices at present connected to networks are usually generalpurpose computers, with their own terminal networks. One reason for networking multiaccess computers, rather than terminals or smaller devices, is that these computer systems already existed when networking was proposed. A second reason is that the protocols used in computer networks are very complex so that only a large computer system would have sufficient spare computing power to implement them. However, terminals can be directly attached to a network, by using a dedicated computer. In the near future computer networks will become as widespread as the telephone network, and large scale integration will enable cheap processors to handle the protocols. The result will be the networking of every sort of computing device. The current trends indicate that powerful, single user, workstations will replace terminals for network use. The workstations will be directly connected to a local area network and use the resources of larger computers via the network.

This chapter is primarily concerned with the technology used to connect the computers and devices that make up a computer network. For the purposes of description the range of technology has been divided into three areas

1. wide area networks
2. Radio and satellite broadcast networks
3. Local networks

The network technology includes the techniques used to interconnect the computing devices and physically transfer information from one computing device to another.

Wide area networks

The term 'wide area network' is applied to a network that covers a large physical area, say a whole country or large area under one administration. Such an area may be worldwide where a multinational organisation owns the network. The basic communication media used are dedicated circuits, usually of about 50 kHz bandwidth. Where digital circuits are available the bandwidth would be 64K bps. The recent introduction of fibre optics in longdistance trunks has make link bandwidth of 2-3M bps available. Wide area networks will be using these links over the next few years. Examples of such networks are PSS, ARPANET, Tymnet, Telenet, etc.; details of some of these networks are given at the end of this section. The physical circuits are usually provided by a PTT, although in the case of PSS the whole network is also run by the PTT.

Although 50 kHz bandwidth seems to be a lot compared with the 3 kHz nominal bandwidth of the voice telephone line, it is not very much when highspeed or large-volume transfers of information are required. Even at these high speeds the channel capacity is a resource that needs to be used efficiently.

It is now necessary to see how information can be transferred from one computer to any other on the network. The problem falls into two parts. The first is that of transferring information via a medium, such as a wire. The second part is concerned with addressing and routing. If there were only two computers on a network, then they could be connected by two channels, one for each direction, and whatever one computer transmitted the other would be bound to receive. When more computers are added, the bidirectional connection solution can be extended by having each computer connected to every other computer by a full duplex connection. To send a message to a particular computer the appropriate connection is selected; thus the routing of a message is carried out by the sender. Using a dedicated connection between every computer on the network is very expensive. If there are n computers on the network then $n(n-1)/2$ lines are needed, and have to be paid for! As a single computer would not normally be communicating with every other computer on the network at the same time, most of the lines would be unused in a fully connected network. Therefore to increase the utilisation of the connection circuits, their number is reduced, and switching is introduced within the network.

There are three forms of switching that can be used in communications: circuit switching, message switching, and packet switching.

Circuit switching

Circuit switching is used on the PSTN to connect telephone subscribers. To use it for a computer network each computer would have a private circuit to a local exchange, and the exchanges would be connected to form a network.

Whenever two computers wish to exchange information, a physical path is established between them via the exchanges. The path is then disconnected when the connection is closed. The circuit has been switched by the exchanges. This method of connection is not used on established computer networks. The major disadvantages of circuit switching are

1. The cost of the equipment is very high, whereas the resulting circuit is not necessarily of high enough quality for computer communications.

2. The resulting circuit can only be used by the two computers on the call, thus the equipment is dedicated to the circuit. In particular the connection from the computer to the exchange is dedicated. To enable a single computer to communicate with more than one other computer at the same time, extra equipment is needed for each simultaneous call. If there are no connections all the equipment is idle but being paid for.

3. The time taken to set up the physical path can be very long in computer terms.

As high-speed connection using good-quality circuits is important for efficient computer networks, circuit switching is discounted in favour of the other methods. Circuit switching is used for some networks connecting computers-for instance, the Nordic Data Network.

Circuit switching has two advantages

1. Charges are made only for the time that a call is connected. If infrequent and short connections are all that is required, then circuit switching may be advantageous to the customer. It is expected that many slower devices, such as terminals, will be connected to national computer networks via the PSTN to gain this advantage.
2. Where a single device is used for long periods, such as a facsimile machine, circuit switching is economically advantageous. This is particularly true where digital facilities, such as X.21, are available.

The above discussion is based on the existing PSTN services offered by the PTTs. When the ISDN service is widely available, then it will be an attractive mechanism for some computer networks. Each host will be able to set up calls, use the 64K bps bandwidth, and quickly close the call, as required. The circuits will still carry packets for the end-to-end data transfer; but circuit switching will be the main link-switching mechanism. In the UK it is intended to bring all the PTT communications together into Integrated Digital Access (IDA). This will combine ISDN, X.25 networking and special digital services into a common access interface.

Message switching

To overcome problems in setting up and taking down physical circuits via exchanges, computer networks use permanent circuits and switch the data, A partially connected network is used in which each computer has a permanent circuit to a number of its neighbours, but not to all computers on the network. An example will illustrate the basic operation of *information switching* where the unit of information is a message.

If the computer at A wishes to send a message to B, the message must pass through either D or C. The points on the network are called *nodes. A will* address the message to B by placing the address of B in the message header. The message and address are then sent on the circuit to D. At D the node inspects the address; if the address is 'D' the message is given to the computer; if the address is not D the message is forwarded on a circuit that the node believes will enable the message to be delivered, In this case D will forward the message to B. Thus the node at D has switched the message on to the appropriate output circuit. In this example two major characteristics of a computer network can be seen.

Addressing

The message is addressed to a remote destination and sent on the next stage of its route.

Store and Forward

Each message is received into the node storage so that it can be processed as a whole unit. Usually an error check is carried out and the whole message has to be received before this can be completed. The message is then inspected for routing information so that the node can decide which output circuit to use to forward the message.

The nodes have been introduced in the network to carry out the functions of routing and store and forward, so the host computer is separated from the network operation as much as possible. The 'hosts' are the user computers which wish to use the network. Often a number of hosts will be attached to a single node.

The node computers are usually minicomputers chosen for their ability to respond in real time to the communications devices. Each node receives incoming messages and stores them. When a complete message has been received the destination address is inspected so that the message can be placed on the output queue of a circuit to forward the message. If the message is for a host attached to the node, the output circuit will be the one connected to the host. If the message is for a distant host the node must forward the message to another node on the route to the distant host. While the message is in the node store, waiting to be processed or waiting for output, it is, of course, being delayed.

The link into any one node may be used to carry messages from several different computers, as may the connection between the node and host. The physical equipment involved is used more efficiently than in circuit switching as a result of this multiplexing. Message multiplexing is the most important advantage of message and packet switching computer networks.

To distinguish between message and packet switching it is necessary to understand what a message is. This has already been introduced in earlier chapters, but a more detailed discussion is given here. The easiest way of defining a message is to say that it is a unit of information which is exchanged by users of a network. This means the characteristics of a message are only dependent on the user or the application. A message could be a few bits or a file, or even a whole database. In a message-switching network the whole message is passed from one node to another as a complete entity. Compared with circuit switching, a message-switching network has the following characteristics.

1. Any computer can communicate with any other computer without having a direct physical connection.

2. Any computer can communicate with several others using the same equipment by multiplexing messages.

3. There is no delay arising from circuit set up, but messages are delayed when they pass through a node *enroute.*

The messages can be transferred between nodes, and nodes and hosts, using an *ARQ* protocol.

Characteristic 3 implies that there is no delay arising from the use of a network other than the store and forward operation of the nodes. This is true in some networks using pure datagram techniques. However, in most networks the internode protocol used within the network introduces some delays. Any network using a virtual circuit protocol, at any level, will introduce a delay when the message or packet is given to the network. In many networks the local node negotiates for resources within the network before actually forwarding a message. This is true of an X.25 network when the call is first set up, and is true of every message on the ARPA network. A user of a message-switching network will pass the network a message, together with a destination address, and the user will receive messages as single units.

Advantages and disadvantages

The advantages of message switching, over circuit switching are

- The sender may dispatch the message when convenient, even if the receiver is not ready, as the network will store the message for delivery, However, if network resources run out, an undelivered message may be deleted and thus lost; this depends on the network protocols.
- Computers can exchange information at different speeds, as the network will buffer the message.
- Broadcasting of a message may be possible.
- Equipment is used more efficiently.
- Messages may be handled by priority.

Each message is treated as a single unit. However, there are also some disadvantages.

- A very long message will hold up other, perhaps more urgent, messages as it monopolises a circuit for the duration of its transmission.
- As a message may be very large, the node computer may not have enough memory to store it before forwarding it; in this case the message is lost. Further, this message will never be delivered as the network does not have the required resources.
- A very large message may monopolise the storage of a node, because it cannot be delivered, so that other messages cannot be received by this node.

Packet switching

The disadvantages of message switching relate to the possible occurrence of *large* messages, where the exact value of 'large' will depend on the network. If a network could be certain of only handling small messages, the disadvantages would disappear. The transfer of messages is a user requirement, so a network that meets user needs must be able to handle very large messages as well as small messages. The solution to these two conflicting requirements is to break the user's message into small *packets* for transfer through the network and have the packets reassembled into the message by the receiver. Note that the message header is included as the data in the first packet and that each packet has its own header. This refinement produces packet switching, which is the most widely used switching technique for computer networks.

The physical organisation of a packet-switching network is the same as for message switching. The network is a partially connected mesh of nodes. For practical reasons most wide area networks use special node computers to perform the switching, with the user computers being attached to the nodes. The term 'host' is now widely used to mean a user computer system attached to a network. The nodes are part of the network, so the hosts use a well-defined interface for accessing the node to enable data transfer across the network. By using a node separated from the host, all of the packet-switching functions, such as storage and routing, are removed from the host. However, the host still needs considerable software to handle the protocols used to access the node and to transfer data to other computers on the network.

The advantages that packet switching has over message switching are

- The small maximum packet size makes storage allocation and management easier in the switching nodes, sufficiently so for minicomputers to be used.
- The multiplexing of packets enables several messages to be interleaved on one circuit, reducing the delay seen by the user.
- The total transmission time through the network is reduced. It shows a message passing from A to B which would normally require 6k + d seconds to reach B, where 3k is the transmission time of the whole message on one link and d is the node delay. If the message is broken into three packets, each taking k seconds to transmit, the whole message arrives at B in 4k + d seconds. The difference increases with the number of links traversed and the size of the message.

It would appear that packet switching solves all the problems of wide area network organisation: it uses fixed highspeed lines and minicomputers for nodes; it is also more efficient and responsive than message switching. However, although packet switching is a better technique with which to implement a computer network, users still want to transfer messages. Packet switching introduces another layer of complexity and translation between the user and the physical network transporting the bits. Fortunately, the cost of processing is falling so the extra cost is outweighed by the practical advantages. A second cost, not so easily overcome, is that each packet will have its own overheads as well as those used by each message; this will reduce the efficiency of the physical circuits.

The conclusion drawn from consideration of these three switching techniques is that packet switching, especially used in a partially connected mesh of nodes with wideband circuits, is currently the best technique for wide area computer networks. Packet switching is also used in other network technologies, rather than message switching, for the same reasons.

Wide area networks have been in existence since the early 1970s. The best known example is the ARPA network in the United States. This network was established by a government research agency to link together computer centres that had contracts for government research so that research workers could share the available computing resources. The network itself also forms part of a research project to evaluate the feasibility of a large computer network, and to investigate techniques that could be used in such a network. The ARPA network has been very successful in showing that the concept of resource sharing by use of a network is feasible. One of the most noticeable advantages that the network has introduced is a mail facility. This allows each user with access to a computer on the network to exchange mail with all the other network users. The mail facility is probably one of the main sources of traffic on the ARPA network and has certainly improved the amount of communication between researchers at different sites.

The basic techniques used within the ARPA network have been influenced by the defence aspects of the research, particularly the need for a fast response and resilience to the failure of any part. The network consists of a mesh of partially connected nodes called Interface Message Processors (IMPs). Each IMP can have up to eight hosts connected to it and may be connected to up to eight other IMPs. Each IMP accepts messages from the hosts of up to 8K bits in length. The IMP breaks the message into IK bit packets which are then forwarded through the network of IMPs to the IMP attached to the destination host. This destination IMP reassembles the message before delivering it to the destination host. If a host wishes to send a message of more than 8K bits it must break the message up itself, into 8K packets, and the destination host must reassemble the message from the 8K packets. Thus the translation between messages and packets takes place at two levels. Within the network of IMPs, packets (1K) are sent individually along whichever route is best at the time, so that packets in a single message may use different routes and may arrive at the destination IMP out of sequence. The destination IMP has to reassemble the message from the packets as they arrive. However, messages passed from the host to the IMP are delivered in the same sequence to the destination host. The technology developed for the ARPANET is now used in a number of commercial wide area networks all over the world.

The British Telecom network PSS (Packet Switching Stream) is an example of a network provided by a PTT as a public service. The design requirements for such a network are different from those of the ARPA network so they have resulted in a network with different characteristics. The network topology consists of a number of *exchanges* which are also partially connected. Each exchange is connected to a number of host computers in its area. The exchanges contain the node computers, the number of node computers in each exchange depending on the number of hosts attached to the exchange. The hosts use an access protocol called X.25 to enable them to make virtual calls to other hosts. A host will give the local exchange the destination address of the host with which it wishes to communicate. The network will route the call to the destination exchange which will then complete the call to the destination host. The call is represented by information kept at all the exchanges on the route. The information is then used to forward the packets transferred on the call. Once the call has been established the hosts may exchange their own information. This is very similar to circuit switching on the PSTN although it is provided using packet-switching techniques. The PSS network techniques are different from those on the ARPA network, where each message is addressed and transferred separately. The hosts can use a single link to the PSS exchange to carry a number of virtual calls to other hosts, thus the link is used to multiplex the calls.

Radio and satellite broadcast networks

These networks differ from wide area networks in the way in which the channel is used for communication between users. Broadcast networks use a channel to which all the users are connected, so all the users receive any transmission made on the channel. At present the two types of channel in use are local radio, covering up to a few hundred kilometres, and satellite channels which are used to span very large distances.

Networks using radio and satellite channels have special problems because noise in the channel can cause errors. There is also the problem of allocating the channel for transmission. The first operational broadcast computer network was built at the University of Hawaii using local radio transmission; many of the techniques and much of the terminology derive from this first network.

Every node receives all packets transmitted on the broadcast channel. When the received packet is complete, the node checks the packet for errors and then checks the destination address. If the address of the receiver matches the packet destination address, it is accepted; otherwise it is discarded. The problems particular to a broadcast network occur in the allocation of the channel to a node for transmitting a packet. Different solutions are used for radio and satellite links. Each node is only able to communicate with each other node via the common channel, so some scheme is needed to coordinate transmission. The schemes that have been proposed and used are discussed here in increasing complexity and are compared for channel efficiency.

The simplest transmission technique is called *pure aloha;* when a node has a packet to transmit it does so immediately. Having transmitted the packet, the node waits for an acknowledgement. This is therefore a positive acknowledgement protocol. If an acknowled-gement is not received within a time out period, the packet is assumed lost. Transmission collisions, which occur when two nodes transmit at the same time and thus interfere with each other's transmission, are detected by the time out mechanism. When a collision is detected, each node waits a period of time of random length before retransmitting the packet to of traffic increases, the rate of collision will increase and more re-transmissions will be needed. As the older packets are re-transmitted, more stations will have newer packets to transmit, causing more collisions, etc. Analysis has shown that a pure aloha scheme can only use a maximum of about 18% of the channel bandwidth. A node may transmit at any time, thus the maximum length of time the channel is wasted as a result of a collision is 2t, where t is the transmission time for one packet. The 2t period is the worst case, where one node begins transmitting just before the previous transmission is complete.

An improvement on pure aloha is *slotted aloha* in which the transmission channel time is divided into time slots of *t.* Each node is then only allowed to begin transmitting a packet at the start of a time slot. The nodes are kept in synchronisation by a time signal on the channel. Now if a collision occurs only one slot *is* wasted, so the maximum efficiency rises to about 34% of the channel capacity. When a collision is detected, a transmitter must wait for a random number of time slots before retransmitting. When the traffic is light the wait can be quite short, but as the traffic load increases the waiting period should be increased.

From the aloha schemes it can be seen that it is collisions that cause problems, so a collision avoidance mechanism should improve efficiency. In packet radio networks a scheme known as Carrier Sense Multiple Access (CSMA) is used. When a node is transmitting all other nodes can receive the transmission, so they can avoid a collision by not transmitting themselves until the channel is free. A transmission is detected by the presence of the carrier signal in the medium. When a node has a packet to transmit it looks for the carrier; if there is no carrier the packet is transmitted. If the carrier is detected the node waits for a random length delay and tries again.

Even in a radio broadcast the signal from a transmitter takes a finite amount of time to reach all the receivers in the network. When two nodes find the channel free, they may both begin transmission because neither has heard the other one. This case is most likely to happen when two stations are waiting for the channel to become free.

The length of time it takes to propagate the signal to all receivers is the time band in which collisions may occur, but it is less than the total packet transmission time. As with the aloha technique, the CSMA technique can be improved by dividing the channel time into slots and only allowing the transmission of packets to begin at the start of a time slot. The slot length is set to the propagation delay, not the packet transmission time.

The CSMA technique has been further refined by modifying the action of the node when the channel is busy. When the node samples the channel again and finds it free, it transmits its packet with a probability p, or waits for a further delay of random length, with a probability (1-p). This is called persistent CSMA or p-persistent transmission. If p is high then the delay before transmission occurs is lower, but the possibility of collision increases if two stations are waiting for another station to finish. In persistent CSMA a trade off is made between channel efficiency and delay with the value of p. Channel efficiencies of about 80% may be achieved using these techniques.

Packet radio networks have a small delay between the start of a transmission and the detection of the transmission by all stations on the network. On a satellite broadcast network there is a very long delay between transmission and receiving, of the order of a quarter of a second. A satellite network operates by each transmitter sending its signal to the satellite. The satellite then broadcasts the signal to all of the Earth stations, which may be spread over a very large area. One satellite system currently used for packet switching connects nodes in England, Norway and North America using a satellite in stationary orbit over the North Atlantic. A different channel allocation technique is used on satellite broadcast networks because of the long propagation delay.

This satellite channel allocation technique involves making reservations for the future use of slots in the channel. The channel is divided into frames consisting of a number of reservation slots and a number of packet slots. Each reservation slot represents a packet slot in the second part of the frame. All ground stations are synchronised to the frame timing by the satellite transmission. During the first part of the frame the ground stations reserve slots for the packets they have ready by transmitting a marker during the reservation slot time. When the reservation slot is heard on the satellite down channel, the ground station inspects the slot to see if it contains its own marker. If so it can transmit a packet in the corresponding packet slot in the second part of the frame. This scheme uses some of the channel capacity to avoid the collisions which could reduce the network to a pure aloha scheme.

Obviously more than one ground station may attempt to reserve a particular packet slot by transmitting during the reservation slot time. There are a number of algorithms to overcome this, including allocating some slots to busy stations. Thus if a station successfully obtained a packet slot in the last frame, the same slot is allocated to that station in the next frame without competition. If an allocated slot is not used then the slot is open for competition in the following frame. Usually there are some slots that all stations can compete for in every frame. Another mechanism involves using a central allocation station to which each station sends its requirements and the central station allocates the slots. This has two disadvantages: firstly, the central station becomes a weakness in the network reliability, and secondly, the delay between requesting an allocation and receiving the allocation may be of the order of 1 or 2 seconds before the packet can be transmitted. A chapter in the book by Kuo is dedicated to broadcast satellite protocols.

Local area networks

A local, or private, network is a communication system connecting computers in a small geographical area, say less than a few kilometres between the furthest points. The network is wholly owned and run by one administration. There are currently two basic types of technology used on such a network: these are cable, or bus, technology and ring technology.

Whereas wide area networks and satellite networks use nodes to separate the internal network switching from the user hosts, local networks are meant to be as cheap as possible and so the separate node computer is omitted. In both local network technologies all the computers are directly attached to the transmission medium by a special interface, and all the interfaces receive all the packets. The difference between a ring and a bus system is the way in which the channel is allocated. Local networks are designed for use in local computing by allowing the interconnection of very small computers, such as microprocessors, personal workstations and peripheral devices. If the local network is to be useful, the cost of the computer interfaces into the network channel has to be low compared with the cost of the computer or peripheral, and microprocessors are very cheap in computer terms. A widely forecast use of local networks is connecting word processors within a set of offices for the exchange of information and electronic mail. The cost constraints, the limited processing power of the small computers and the protocols used on a local network are different from those used in wide area networks. A local network usually has a very high bandwidth channel of between I and 10 MHz and a very low error rate say one bit in several million might be corrupted. These characteristics permit the use of simple protocols. The lowest level protocol for using the transmission medium is built into the computer interface.

Cable or bus networks

These networks usually use a length of coaxial cable, or an existing cable such as that used for closed circuit television (CCTV). The medium is used in a broadcast fashion, exactly as described in the previous section on broadcast networks. The channel allocation techniques vary slightly on the theme of the CSMA techniques, or on a centralised slot allocation. The most popular broadcast local network is the Ethernet system developed by Xerox. The Ethernet principles can be used on any broadcast medium: radio, telephone lines, coaxial cable and optical fibres have all been used successfully. The Ethernet uses a base band signal, rather than a modulated signal, to simplify the broadcast transmitter and receiver, with a modified CSMA channel access technique. To obtain the maximum efficiency from the broadcast medium an Ethernet transmitter can listen to its own broadcast to detect a collision and abort the transmission. This extra complexity is known as CSMACD (CD = collision detection) or listen-while-talk. As with the other CSMA techniques a station does not begin transmitting until the broadcast medium is free. Two stations waiting for another station to finish a transmission will begin transmitting together, and thus interfere with each other. The collision is detected by the stations and they both abort the transmission immediately. To enforce the protocol a station that aborts a transfer then jams the ether. After a collision each station waits for a random time before trying again.

The CSMA-CD technique enables the Ethernet system to obtain up to 95% of the broadcast channel bandwidth. The improvement in performance over ordinary CSMA is due to the stopping of transmission as soon as a collision is detected. Note that no slots are used so a network-wide timing signal is not required. The transceiver handles all of the CSMACD access, including the retries and delay calculation which is varied with the traffic load. Thus only complete, and checked, packets are passed up to the station interface and only one request is made for a packet to be sent. The checksum generation and checking are carried out within the hardware: bad packets are discarded. A time out mechanism is used to retransmit packets that may have been lost as a result of errors.

Ring networks

The ring technique originated in the USA. The idea was then developed in parallel at Cambridge University in the UK and at two research centres in the USA. The version developed at Cambridge is known as the Cambridge ring in the UK. The computer interface is divided into two parts: the repeater and the interface proper. A ring uses a twisted pair of wires as the transmission medium. However, to improve reliability, the repeater is powered from the ring and electrically isolated from the computer interface, so four wires are used to connect the repeaters. The four wires are used as two pairs for signalling and carry sufficient power for the repeaters. In this way the computer can be switched off and removed from the ring without switching off the repeater. With the ring the medium is terminated at each station, whereas in the cable network it is not. Each station is represented by a repeater, several of which are then connected together into a ring. The repeater is a simple device containing a shift register and some logic to detect certain conditions in the information being passed around the ring. The repeater normally passes any information received on to the next repeater, so transmission only occurs in one direction. When a station transmits data, the repeater transmits the information from the station instead of the information received from the previous repeater.

Slotted ring

There are slight differences in the channel allocation mechanism used in the Cambridge ring and in those rings developed in the USA. In the Cambridge ring a fixed-size mini-packet is used which constantly circulates in the ring, and a special station called a monitor is used to generate and maintain the mini-packet and provide the power for the repeaters. In the American versions a variable-size packet is used which may be lost and regenerated as required by each repeater. The current format of the Cambridge mini-packet. Note that only 16 bits of information are carried in a ring mini-packet whereas the broadcast network packet may contain several hundred bytes. The assembly of information into a block has to be done by the computer. The monitor station also provides a buffer if the ring is not physically long enough to hold a complete mini-packet. The monitor performs a check on the mini-packet each time it passes to ensure that it is intact, and to replace it if not. The monitor is an obvious weakness in the Cambridge ring design so far as reliability is concerned; however, experience so far has shown that monitor failures are rare. The advantage of the monitor is that the repeaters can be very simple as well as cheap, which is the purpose of a local network.

To use the ring to send a packet of information, the station will wait until an empty mini-packet is detected by the repeater. When the full/empty bit in the mini-packet passes the repeater it is set to one. If the packet was already full no change has been made to the bit; if the packet was empty (full/empty bit = 0) the mini-packet is now reserved by this station, The repeater will use this mini-packet if the full/empty bit was received as 0. The addresses of the source and destination stations are placed in the address fields followed by the next 16 bits of the information that the station wishes to send; these are placed in the data field from the station buffer. The reserved mini-packet then travels round to all the other stations on the ring. Each station has a source select register in which an address is placed. If the source address in a mini-packet matches the contents of the source select register, and the destination address matches the station address, the data field is copied into the station receive buffer and the accept status is set at the end of the packet. If the packet is refused, or the destination station is busy, the destination repeater will set the appropriate value in the status bits at the end of the mini-packet. No other change is made by the receiving repeater, and all other repeaters will pass on the mini-packet unchanged. Special values which can be used in the source select register are: all ones, which means accept any source station address, and all zeros, which means do not accept the data from any mini-packets.

When the mini-packet returns to the sending station the full/empty bit is reset to 0 and the status bits are checked to see if the information was accepted. As an error check, the station also reads back the 16 data bits and checks them against the data in its buffer. Having reset the full/empty bit, the station must now wait for another empty mini-packet before it can send the next 16 bits of information. In this way the now empty packet becomes available to successive stations around the ring and the packet slot is allocated in a round robin fashion.

The variable nature of packet traffic in a local network makes it difficult to design a system that will provide a very fast response, especially when there is little traffic, and yet not become overloaded or unfair when the traffic becomes heavy. The broadcast techniques provide a low delay, especially in low-volume traffic, as the transmitter can usually send a packet as soon as one is available. However, as the volume of traffic increases, the broadcast system suffers from collisions and longer delays which can eventually lead to an unstable situation. In the slotted ring the channel is allocated by means of a round robin mechanism so collisions never occur, and during a burst of traffic each station is able to continue transmitting with only a larger delay. During periods of low traffic volume the ring does introduce a delay while a station waits for the empty packet to come round.

Proponents of both systems argue that because of the very high bandwidth available on the channel, and the low processing power of the computers attached to the local network, the volume of traffic is nearly always low in a broadcast network and the delay is negligible in a ring.

Token Ring

The token ring attempts to provide the advantages of broadcast access in low-volume traffic periods, with the inherent sharing of the slotted ring during high-volume traffic periods. The physical topology of the ring is the same, but instead of a circulating mini-packet there is a circulating token. Any host requiring access to the ring waits for the token to arrive; it then changes the token to indicate that a packet is following. The modified token is then followed immediately by the data packet, which can be of any size up to some system maximum. All hosts detect the modified token and examine the packet to see if it is addressed to them; if it is the packet is copied off the ring. The receiving host still sends the packet on though, so the data packet goes all the way round the ring to the sender. The sender takes the packet off the ring. Normally the sender receives the front of the data packet before it has finished transmitting the rest of the packet, owing to the short length of the ring. When the receiver detects the end of the data packet it marks its status by changing the last few bits, as in the Cambridge ring mini-packet; thus the sender knows if the packet was accepted or not. Immediately the sender has finished the packet it puts a token on the ring so another host may have a go.

The token ring is a simple idea, but it is more complex than the Cambridge ring and the interfaces are more expensive. The initialise sequence which is required to start the ring is quite complex as the token has to be put on the ring to start data transfer; of course there can only be one token. The mechanisms for detecting duplicate tokens and lost tokens, without the use of a monitor station, add to the cost of the computer interfaces. IBM carried out extensive tests and simulations of all the local area network technologies, and decided that the token ring was the best available. The company now intends to use the token ring as the basis of its local area network products.

File management utilities

Unlike a manual filing system in which one can glance at documents for information, electronic storage of data means that files must be retrieved from disk and read into memory to review their contents. Thus, electronically stored files can be difficult to identify and access without some sort of file management system. Periodically, old or infrequently used files must be archived to make room for new ones. Such tasks are the "housekeeping" functions with which every user must contend. The File Management utilities are basic functions used in the maintenance and "housekeeping" functions of a hard disk system.

There are six File Management utilities. They include routines for:

- copying files
- moving files from one directory to another
- combining files and performing text searches for character strings
- locating a file on the hard disk
- assigning files as Read-Write or Read-Only access

Why are they used?

Although routine "housekeeping" functions are not difficult to perform, they require a working knowledge of many DOS commands. As a result, some functions are not performed as often as they should be. The File Management utilities are designed to provide the user with a standard set of easy-to-use routines for maintaining a hard disk system.

How to use the utilities

The File Management utilities are accessed when selection 5 is chosen from the *Hard Disk Manager* main menu. This selection changes the directory to \HDU\FILE and displays the File Management menu. Any of the six selections on the screen can be chosen simply by typing the number of the desired utility. After the selection is made, the utilities prompt the user for any required input; informational screens, when necessary, guide the user through the utility. If at any time the user chooses not to proceed with a utility, the < F1 > key can be pressed to return to the previous menu.

For the user who would like additional information on file management and hard disk maintenance, overviews of these topics can be found at the end of this chapter.

Organization of the file management utilities

The batch files and information screens for all of the File Management utilities are found in a single directory: \HDU\FILE. There are no subdirectories for any of the File Management utilities. Because there is no multiple usage of the "Continue (Y/N)?" prompt by these utilities, there is no need for separate directories for the corresponding Y.BAT and N.BAT files.

The contents of the \HDU\FILE directory are shown in Figure 1. As can be seen in Figure 1, there are only three types of files in the \HDU\FILE directory. The numbered batch files start the individual utilities. Each of these displays an appropriate instruction screen (the SCR files). Finally, as indicated by the instruction screen, the user activates the specific utility by entering a command followed by any required parameters. This command is the name of a batch file that performs the given operation (e.g., ARCHIVE.BAT).

```
C:\HDU\FILE <DIR>

1. BAT    ARCHIVE. BAT ARCHIVE. SCR

2. BAT    COMBINE. BAT COMBINE. SCR

3. BAT    MOVE. BAT          MOVE. SCR

4. BAT    SEARCH. BAT   SEARCH. SCR

5. BAT    LOCATE. BAT   FILEMENU. SCR

6. BAT    DOLOCATE. BAT       LOCATE.SCR

7. BAT    DODCOPY. BAT        NOINPUT. TXT

C:\HDU\PROTECT  <DIR>

   PROTECT.BAT   PROTECT.SCR

   UNPROTEC.BAT INSTRUCT.SCR

   Y.BAT        N.BAT
```

Figure 1: Directory and file structure for the file management utilities

Activation of the uilities

Selection 5 on the main menu accesses the File Management utilities by activating the 5.BAT file in the \HDU\FILE directory. It contains the following commands:

```
5. BAT

echo off
cls
cd file
type filemenu. scr
echo ENTER SELECTION:
prompt $e[22;18H
setscrn
```

As can be seen from the above commands, the principal function of this batch file is to change the current directory to the \HDU\FILE directory and to display the File Management screen (FILEMENU. SCR). The last line resets the screen display attributes with SETSCRN. BAT. The File Management menu screen is shown in Figure 2.

File Management Menu

1.	File Archive	4.	Text Search
2.	Move File	5.	Locate File
3.	File Combine	6.	Diskcopy (A: to A:)
			7. File Protect/Unprotect

(Dos 3.0 or higher)

<<Press F1 to Return>>

Figure 2: File management utilities menu

The file management utilities

The file archive utility

The File Archive utility allows the user to copy hard disk files onto a floppy disk in drive A. It provides a structured approach to the DOS COPY command. When a 1 is entered by the user from the File Management screen, an information screen is displayed. Figure 3 shows the text of this screen.

As can be seen from Figure 3, the user is given instructions on how to enter the ARCHIVE command and directions and suggestions in the use of pathnames and global filename characters. The user must enter the command ARCHIVE followed by the pathname/filename of the file(s) to be archived. Before the copy is attempted, a message is displayed showing the user what filename was entered.

Normal DOS messages are displayed if the copy is successful or unsuccessful. The File Management menu is redisplayed regardless of the outcome.

With this utility, you may copy one or more files from the hard disk to a floppy disk in drive A. If the file is too large for one floppy disk, or you wish to copy more files than will fit on the floppy, use the Partial Backup option under the Backup/Restore Utilities.

To archive a file, enter the command ARCHIVE followed by the path and filename. To archive more than one file, use global filename characters.

For example, to archive a file in the \WP directory called MEMO. DOC, the command is entered as

archive \wp\memo.doc

<<<<< Press F1 to Return >>>>>

Figure 3: File archive information screen

Undoubtedly, experienced users will find it easier to simply go straight into DOS to run the COPY command. However, for the less experienced, the information screen in the File Archive utility can be a useful reminder of the necessity of using directory paths, and of the convenience of using global filename characters.

The file archive program files

Two batch files and one information screen make up the components of the File Archive utility. Its execution begins when the user enters 1 from the File Management menu. This causes the 1.BAT file in the \HDU\FILE directory to be executed. The commands in this file are as follows:

```
1. BAT

1:   echo off
2:   cls
3:   type archive.scr
4:   echo ENTER COMMAND:
5:   prompt $e[22;16H
```

The above batch file simply displays an information screen (ARCHIVE.SCR) and positions the cursor after the ENTER COMMAND prompt. The information contained on ARCHIVE.SCR is shown in Figure 3.

When the user enters the command ARCHIVE along with the pathname/filename of the file to be archived, this executes the ARCHIVE.BAT file. This file contains the following commands:

```
     ARCHIVE.BAT
1:   echo off
2:   cls
3:   if "%1 "=="" goto ERROR
4:   echo Copying %1 to disk in drive A...
5:   copy %1 a:
6:   goto DONE
7:   :ERROR
8:   echo You must specify the name of the file with the ARCHIVE command. Try
     again.
9:   pause
10:  cls
11:  type archive.scr
12:  echo ENTER COMMAND:
13:  goto END
14:  :DONE
15:  pause
16:  cd \hdu\file
17:  cls
18:  type filemenu.scr
19:  echo ENTER SELECTION:
20:  prompt $e[22;184
21:  setscrn
22:  :END
```

The IF command in line 3 checks to see if the user has included the argument with the command. The ECHO command in line 4 is a confirmation of the filename the user is attempting to copy. The pathname/ filename that is entered with the ARCHIVE command is substituted for the %1 replaceable parameter in this line as well as the COPY command in line 5.

There is no suppression of output so all DOS messages are displayed if the COPY is successful or unsuccessful. The last five lines redisplay the File Management menu.

The move file utility

Using the Move File utility, a user can copy a file from one location on the hard disk to another location, and then erase the file from the original location. This routine combines the DOS commands COPY and ERASE into one operation.

The process begins when 2 is entered at the File Management menu. This activates the display of an information screen. The user must enter the command MOVE together with two arguments: the source directory/filename and the target directory. The filename is not allowed as a part of the target directory specification; a file automatically will be assigned the same filename in the new location.

Multiple files may be moved using global filename characters in the source information. For example, the following command would move all .WKS files from \123DATA to \NEW123:

```
move \123data\*.wks \new123
```

File Move

With this utility, you may move one or more files from one directory to another. The file is first copied into the target location and then erased from the source location. Multiple files may be moved by using global filename characters in the source filename designation.

To move files, enter the command MOVE followed by the path and filename of the source file, and then the target directory.

For example, to move a file in the \WP directory called REPORT.DOC to the \WP\DATA directory, the command is entered as

```
move \wp\report.doc \wp\data
```

<<<<< Press F1 to Return >>>>>

Figure 4: File move screen

After the MOVE command is entered, a confirmation message appears that displays the source and target arguments entered by the user. For example, the above command produces the following message:

```
Moving \123data\* wks file(s) to \new123..
```

The user must enter the MOVE command with both arguments. If the first argument is absent or invalid, DOS error messages are displayed. If the second argument is absent or invalid, in addition to DOS error messages, the following additional message appears:

Target directory invalid or not specified. Try again.

The user is then returned to the Move Utility Instruction screen. When the file has been successfully moved, the File Management menu is redisplayed.

The move utility program files

The Move File utility is composed of two batch files and one instruction screen. The operation begins with the entry of 2 on the File Management menu. This executes the 2.BAT file in the \HDU\FILE directory. This file has the following commands:

```
2. BAT

1:    echo off
2:    cls
3:    type move.scr
4:    echo ENTER COMMAND:
5:    prompt $e[22;16H
```

The TYPE command (line 3) displays the instruction screen, MOVE.SCR, and positions the cursor after the ENTER COMMAND prompt.

When the user enters the MOVE command, the MOVE.BAT file is executed. The commands in this file are as follows:

```
MOVE.BAT

1:    echo off
2:    cls
3:    if "%2" "= ="" goto ERROR
4:    echo Moving %1 file(s) to %2 . . .
5:    cd %2
6:    if exist move .bat goto ERROR
7:    copy %1 %2
8:    del %1
9:    pause
```

```
10:   cls
11:   cd \hdu\file
12:   type filemenu.scr
13:   echo ENTER SELECTION:
14:   prompt $e[22;18H
15:   setscrn
16:   goto END
17:   :ERROR
18:   echo Target directory invalid or not specified. Try again.
19    pause
20:   cls
21:   type move.scr
22:   echo ENTER COMMAND:
23:   prompt $e[22;16H
24:   :END
```

Line 3 uses the IF command to ensure that the user entered the second argument. This prevents the DEL command (line 8) from erasing the source file without it first being copied. Line 4 generates the confirmation prompt. The %1 and %2 replaceable parameters are obtained from the arguments that the user supplies when the MOVE command is entered.

The function of the CD and IF commands in lines 5-6 is to check that the user has entered a valid directory for the second argument. This prevents the disastrous course of events in which the DEL command (line 8) erases the source file without it first being copied. If the specified directory is not valid, the current directory remains \HDU\FILE. Then, if the MOVE.BAT file is found to exist in the current directory, this means that the current directory has not been changed and an error has occurred; control is then passed to the ERROR portion of the batch file. Otherwise, it can be assumed that the %2 parameter has been entered correctly; DOS thus executes the COPY and DEL commands in lines 7-8.

There are two different "endings": If the ERROR condition occurs, the error message is displayed and the user is returned to the Move File instruction screen. Note that this does not occur if there is a problem with the first argument: DOS error messages are displayed and the File Management menu is redisplayed. This menu is also displayed when the operation is completed successfully.

In all cases, a pause occurs with the message "Strike a key when ready" before the screen is cleared.

The file combine utility

This utility allows the user to utilize the file concatenation abilities of the DOS COPY command. A lesser known function of the COPY command is its file combination or concatenation facility. Using conventional file specifications, several of the COPY command switches, and " + " signs, any number of files may be linked together. With this utility, the user may combine two ASCII (text) files.

The utility is activated when 3 is entered on the File Management menu. This displays the information screen shown in Figure 5. As indicated in the instructions, the second file is appended to the first. The user must enter, the command COMBINE followed by the two arguments: the source file and the file that is to be appended to it.

When the file combine is complete, the following message is displayed:

File combine is now complete. Combined files are stored in

File Combine

This routine will combine two ASCII (text) files. The files will be combined in the first (source) file and stored under that filename. If you wish to combine more than two files, repeat the process with the results of the first combination.

To combine the files, enter the command COMBINE followed by source file, and then the other file that is to be appended to the to the source file. Include any necessary drives and/or paths.

For example, to combine two files in the \123DATA directory called REPORT.PRN and SUMMARY.PRN, where the first file is added to the second, the command is entered as combine \123data\summary.prn\123data\report.p rn

<<<<< Press F1 to Return >>>>>

Figure 5: File combine screen

The file combine program files

The File Combine utility is comprised of two batch files and one information screen. It is activated by the 3.BAT file in the \HDU\FILE directory. This file contains the following commands:

3.BAT

```
1:  echo off
2:  cls
3:  type combine.scr
4:  echo ENTER COMMAND:
5:  prompt $e [22; 16H
```

The above commands display the COMBINE.SCR information screen (fine 3) and position the cursor after the ENTER COMMAND prompt (fines 45).

The program continues when the user enters the COMBINE command with the two required arguments.

COMBINE.BAT

```
1:  echo off
2:  cls
3:  if "%1"= ="" goto ERROR
4:  if "%2"= ="" goto ERROR
5:  copy %1 + %2 %1
6:  echo File combine is now complete. Combined files are stored in %1
7:  goto DONE
8:  :ERROR
9:  echo You must specify both arguments after the  command. Try again.
10: pause
11: cls
12: type combine.scr
13: echo ENTER COMMAND:
14: goto END
15: :DONE
16: pause
17: cd\hdu\file
18: cls
```

```
19:  type filemenu.scr
20:  echo ENTER SELECTION:
21:  prompt $e[22;184
22:  setscrn
23:  :END
```

The two IF commands in lines 3 and 4 check for inclusion of the two required arguments. The COPY operation in line 5 uses the two arguments entered by the user with the COMBINE command for the replaceable parameters %1 and %2. The last five lines redisplay the File Management menu. Line 22 resets the screen display attributes with the SETSCRN.BAT file.

The text search utility

With the Text Search utility, the user may search ASCII files (text files) for specific character strings. It utilizes the DOS FIND filter. A filter is a command or program that transforms input data and outputs the results to a file or a device such as a printer. Through the use of global filename characters and the FOR command, more than one file can be included in the search. It is important to note, however, that this routine is upper and lowercase sensitive (e.g., the letters "a" and "A" are considered different characters).

Text Search

This routine will search through one or more ASCII (text) files for the occurrence of a specified string. To search more than one file, use global filename characters in the filename specification (e.g., *.prn).

The command is entered in the following format: SEARCH<directory location> <filename> <string>

For example, to search all batch files (*.BAT) in the \UTILITY directory for the occurrence of the string "a:", the command would be entered as

search \utility *.bat a:

String may not have spaces. To print results, press [Ctrl) (Prt3c] before entering command; repeat when done to turn off printing.

<<<<< Press F1 to Return >>>>>

Figure 6: Text search screen

The utility begins when 4 is entered from the File Management menu. The user must enter the command SEARCH followed by three arguments: the directory location of the file(s), the filename(s), and the character string that is the subject of the search.

The command is entered in the following format:

SEARCH <directory Location> <Filename> <string>

Each argument is separated by spaces, and the specified string may not contain any space characters. For example, if the user wished to search all .PRN files in the \123DATA directory for the occurrence of the word "Budget," the command would be entered as:

search \123data *.prn Budget

A confirmation of the arguments entered by the user is displayed at the top of the screen.

Searching...Directory: \hdu\protect FILE: *.scr STRING: "example"

-------- INSTRUCT.SCR

[5] (if any) and the name of the file. For example, to protect a

-------- PROTECT.SCR

Search is now complete.

The numbers in brackets are line numbers in the file(s).

Figure 7: Screen output from search utility

Searching ... DIRECTORY: \123data FILE: *.prn STRING:

"Budget"

If the specified directory or filename is not valid or does not exist, an error message is displayed and, after a pause the Text Search information screen is redisplayed.

If the directory and filename entries are valid, the search process begins. The file is listed on the screen as it is searched. Under the filename is listed each line in the file that contains the specified string. The line number appears in brackets at the beginning of each line. Figure 7 shows the screen output generated by search through all SCR files in the \HDU\PROTECT directory for the string "example." Note that the second file had no occurrences of the "example" string, but the filename is listed anyway. When the search is finished, the message "Search is now complete" appears. After a pause, the File Manage-ment menu is redisplayed.

The text search program files

The Text Search utility is made up of two batch files and one information screen, all located in the \HDU\FILE directory. The utility is activated by the 4.BAT file, which contains the following commands:

4. BAT

```
echo off
cls
type search.scr
echo ENTER COMMAND
prompt $e[22;16H
```

There are no special tricks in the above batch file; its main function is to display the SEARCH.SCR file. The program continues when the user enters the SEARCH command and the required arguments. This activates the SEARCH.BAT file.

How SEARCH.BAT works

Refer to Figure 8 to see a listing of the SEARCH.BAT file. Lines 35 check for user input of the required arguments; control is passed to the ERROR1 section if all three have not been entered with the command. Line 6 provides a confirmation prompt that displays the arguments, using replaceable parameters.

SEARCH.BAT

```
1:  echo off
2:  cls
3:  if "%1"= ="" goto ERROR1
4:  if "%2"= ="" goto ERROR1
5:  if "%3"= ="" goto ERROR1
6:  echo Searching DIRECTORY: %1 FILE: %2 STRING:  "%3"
7:  cd %1
8:  if exist search.bat goto ERROR2
9:  if not exist %2 goto NOFILE
10: for %%x in (%2) do find /n "%3" %%x
11: echo?
12: echo End of search.
13: echo The numbers in brackets are line numbers in the  file(s).
14: pause
15: cd \hdu\file
```

```
16:  cls
17:  type filemenu.scr
18:  echo ENTER SELECTION:
19:  prompt $e[22;IBH
20:  setscrn
21:  goto DONE
22:  :ERROR1
23:  echo You must specify all three arguments after command. Try
     again.
24:  goto END
25:  :ERROR2
26:  echo ... your directory does not exist. Try again.
27:  goto END
28:  :NOFILE
29:  echo Specified file(s) not found. Try again.
30:  :END
31:  pause
32:  cd \hdu\file
33:  cls
34:  type search.scr
35:  echo ENTER COMMAND:
36:  prompt $e[22;16H
37:  :DONE
```

Figure 8: SEARCH.BAT File Listing

The CD and IF commands in lines 79 of SEARCH.BAT are attempts at making the routine somewhat "idiot-proof." If the directory argument is not valid, then the current directory remains \HDU\FILE and the subsequent IF command finds SEARCH.BAT to exist. Control then is passed to the ERROR2 section of the batch file and an error message is displayed. Likewise, the second IF command checks to see if the specified file exists; if not, control is passed to the NOFILE section for the display of an appropriate error message. In both cases, the SEARCH.SCR file and prompt are redisplayed.

If the specified arguments pass these little tests, the search is performed with the

FIND command that is embedded in the FOR command (line 10 of SEARCH.BAT). The FOR command is used so that multiple files may be searched when global filename characters appear in the filename parameter. Each filename is displayed on the screen as it is searched. Lines containing the specified string appear under the filename. Nothing is displayed if the string is not found in a file.

When the search is finished, the ECHO commands display some messages, a pause occurs, and the File Management menu is redisplayed (lines 12-19 of SEARCH.BAT). Line 20 resets the screen display attributes with SETSCRN.BAT. Control is shifted to the last line in the file with the GOTO command in line 21 of SEARCH.BAT so that the error conditions are not executed. The ECHO command in line 11 forces a blank line; the "text" of the command is actually an unprintable character, <Alt> 255.

The file locate utility

Every hard disk user suffers the frustration of misplacing a file in the hard disk occasionally. (" . . . I know it's here somewhere.") This utility eliminates the necessity of wading through one directory listing after another in search of the elusive file. It works by using two DOS commands: the CHKDSK (Check Disk) command, and the FIND filter. Using the /V switch with the CHKDSK command generates a list of files (and their paths) on the hard disk; this output is redirected to a file that is then searched by the FIND filter.

The program begins when 5 is entered on the File Management menu. This produces the information screen shown in Figure 9. The user must enter the command LOCATE followed by the filename. The filename must be specified in uppercase letters. This is because the CHKDSK commands generates its output in uppercase; the FIND command is case sensitive (i.e., it differentiates between an "A" and an "a").

Locate file

This routine searches directories on your hard disk for a specified file or files. The filename MUST be entered in upper case.

The command is entered in the following format: LOCATE <filename>

The filename may be with or without extension. If only the extension is entered, all files with that extension will be located. For example, to locate a file called TCRESUME.WK1, the command would be entered as locate TCRESUME.WK1

Again, note that uppercase letters must be used for the filename.

<<<<< Press F1 to Return >>>>>

Figure 9: File locate screen

The command is entered in the following format:

LOCATE <FILENAME>

Global filename characters are not permitted. However, by entering only an extension, or other portions of the filename, a list of all files containing those characters is displayed. For example, to locate all files whose first four characters are MEMO, the command is entered as

locate MEMO

Or, to find all files with extensions of ..DAT, the command is

Locate DAT

After the command is entered, a confirmation prompt appears at the top of the screen. If the specified directory or filename is not valid or does not exist, an error message is displayed and, after a pause, the Text Search information screen is redisplayed.

Starting search. A full disk may take a few minutes; be patient... Looking for file 3CH8C.

--------- Result

C:\123DATA\3CH8C.WKS

C:\123DATA\3CH8C.WK1

End of search.

Strike a key when ready . . .

Figure 10: Screen output from locate utility

If the directory and filename entries are valid, the program begins the attempt to locate the file(s). The drive, path, and filename will be listed for every file on the disk that matches the input specified by the user. If no match is found, no file will be listed, only the message "End of search. Press Enter to continue." Figure 8. 10 shows the output when a file called 3CH8C is located on the hard disk. Note that two entries are displayed because there are two different extensions on this filename.

When the search is finished, the File Management menu is redisplayed.

Printing the results

If the output of the Locate File utility exceeds a single screen, the user may send the output to the printer by pressing < Ctrl > < PrtSc > before the command is entered. Be sure to press these keys again when finished to turn off this "slaving" of the printer (as it's called); otherwise, it will continue to print everything that appears on the screen.

The locate file program files

The Locate File utility is made up of three batch files and one information screen, all located in the /HDU/FILE directory. The utility is activated by the 5.BAT file, which contains the following commands

5.BAT

```
echo off
cls
type locate.scr
echo ENTER COMMAND:
prompt $e[22;16H
```

The purpose of this file is simply to display the LOCATE.SCR information screen, shown in Figure 8.9. The program continues when the user enters the command LOCATE.

How LOCATE.BAT works

When the user enters the command LOCATE, followed by the specified filename, the batch file LOCATE.BAT is activated. This contains the following commands:

LOCATE.BAT

```
echo off
cls
if "%1 "==" goto BADINPUT
command /c dolocate %1
echo off
goto DONE
:BADINPUT
echo You must specify a filename after the command. Try again.
pause
cls
type locate.scr
echo ENTER COMMAND:
prompt $e[22;16H
goto END
:DONE
```

```
16:  cls
17:  type filemenu.scr
18:  echo ENTER SELECTION
19:  prompt $e[22;18H
20:  setscrn
21:  :END
```

Line 3 in the above batch file checks if the user entered an argument with the command. If no argument has been entered, control passes to the BADINPUT section, lines 7-14. Note that in line 4, a batch file subroutine is called. It is DOLOCATE.BAT that contains the heart of the location routine. The program has been structured in this way so that a menu will be redisplayed in the event < Crtl > < Break > is pressed before execution is completed. The DOLOCATE.BAT file contains the following commands:

```
DOLOCATE.BAT
1:   echo off
2:   cls
3:   echo Starting search. A full disk may take a few minutes; be patient.
4:   chkdsk /v <no input.txt>result
5:   echo Looking for file %1.
6:   find "%1" Result
7:   echo
8:   echo End of search
9:   pause
10:  exit
```

The CHKDSK command in line 4 has its output redirected to the file RESULT. The ECHO in line 5 uses a %1 replaceable parameter to display the user's input in the message. In line 6, the FIND command performs the search on the RESULT file for the user filename, which is %1. Line 7 forces a blank line to be displayed (the "text" is the unprintable character, <Alt > 255). At the end of DOLOCATE.BAT, the EXIT command returns control to LOCATE.BAT, line 5.

The diskcopy utility

The Diskcopy utility allows the user to duplicate an entire disk. It uses the DOS command DISKCOPY, and it requires the use of only one disk drive (drive A). It is also one of the simplest routines on the program disk.

It is started by entering 6 at the File Management menu. The screen clears, and the following messages are displayed.

```
This routine duplicates diskettes using a single drive (A) . You will be prompted to
    insert the source and target disks . . .
```

After a pause, the operation begins. This user is prompted by DOS to insert the source disk and target disk at various intervals. The target disk is formatted if it is not already. When the diskcopy is finished, DOS displays the message:

```
Copy another (Y/N) ?
```

A response of Y repeats the operation; N redisplays the File Management menu.

The diskcopy program files

There are only two files in this utility: The 6.BAT and DODCOPY.BAT files in the \HDU\FILE directory. The 6.BAT file contains the following commands:

```
6. BAT
1:    echo off
2:    cls
3:    command /c dodcopy
4:    echo off
5:    cls
6:    type filemenu.scr
7:    echo ENTER SELECTION
8:    prompt $e[22;18H
9:    setscrn
```

In line 3 of the above file, a subroutine batch file, DODCOPY.BAT, is called, using the COMMAND command. This ensures that a menu is redisplayed if the user does a < Ctrl > < Break > before the program is completed. DODCOPY.BAT contains the following commands:

```
DODCOPY.BAT
1:    echo off
2:    cls
3:    echo This routine duplicates diskettes using a single  drive  (drive A) .
```

4: echo You will be prompted to insert the source and target disks . . .

5: pause

6: diskcopy a: a:

7: exit

The DISKCOPY command is performed in line 6 of DODCOPY.BAT. In line 7, control is returned to 6.BAT, line 4. The last five lines redisplay the File Management menu when the diskcopy is complete.

The file protect/unprotect utilities

The File Protect/Unprotect utilities can be used to change the status of a file from Read/Write to Read Only, and vice versa. Note that they can be used only if the system is using DOS 3.0 or higher. This is because these utilities use the DOS command ATTRIB (Attribute), which is not available in earlier versions of DOS.

File Protect/Unprotect Utility

(DOS 3.0 or higher)

This routine allows you to protect files from inadvertent erasure or alteration. Files that have been "protected" are marked as Read-Only, and cannot be erased or changed without first "unprotecting" them marking them as Read/Write.

You MUST be using DOS 3.0 or higher. Do not continue if this is not the case

Figure 11: File protect/unprotect screen

The utilities are accessed by entering 7 from the File Management menu. This displays an information screen that describes the utility and the requirement for DOS 3.0 or higher. The text of this screen is shown in Figure 11. If the user responds to the "Continue (Y/N)? " prompt with N the File Management menu is redisplayed. If Y is entered, an instruction screen is then displayed.

To protect a file, the user is required to enter the PROTECT command followed by the pathname/filename of the file. This makes the file Read Only. Similarly, when the UNPROTECT command is entered followed by the pathname/filename specification, the status of the file is changed to Read/Write. In either case, global filename characters may be used to run the utility on multiple files.

Instructions

To protect a file, enter the command PROTECT followed by the drive and/or path, and the name of the file. For example, to protect a file in the \123\DATA directory called RESUME.WKS, the command is entered as protect \123\data\resume.wks

To unprotect a file, enter the command UNPROTECT followed by the drive and/or path, and the name of the file, as in

unprotect \123\data\resume.wks

<<<<< Press F1 to Return >>>>>

Figure 12: File Protect/Unprotect Instructions

For both utilities, if the directory or filename is not valid, the following error message is displayed:

Invalid directory or file does not exist. Try again.

The instruction screen then is redisplayed. If there is no problem with the pathname/filename parameter, then a message is displayed indicating that the file has been marked either Read Only or Read/Write. In this case, the user then is returned to the File Management menu.

The protect/unprotect program files

There are a few more files involved in the Protect/Unprotect utilities than others in the File Management section. This utility includes five batch files and two information screens. The utility is activated by choosing selection 7 on the File Management menu. The contents of this file are as follows:

```
7. SAT

1:    echo off
2:    cls
3:    cd ..\protect
4:    type protect.scr
5:    echo Continue (Y/N)?
6:    prompt $e [.14; 18H
```

With the exception of this batch file, a other files associated with these utilities are located in the \HDU\PROTECT directory. The above batch file makes \HDU\PROTECT the current directory (line 3), displays an information screen (PROTECT.SCR in line 4), and positions the cursor at the end of the "Continue (Y/N)?" prompt (line 6). The Y.BAT and N.BAT files that are activated by the user in response to this prompt are shown below.

Y. BAT

```
echo off
cls
type instruct.scr
echo ENTER COMMAND
prompt $e[17;16H
```

N. BAT

```
echo off
cls
cd \hdu\file
type filemenu.scr
echo ENTER SELECTION
prompt $e[22;18H
setscrn
```

The N.BAT file redisplays the File Management menu, whereas the Y.BAT file displays the instructions for entering the PROTECT and UNPROTECT commands. When the PROTECT command is entered, the PROTECT.BAT file is executed. This file contains the following commands:

PROTECT.BAT

```
echo off
cls
if not exist %1 goto ERROR
attrib + r %1
echo File(s) now marked Read-Only.
pause
cls
cd \hdu\file
type filemenu.scr
echo ENTER SELECTION:
```

```
12:  setscrn
13:  goto DONE
14:  :ERROR
15:  echo Invalid directory or filename does not exist. Try again.
16:  pause
17:  cls
18:  type instruct.scr
19:  echo ENTER COMMAND:
20:  prompt $e[17;16H
21:  :DONE
```

The IF command in line 3 checks for the existence of the specified file. (A directory path can be used because DOS versions 3.0 and later accept pathnames as part of the EXIST conditions.) If the file is not found, control is shifted to the ERROR section (line 14) of the batch file There an error message is displayed and, after a pause, the instruction screen is redisplayed. If the filename parameter is valid, then the ATTRIB command in line 4 is executed on that file, using the file specified for the %1 replaceable parameter. The confirmation message is displayed and, after the pause, the File Management menu is redisplayed. Line 12 executes SETSCRN.BAT, which resets the screen display attributes.

The UNPROTECT command activates the UNPROTEC.BAT file. (The ending "T" in the command is ignored since filenames cannot exceed 8 characters.) The contents of that file are exactly the same as the PROTECT.BAT file except for lines 4 and 5. In line 4, the ATTRIB command is written as

attrib - r %1

The use of the minus sign in front of the "r" gives the file a Read/Write status. In line 5, the confirmation message indicates that the file is now marked as Read/Write.

Modifying the file management utitlites

File management has different requirements for different users. The authors have no expectations that the utilities included in the File Management Utilities will cover the needs of all users. The utilities that were chosen for inclusion generally met one or both of the following criteria:

the DOS command in its native state is somewhat complicated, easily forgotten, or overlooked

several, DOS operations are required to accomplish the specific task

For this reason, standard DOS file management operations such as COPY, ERASE, and RENAME are not included. These are relatively straightforward operations (for DOS) that are easily executed without the aid of a structured utility. Experienced users will probably find it easier to execute these commands outside of a menu or batch-file environment. (When setting up a main menu, it can be useful to have an "Exit to DOS" menu choice for such situations.)

However, it may be necessary or desirable to totally structure all aspects of file management, particularly if the system is to be used by PC novices. The following section is a "how to" for adding, deleting, or modifying the File Management utilities.

Some *points to* keep *in* mind

Here are a few general suggestions and reminders for commands and operations that may be involved in modifying or creating File Management utilities:

1. When using the COPY command, if the drive or path parameters are not specified in either the source or target files, the default drive is assumed. If the target filename is not specified, the file is given the same filename as the source file.
2. The use of global filename characters can be helpful when applying an operation to multiple files in a directory. This is particularly true for commands such as COPY, ATTRIB, etc. Instruction screens should remind users of the availability of these utilities. Standardized filenaming conventions greatly enhance the applicability of global filename characters.
3. The EXIST and NOT EXIST conditions of the IF command are useful for checking the validity of filename parameters entered by the user. It must be remembered that pathnames cannot be used in this command in DOS versions earlier than 3.0. In such cases, it is necessary to change the directory to the current directory containing the file before the IF command is executed.
4. If it is necessary to make sure that the user has supplied the necessary arguments with a command, the IF command can ne used for this purpose, as in:

   if "%1" =="" got ERROR

   In other words, IF is checking for a blank (or nonexistent) %1 replaceable parameter; if this is true, the GOTO command is executed.
5. The ATTRIB command in DOS 3.0 and later is useful for protecting files from inadvertent erasure.
6. The COPY command can be used to combine files. Files may be appended to a source file, or they may be combined together into an new summary file. Both binary and ASCII (text) files can be combined, using different switch settings in the command.

7. Execution of the main body of a batch file program through a subroutine batch file is advisable if it is possible that the user may press < Ctrl > < Break > during program execution. This ensures that the utility will return to menu and not leave the user stuck in DOS somewhere.

Adding and deleting menu selections

Adding and deleting menu choices on the File Management menu does not require a great deal of effort. There are only a few preliminary points that need to be made before the reader proceeds to that chapter.

The File Management menu is named FILEMENU.SCR and is located in the HDU\FILE directory. All batch and screen files are located in that directory. When adding new menu choices, all batch and screen files should be placed in the \HDU\FILE directory.

There are no Y.BAT and N.BAT files in HDUFILE. This means that the "Continue (Y/N)?" prompt can be used in one new utility that occupies that directory. If more than one utility requires this feature, then it is necessary to create subdirectories for those utilities. This is because only one set of Y.BAT and N.BAT files can occupy the same directory. Likewise, there are no INSTRUCT.SCR files in this directory.

When creating utilities that use the ERASE command, be particularly alert to the possibility of error or misuse by the novice user. Try to anticipate every possible blunder someone might make in using the utility. Then try to build some controls into the batch file to account for these mistakes.

Some possible modification and enhancements

A number of changes can be suggested for the File Management utilities. In addition, depending on the user's needs, more utilities can be developed that build upon the existing ones. The user may modify, delete, or add menu selections to the existing routines. This section describes some suggestions for additional menu choices.

Creating an audit trail of file manipulations

The File Management utilities allow the user to archive files, move files, and combine one or more files. In order to keep track of these modifications, the utilities can be altered to automatically print the changes. This can be done by using DOS's redirection of output facilities.

DOS's redirection facilities allow output to be sent to a number of devices, including the printer. PRN is the reserved device name used by DOS to specify the printer. To direct the output to a printer the symbols >PRN must follow the command. For example, entering the command at the system prompt:

C>DIR>PRN

produces a directory listing of the current directory and outputs the contents of the disk to a printer instead of the display. Consider the first 5 lines of the batch file for the File Archive utility described previously:

```
ARCHIVE.BAT
1:    echo off
2:    cls
3:    if "%1"=="" goto ERROR
4:    echo Copying %1 to disk in drive A ...
5:    copy %1 a:
```

Functionally speaking, the filename(s) that are entered after the command ARCHIVE are inserted as the %1 replaceable parameter. Thus, by using DOS's redirection features, the names of the files that are archived can be sent to the printer by changing line 5 to read:

```
copy %1 a:>prn
```

This same technique can be used on other utilities included in the File Management programs. For example, the user can obtain a printout of the names of files that have been moved, the names of files that have been combined, etc.

Creating an archived file inventory

DOS's redirection facilities also permit the user to output data to a text file. In a process similar to that described above, one can maintain an inventory file of all filenames that have been archived. Using the COPY command, one can continually append newly archived files to an Archived Files Inventory. Consider again the ARCHIVE.BAT file shown above. The output of the archive command can be redirected into a text file (ARCHIVE.TMP):

```
copy %1 a:>archive.txt
```

This temporary file will always hold the most recently archived filename(s).

The " > > " symbols could be used instead of of " > " to append output to an existing file:

```
copy %1 a :>>archive.txt
```

If the output is sent to the file ARCHIVE.TXT, the user then may go to this file and view a list of all files that have been archived. This file can be sorted into ascending or descending alphabetic order.

The user can also "time stamp" the last time/date that files were archived by using another feature of the COPY command. This feature allows the user to change the time and date on the file entry (normally, the time and date are NOT changed when the COPY command is used). Another line is added to the batch file after the append operation:

```
copy archive.txt +,,
```

The two commas in the example are used to define the end of the source file (ARCHIVE.TXT). Otherwise, DOS would expect another filename to follow the " + " sign.

Finally, if one wants to be super-organized, the floppy disks that contain the archived files can be numbered. Then, the user can manually edit (with EDLIN or another text editor) the ARCHIVE.TXT file and insert the number of the disk on which the archived file is located.

A few other short utilities

This section describes some possible additions to the File Management menu. These are utilities that use DOS features not covered in the existing utilities or commands found in the later versions of DOS. The descriptions basically only cover the actual program files.

Copy, erase, and rename utilities

These utilities might be helpful for users who wish to structure all aspects of file management in a menu and batch file environment. This may be a necessity if the hard disk system is being used by DOS novices. In the case of ERASE, the user may wish to build into it an audit trail such as the one described for the File Archive utility.

The batch file that runs these routines would not have to be very complicated. For example, the following commands would suffice for a rename routine:

```
echo off
cls
if "%2"=="" goto ERROR
echo Renaming %1 to %2 . . .
rename %1 %2
goto DONE
: ERROR
echo You must enter two arguments with the command. Try again.
```

```
9:   :DONE
10:  pause
11:  cd \hdu\file
12:  cls
13:  type filemenu.scr
14:  echo ENTER SELECTION:
15:  prompt $e[22;18H
16 : setscrn
```

The use of the replaceable parameters would require the use of a preliminary instruction screen to prompt the user for input. The name of this batch file would be the command that preceded the arguments. The IF command in line 3 checks for the required arguments.

A Copy utility could use the same batch file, substituting a COPY command for the RENAME command. The routine for an Erase utility also could follow the same format. Instead of the RENAME command in the above batch file, the ERASE command would be used, with only one replaceable parameter. For users concerned about inadvertent erasure, the ERASE command could be preceded by a "Y/N" prompt asking users if they wish to copy the file to an archive directory. (Or, for the truly paranoid, the files could be copied automatically.) However, if disk space usage is an issue, this may not be a desirable feature.

A multiple directory copy utility

For users with DOS 3.2 or later, a utility can be added that uses the DOS command XCOPY. This command was introduced in DOS 3.2. It allows the user to copy all files in a directory plus the files of any subdirectories of that directory. This command can be particularly useful if the user is copying an entire floppy diskette with multiple directories to a hard disk. Or, if a system has two hard disks, one can use this command to copy large chunks of one disk to another. A final use of the XCOPY command might be to create a backup disk on a removable cartridge (when the BACKUP format is not desired). The XCOPY command has many switches that involve the use of dates, prompting, the archive bit, and the creation of subdirectories. No attempt is made here to use all of these in the suggested utilities.

A utility that copies a floppy diskette with subdirectories might have the following format:

```
1:   echo off
2:   cls
```

```
3:   echo Insert the floppy diskette in Drive A . . .
4:   xcopy a: \ c:\ /s /w
5:   cd \hdu\file
6:   cls
7:   type filemenu.scr
8:   echo ENTER SELECTION
9:   prompt $e(22;18H
10:  setscrn
```

This utility might be called something like "Copy Entire Floppy To Drive C." The XCOPY command in line 4 copies all files on the floppy diskette to drive C. The /S switch includes files in any subdirectories, creating the necessary directories on the hard disk if they do not already exist. The /W switch makes the XCOPY command wait for the user to insert the floppy diskette in the drive before beginning the search for the source files. Together with the ECHO command preceding it, the following message is displayed:

Insert the floppy diskette in Drive A ...

Press any key to begin copying file(s)

A /P switch could be added that would produce a DOS "Y/N" prompt before each file copied. This would permit copying on a file-by-file basis.

Some background information on file management and hard disk maintenance

When it comes to performing hard disk housekeeping tasks, it is particularly important to be able to quickly locate and identify files. This is because a substantial portion of a user's time must be spent on housekeeping (i.e., moving files from one area of the disk to another, renaming files, combining files, and so on). Since the user is dealing with a fixed-capacity disk, he or she also will periodically want to weed out seldom-used or duplicate files. This can be a tedious, time-consuming task if the user must retrieve every file to determine its contents.

A hard disk system can be organized so that files can be easily identified, located, and manipulated. Using filenaming conventions and a hierarchical directory structure, files can be organized in two fundamental ways:

1. Files may have common identifiers in their filenames so that it is apparent to the user that they have some commonality in content.
2. Files can be logically grouped together in one or more subdirectories, each subdirectory containing files with similar contents.

Using filenaming conventions

Filenaming conventions refer to a general agreement on the usage of filenames to identify and describe the contents of files. A carefully designed filenaming scheme is essential to a well-organized hard disk system for three reasons:

1. Well-designed filenaming conventions describe and/or abstract the contents of a file so that it is meaningful to multiple users. Filenaming conventions also provide a framework for naming subsequently created files.

2. Filenaming conventions greatly increase the efficiency of file management and maintenance if they are used in conjunction with DOS commands and global filename characters.

3. Filenaming conventions allow the user to sort his or her directories and obtain an inventory of relevant files. For example, if date information is included in the filenaming scheme, sorting the directory will provide a list by file type in the date order. Although DOS includes its own date information in the directory listing, the date changes with each update to a file. In contrast, the date information in the filename always reflects the creation or start date of a file.

Filenaming conventions are best established at the time the machine is first installed. This allows one to define a scheme that can be readily understood by multiple users. Users can name new files in accordance with the filenaming conventions, and more importantly, they can quickly locate and identify preexisting files. As the volume of files increases over time, filenaming standards reduce the amount of time required to perform many managerial tasks associated with disk organization and file maintenance.

Using column positions in filenames

Filenaming conventions can be designed in a number of different ways, depending on the needs of the end user and the various types of applications. Perhaps the best way of establishing filenaming conventions is to assign meaning to each of the eight column positions in a filename.

To design a filenaming scheme using column positions, a number of decisions have to be made. Most importantly, the user must decide how to categorize application types (and subtypes, if necessary). Once types and subtypes have been identified, each one must be assigned a unique code (either alpha or numeric).

The user must also decide the detail level that he or she wants to build into the filename. For example, a filename could simply indicate that the file is a memo written on a particular date. Or the filename could contain a reference number to indicate the subject of the memo, the recipient of the memo, and so on.

In designing a filenaming scheme, it is important to construct it with enough flexibility so that more detail may be added at a later time. This could be accomplished by including several "open" positions within the eight-column limitation. When not necessary to the identification of a file, the position(s) could always contain the number "0." If this type of strategy is used, the detail level of the filenaming scheme can be easily modified. Another code number or letter can be added rather than adding or deleting the position itself.

Finally, the user must decide on a logical order of the codes for the various column positions. This order must be consistent for all files on the hard disk. The user then is able to gain maximum benefit from DOS file management features such as directory sorts and global filename characters. This order also should be meaningful to the user. For example, if the most critical identifier of the data files is application type, then this code should precede all others.

Using meaningful syllables in filenames

An alternative to using column positions to establish a filename convention scheme is to use short, meaningful syllables within the filename. Thus, documentation files may be labelled "DOC," model-related files "MOD," and so on. For example, a file containing expenses accrued for the month of February 1987 might be called "EXP0287." Meaningful syllables can be used very effectively under certain circumstances:

1. When all files to be stored on the hard disk are known at the onset; therefore, a great deal of flexibility for handling new filenames is not required.
2. When they are used in conjunction with a highly organized, many-layered, tree-structured directory. In this case, files can be organized into directories and subdirectories by file type, subtype, date, and so on. If the tree-structured directory contains too many levels, however, DOS search and retrieval time will be quite sluggish.
3. The meaningful syllable always appears in the same column positions for each filename. This permits the use of DOS utilities with global filename characters.

The greatest advantage of using this type of filenaming convention is that the first-time user can readily recognize filenames and identify file contents. Extensive documentation on the meaning of each filename column position is not required.

Using global filename characters with filenaming conventions

DOS provides the user with two characters that can be used to perform operations on groups of files rather than individual files. These characters (the symbols? and *) are called Global Filename Characters or wild cards. Use of the? character in a filename or extension means that any character can occupy the position. Use of the * character in a filename or extension means that one or more characters can occupy the position.

Used with a hard disk in which filenaming conventions have been established, global filename characters can be extraordinarily useful when performing operations on groups of like files.

Consider a filenaming convention in which monthly expense files are labelled with the prefix EXP followed by a two-digit month and a two-digit year. For example, the file for February 1987 expense data would be called EXP0287. If one wants to archive all expense files for 1986 from a subdirectory called EXPENSE into a subdirectory containing only expense data for 1986 (called EXPENSE6), the following command would be issued:

COPY C: \EXPENSE\EXP?? 86. * C: \EXPENSE6\EXP?? 86.*

Once the 1986 expense files are copied into the archive directory (EXPENSE6), they can be erased in the current EXPENSE directory:

ERASE EXP?? 86.*

Using the? global filename character, the user must include only the prefix code for file type ("EXP") and the year ("86") in the command specification. If, for example, 50 or more files are included in this population, performing this function without using global filename characters could be a highly time-consuming process.

Setting up a hierarchical file and directory structure

Information stored on the fixed disk of the XT and AT can be organized by function and type. This is one of the most important features of DOS, since thousands of files may be placed on the fixed disk. The storage capacity of a 20-megabyte fixed disk is approximately 56 times greater than that of a single 360-KB floppy disk and 17 times that of a high-capacity disk. With a large amount of information stored on the fixed disk, locating a specific file could be a slow process. However, with DOS, quick access of information on the fixed disk can be achieved through the use of hierarchical directories.

The first task in designing a hierarchical directory system is deciding how the directory system is to be structured. DOS gives the user a great deal of flexibility in setting up a hierarchical directory. When a disk is formatted, DOS starts the basic organization of the directory system by creating one main directory. The structure of the directory system after this point is determined by the user.

Structuring a hierarchical directory

The starting point for all hierarchical directories is the root directory. All formatted disks contain a root directory; in DOS versions 2 and 3 the root directory may contain programs, data files, or the names of other directories (subdirectories). However, most individuals prefer to limit the root directory to system or program files. Each directory within the root directory may contain its own set of programs, data files, or directories (subdirectories). This type of organization is referred to as a tree-structured directory. The branching of directories into subdirectories may be extended out as far as necessary.

Hierarchical directories may be structured in any manner that is convenient for the user. To demonstrate how a directory might be organized, consider the following example. The fixed disk on a PC-AT is used to store DOS files, a word processing program, and a spreadsheet program.

The word processing directory (WP) might contain all the files necessary to run *DisplayWrite3* as well as three further subdirectories of its own.

\WP\DOC (Documentation Subdirectory)

\WP\MEMO (Memo Subdirectory)

\WP\ADMIN (Administrative Reports Subdirectory)

Each of the word processing subdirectories might in turn contain fur. ther subdirectory divisions. For example, the \WP\MEMO subdirectory might contain separate subdirectories by month. Thus, the subdirectory structure might contain:

\WP\MEMO\JAN

\WP\MEMO\FEB

\WP\MEMO\MAR

etc.

Hierarchical directory paths

Hierarchical directories allow DOS to quickly locate a specified file. This is because DOS sees only the files contained in the specified directory when it is searching for a file. The system is able to do this by using a pathname that precedes the filename. A pathname specifies each directory through which DOS must move in order to access the specific file. Each directory in the pathname is separated by the backslash symbol (\). For example, using the hierarchy described above, the path from the Root Directory to a January 19, 1987 memo would be:

C:\WP\MEMOS\JAN\NCFX0119.TXT

Note that a backslash also separates the directory name from the filename.

Hard disk supervision

This chapter is not just a description of the installation steps. It is important to understand exactly what operations are being performed during installation. This does not mean that anything radical is being done to your hard disk. On the contrary, the routines are fairly uncomplicated. This chapter is for those users want to know what is happening when anything, no matter how minor, is being done to their systems. Many experienced users will say that they never run the installation routine of an unknown program without first checking to see what it does. This chapter explains the process.

Requirements

The system requirements for the use of these programs are minimal. There are no system memory requirements because none of these routines is memory resident. The only requirements are as follows:

1. The user's hard disk must contain all of the DOS programs (the DOS disk and the Supplemental Programs disk). The user must know the directory location of DOS on the hard disk. The DOS version may be 2.0 or later.
2. It is assumed that all individuals using *Hard Disk Manager* are using a hard disk system with a C drive.

If the user can answer "yes" to the above requirements, the installation of all of *Hard Disk Manager* is a straightforward process. If the hard disk does not contain the DOS programs, the DOS manual should be consulted for instructions on how to install all of the DOS programs on the hard disk.

It should also be noted that the program disk does not contain any operating system files; the computer cannot be started using this program disk as a "boot" disk.

Installing the entire program

The amount of disk space occupied by the *Hard Disk Manager* varies with the size of the hard disk. For example, on a 20-MB hard disk, the program uses approximately 700 KB of disk space. A directory structure is created and the files are copied into these directories. There should be no overlap with any existing directories since there is only one directory created at the second level under the root directory: \HDU. All of the other directories created are subdirectories of \HDU.

Steps

The only information required of the user is the directory containing the DOS files. During the installation process, the user is prompted for this information. Otherwise, the process is as follows:

1. Turn on the computer. After the DOS system prompt (the C > symbols) is displayed, insert the *Hard Disk Manager* disk in drive A.
2. Enter the following command:

   a: install

3. An information screen that describes the installation process will be displayed. A "Strike any key when ready" message appears at the bottom of the screen; press a key for the installation process to proceed.

4. After a few moments, a prompt for the name of the directory containing the DOS program files appears. You must:

Enter the directory name (including the drive and path). The path should include all path parameters currently on your disk.

Press the < F6 > function key.

Press < Enter >.

Pressing the < F6 > key causes the symbols ^ Z to be displayed; this is normal. The installation process then continues.

5. A check is made to determine if the DOS directory input is valid (i.e., if the specified directory does indeed contain the DOS program files). If the input is not valid, an error message is displayed and the installation is aborted.

6. If the DOS directory specification is valid, the installation proceeds to create the necessary directories and to copy program files into them. This section takes about 5 to 10 minutes, depending on the speed of ones system.

7. A message is displayed when the installation is complete.

8. You must then reboot the computer (press < Ctrl > < Alt > < Del >).

9. To start the program, change the current directory to the root directory (by entering the command CD\).

Then, enter the command

hdu

to display the *Hard Disk Manager* main menu.

That is all there is to the installation of *Hard Disk Manager.* Be sure you make a backup copy of the program disk. The program is always started by executing the command hdu from the root directory. The following section describes the action that is taken during the installation process.

The installation of all of *Hard Disk Manager* begins with INSTALL.BAT and is completed with CONTINUE.BAT.

Installation is now complete. To start the program...

1. Remove disk from drive A

2. Reboot the system (by pressing [Ctrl] [Alt] [Del])
3. Enter the command CD\
4. Then, enter the command HDU

Figure 1. Hard Disk Manager Final Installation Message

Basically, the installation can be divided into the operations listed:

1. The directory containing the DOS program files is specified by the user.
2. The user's DOS directory input is added to a file that becomes CONTINUE.BAT.
3. The validity of the DOS directory information is checked.
4. The ANSI.SYS file is copied to the root directory.
5. The necessary directories are created.
6. The *Hard Disk Manager* programs are copied into the new directories.
7. A check is made to determine if a CONFIG.SYS file exists. (CONFIG.SYS is a configuration file required to run some of the *Hard Disk Manager* utilities.) If CONFIG.SYS does not exist, this file is copied to the root directory; if it does exist, then the command DEVICE= ANSI.SYS is appended to the existing file.
8. The DOS directory information is appended to a PATH command that is stored in a separate file for future use. This PATH command also is added to the beginning of the HDU.BAT file. This is the batch file that calls up the *Hard Disk Manager* main menu.

Installing part of Hard Disk Manager

For users interested in installing only certain components of *Hard Disk Manager,* the installation process is somewhat different. A directory structure is created, but only the directories necessary for the desired utility are created. Like the complete installation, there should be no overlap with any existing directories since there is only one directory created at the first level under the root directory: \HDU The other directories created are subdirectories of the \HDU directory.

The partial installation process can be divided into two parts. The first part is automated, whereas the second part is menu driven. The automated process performs the initial configuration routines that are necessary for all the programs on *Hard Disk Manager.* It is executed only once.

Steps

The first part of the installation performs the following operations: The user is asked to specify the location of the DOS program files; the validity of the user's entry is checked; a CONFIG.SYS file is created or the command DEVICE= ANSI.SYS is appended to an existing one; the \HDU directory is created; and some key files are copied to the new directory. Here are the specific steps.

1. Turn on the computer. After the DOS system prompt (the C > symbols) is displayed, insert the *Hard Disk Manager* disk in drive A.

2. Enter the following command:

   a: partial

3. You are prompted for the name of the directory containing the DOS program files. You must:

   Enter the directory name (including the drive and path).

   Press the < F6 > function key.

   Press <Enter >.

   Pressing the < F6 > key causes the symbols ^ Z to be displayed; this is normal. The preparation routine then continues.

4. A check is made to determine if the user's DOS directory input is valid (i.e., if the specified directory does indeed contain the DOS program files). If it is not valid, an error message is displayed and the preparation process is aborted. (The user should refer to the "Troubleshooting" section of this chapter.)

5. If the DOS directory specification is valid, the necessary directories are created and certain files are copied into them. This section takes a few minutes. A message informs the user when the preparation routine is complete. Pressing any key will display a menu of installation options.

6. The Installation Menu contains the following options:

   Install Disk/Directory Utilities

   Install Customized Display Utilities

   Install Screen Design Utility

   Install Backup/Restore Utilities

   Install File Management Utilities

   Install HELP Utilities

   Install All Utilities

   Exit To DOS

You may select one or more of these components of *Hard Disk Manager* for installation. All utilities may be installed even if individual components have previously been installed.

7. When the desired portions of *Hard Disk Manager* have been installed, select the Exit To DOS option.

8. Each selected utility is now installed. The following commands call tip the menu associated with the specific utility from the \HDU directory:

Disk/Directory:	DISK
Display:	DISPLAY
Screen Design:	DESIGN
Backup/Restore:	BACK
File Management:	FILE
Help Utilities:	HELP

9. *You must then reboot the computer* (press <Ctrl> <Alt> <Del>).

10. Then, change the current directory to C:\HDU and execute the appropriate command.

Installation Menu

1. InstallDisk/Directory Utilities
2. InstallCustomized Display Utilities
3. InstallScreen Design Utility
4. InstallBackup/Restore Utility
5. InstallFile Management Utilities
6. InstallHELP Screen Utilities
7. InstallALL Hard Disk Utilites
8. Exit to DOS

Troubleshooting

This section briefly covers some problems that may be encountered during installation and use of *Hard Disk Manager*.

Invalid directory specification

This is the problem when the user encounters the error message "Your DOS directory specification was not specified correctly." Here are some possible errors:

1. The specified directory does not contain DOS. Check to make sure that the directory really contains DOS. Run the DIR command and look for files such as

FORMAT, TREE, DISKCOPY, and EDLIN. If DOS is not found, you must copy the DOS program files into a directory on the hard disk and rerun the installation.

2. The pathname entered with the directory name was invalid. The complete path must be specified. For example, if the directory containing DOS is \DOS, the directory should be entered as

   C:\DOS

   If the root directory contains DOS, the directory would be specified as

   C:\

   Also, be careful of typing errors.

Strange characters after the prompt

Odd characters may appear at the bottom of the menu as a prompt, below the ENTER SELECTION line, such as

[1, 59; "return", 13p; [22; 18H

This is a result of an absent CONFIG.SYS file. If this file does not exist on your system when *Hard Disk Manager is* installed (either partially or totally), the installation routines should create it. If you have just installed *Hard Disk Manager* utilities, you must restart (reboot) your system before using any of the utilities. The CONFIG.SYS file is only read by DOS at start-up time. If you have already done this, here are some possible solutions:

1. Enter the following command:

   type c:\config.sys

   The contents should contain the following line:

   device = ansi.sys

2. If DOS responds with a "File not found" message, then place the *Hard Disk Manager* disk in drive A and enter this command:

copy a:\hdu\disk\auto\config.tmp c:\config.sys

3. If the CONFIG.SYS file exists, but does not contain the line shown above, the~ place the *Hard Disk Manager* disk in drive A and enter this command:

copy c:\config.sys + a:\hdu\disk\auto\config.tmp

4. If the CONFIG.SYS file exists and contains the required line shown above, then try entering this command:

   dir c:\ansi.sys

If a "File not found" message is the response, then you must copy the ANSI.SYS file from your DOS directory to the root directory, as in:

copy c:\dos\ansi sys c:\

One of the above steps should solve the problem. Be sure to reboot the system after performing any of the above steps.

Conflicts with additional PATH Commands

In order for Hard *Disk Manager* to work, it is necessary for the user to specify the directory containing the DOS programs. This information is placed in a PATH command at the beginning of a file called HDU.BAT. (This is the command file that calls the *Hard Disk Manager* program.)

If the user's system contains an AUTOEXEC.BAT file, and that file also contains a PATH command, there may be problems if the specified paths are not the same in both files. The problems will only be evident when the other programs are executed after *Hard Disk Manager* has been run. Here are the steps for investigating this possibility.

1. Enter the following command:

type c:\hdu\ hdu.bat

The first line of this file should contain the PATH command.

2. Now enter this command:

type c :\autoexec.bat

If your system responds with the message "File not found," or no PATH command is found in the displayed file, then the PATH command is not causing a problem.

3. However, if there is a PATH command in the AUTOEXEC.BAT file, compare its contents to the same command in the HDU.BAT file. Disregard differences in upper- and lowercase letters or the presence or absence of the "equals" (=) sign.
4. If any directories are shown in the AUTOEXEC.BAT file's PATH command, these should be added to the HDU.BAT file. For example, suppose the HDU.BAT file contains the command

path c:\; c:\dos

and the AUTOEXEC.BAT file contains this PATH command:

path c:\; c:\dos; c:\utility

5. The additional directory (c:\utility) must be added to HDU.BAT. Here is the procedure for editing HDU.BAT

a. Change your current directory to the directory containing your DOS program files.

b. Enter the following command:

edlin c:\hdu.bat

EDLIN will respond with the message "End of file."

c. To edit the first line, enter the number 1. EDLIN will display the contents of the existing line 1.

d. Type the existing line exactly as it appears, and add the additional directory at the end of the line; then press <Enter>.

e. End the EDLIN session by entering the command

E

Pressing <Ctrl> <Break>: No Menu, No Prompt

The user may encounter problems when the < Ctrl > < Break > is activated during the running of some of the utilities. Under normal execution, all the utilities will return to a menu screen. However, if <Ctrl> < Break > is pressed during the execution of a utility and a menu does not reappear, the user can press the < Fl > key to redisplay the menu.

Removing all utilities from the hard disk

If the user, alas, wishes to remove all of the *Hard Disk Manager* from his or her hard disk, a batch file has been included on the program disk that will do the entire process. This routine will erase all files in the directory system of the *Hard Disk Manager.* If any nonprogram files are stored in those directories, they too will be erased. After the directories are emptied, they will be removed. There will be no trace of Hard *Disk Manager* on the user's system.

Hard Disk Manager is removed by placing the *Hard Disk Manager* program disk in drive A, and entering the following command:

a:remove

Of course, if the user later decides that this was folly, the *Hard Disk Manager* can simply be reinstalled.

INSTALL.BAT

1: echo off

2: cls

```
type a:title.scr
pause
cls
a:
echo    This routine installs all of Hard Disk Manager on your
echo    hard disk. The program is installed on drive C.
echo    DOS must already be installed on the hard disk. You will
echo    be prompted to enter its path and directory name.
echo    Those unfamiliar with DOS should read Chapter 3 prior to
echo    proceeding. The installation process is explained in this chapter.
echo    To abort the installation, press [Ctrl] [Break], and
echo    then a "Y" in response to "Terminate batch job (Y/N)?"
pause
cls
type dospath.scr
copy con:dospath.tmp
if not exist dospath.tmp goto ABORT
copy dospath1.txt + dospath.tmp + continue.txt continue.bat
continue
:ABORT
echo    DOS directory information was   not specified correctly;
echo    installation aborted.
echo    Please refer to Chapter 3 for installation procedures.
c:
```

Install.Bat Batch File

Disk organisation utilities

How much data can be stored on a disk and how those data are stored are issues of primary concern to users. When a vast amount of data are stored electronically, the user wants some assurance that the data can be retrieved reliably and with a minimal amount of effort. Although the operating system manages how the data are physically stored, it is up to the user to determine the media (hard disk, floppy disk, tape, etc.) and the logical groupings of the data into directories, subdirectories, and files. The Disk/Directory utilities guide users through the development of a logical directory structure and assist in the management and organization of their storage media.

There are five Disk/Directory utilities. They include routines for:

- setting up a logical directory structure and linking it to a master menu for easy access to any subdirectory
- viewing and/or printing the contents of directories and subdirectories
- formatting floppy disks under a number of different conditions

The key to a well-managed hard disk system is having an easily accessible and well-organized directory and file structure. Particularly when a number of different users will be retrieving and storing data, the administrative tasks associated with maintaining many data files can be overwhelming.

The Disk/Directory utilities address this problem. They provide menu-driven access to all of the necessary directories, subdirectories, and software programs. Such menu-based programs can navigate even the most inexperienced user through a hierarchical directory structure.

In addition, these utilities eliminate the need to memorize complicated DOS commands and minimize potential errors associated with using certain disk-related commands.

The Disk/Directory utilites are accessed when selection 1 is chosen from the *Hard Disk Manager* main menu. This selection changes the directory to \HDU\DISK and displays the Disk Directory Menu.

Any of the five selections on the screen can be chosen simply by entering the number of the desired utility. After the selection ' is made, the user is prompted for any required input; informational screens, when necessary, guide the user through the utility. If at any time the user chooses not to proceed with a utility, the < F1 > key can be pressed to return to the previous menu.

Organization of the disk/directory utilities

The disk organization utilities contained on the *Hard Disk Manager* program disk are made up of numerous files in several different directories. The principal directory is the \HDU\DISK directory. It contains the routines for all the Disk/Directory utilities except the second menu choice on the Disk/Directory menu.

Although there are over 70 files in the \HDU\DISK directory, most of these are used by the Menu/Directory Setup utility. This is a fairly extensive program, and there are two subdirectories also used by this utility: \HDU\DISK\MP and \HDU\DISK\AUTO. The first of these contains the programs for installing the Miscellaneous Programs option on the main menu. The \HDU\DISK\AUTO directory contains the files used for installation of the main menu onto the system.

C:\HDU\DISK <DIR>			
1. BAT	1DBINPUT. TXT	3DBINPUT. TXT	5DBINPUT. TXT
2. BAT	1EXINPUT. TXT	3EXINPUT. TXT	5EXINPUT. TXT
3. BAT	1HDINPUT. TXT	3HDINPUT. TXT	5HDINPUT. TXT
4. BAT	1MPINPUT. TXT	3MPINPUT. TXT	5MPINPUT. TXT
5. BAT	1SSINPUT. TXT	3SSINPUT. TXT	5SSINPUT. TXT
	1WPINPUT. TXT	3WPINPUT. TXT	5WPINPUT.TXT
A. BAT	2DBINPUT. TXT	4DBINPUT. TXT	6DBINPUT. TXT
B. BAT	2EXINPUT. TXT	4EXINPUT. TXT	6EXINPUT. TXT
C. BAT	2HDINPUT. TXT	4HDINPUT. TXT	6HDINPUT. TXT
D. BAT	2MPINPUT. TXT	4MPINPUT. TXT	6MPINPUT. TXT
E. BAT	2SSINPUT. TXT	4SSINPUT. TXT	6SSINPUT. TXT
F. BAT	2WPINPUT. TXT	4WPINPUT. TXT	6WPINPUT. TXT
G. BAT			
	DBBEGIN. TXT	EXIT 2DOS. BAT	SSBEGIN. TXT
	DISKMENU. SCR	MAINMENU. TMP	WPBEGIN. TXT
	END. TXT	MENU. BAT	SETUP. SCR
	CR. TXT		
	DOCOPYC1. BAT	DOFORM3. BAT	DOFORM5. BAT
	DOCOPYC2. BAT	DOFORM4. BAT	
	SSSTART. TXT	WPSTART. TXT	DBSTART. TXT
	SSSTART. BAT	WPSTART. BAT	DBSTART. BAT
C:\HDU\DISK\VIEW		<DIR>	
1. BAT	INSTRUCT. SCR	VIEW. BAT	DOTREE2. BAT
2. BAT	VIEW. SCR	DOVIEW. BAT	DOTREE3. BAT
3. BAT	PRINT. BAT	DOPRINT. BAT	
C:\HDU\DIST\AUTO		<DIR>	
Y. BAT	MANUAL.BAT	INSTRUCT. SCR	AUTOEXEC. TMP
N. BAT	AUTO.BAT	MAKEAUTO. SCR	RETURN. TMP
	CONFIG.TMP	NURETURN. TMP	

C:\HDU\DISK\MP		<DIR>	
Y. BAT	MP2BEGIN.TXT	MP2. SCR	MISCPROG. SCR
N. BAT	MP3BEGIN.TXT	MP3. SCR	DOCOPYC3. BAT
1. BAT	MP4BEGIN.TXT	MP4. SCR	
MISCPROG. BAT		MP5BEGIN. TXT	MP5. SCR
		MP6BEGIN. TXT	MP6. SCR
		MPBEGIN. TXT	MPLINE. SCR
		MPEND. TXT	MPINSTRU. SCR

Figure 1: Directory and file structure for Disk/Directory Utilities

The \HDU\VIEW directory contains the files that run the second menu choice, Disk and Directory View/Print Utilities.

Above figure shows the structure of the files and directories for the Disk/Directory utilities. As is shown in figure, there are basically three file types used by the Disk/Directory utilities: the batch files (.TXT extensions), information/instruction screens (.SCR extensions), and EDLIN input files (.TXT extensions). The .TXT files serve as input to batch files where the EDLIN program is executed inside the batch file.

Activation of the utilities

Selection of choice 1 on the main utility menu accesses the Disk/Directory utilities by activating the 1.BAT file in the \HDU directory. It contains the following commands:

1. BAT

1: echo off

2: cls

3: cd disk

4: type diskmenu. scr

5: echo ENTER SELECTION:

6: prompt $e [22;18H

7: sctscrn

DISK/DIRECTORY MENU

1. Main Menu and Directory Setup Utility
2. Disk and Directory View/Print Utilities
3. Format a Floppy (Data Disk)

4. Format a Floppy (System Disk)
5. Format a 360 KB Floppy in High- Capacity Drive

<< Press F1 to Return >>

Figure 2: Disk/directory Utility Menu Screen

The functions of this file are to change the current directory to \HDU\DISK, display the Disk/Directory menu (DISKMENU.SCR), position the cursor at the end of the ENTER SELECTION: prompt, and to reset the screen display attributes (setscrn). Figure 2 shows the Disk/Directory screen.

The disk/directory utilities

The menu/directory setup utility

This is one of the key utilities in the *Hard Disk Manager.* This utility allows the user to create a directory structure for common microcomputer applications (such as spreadsheet and word processing programs), and a menu system that accesses these applications. The user decides what the contents of the main menu should be.

The menu choices

The choices that can appear on the main menu include: Word Processing, Spreadsheet, Database, Exit To DOS, Hard Disk Manager, and Miscellaneous Programs. The menu choice Miscellaneous Programs is a submenu to which the user can add any program or application not found on the main menu. The user selects one or more of these six items (in any order) for inclusion in the main menu. The main menu can be installed in the system so that it is displayed automatically every time the system is turned on or restarted, or it may be installed so that it is displayed whenever the user manually enters the command MENU at a DOS prompt. Figure 3 shows the appearance of this main menu when all six menu choices have been placed on the menu.

Main Menu

1. Word Processing
2. Spreadsheet
3. Database
4. Hard Disk Manager
5. Miscellaneous Programs
6. Exit to DOS

Figure 3: Main menu screen with six options

It should be noted at the onset that this simple menu system is just that--it is a simple menu structure that is created entirely with DOS commands and utilities. Because it involves no compiled code, it can be modified to meet the needs of individual users. Without the cost of purchasing a menu-creation program, one can create a menu system that gives the average hard disk user the ability to organize and easily access hard disk applications.

Choosing menu selections

The Main Menu Setup Utility screen is displayed when selection 1 is chosen on the Disk/Directory menu. From here, the menu and directory structure is created in a two-step process.

Main Menu Setup Utility

This utility creates and installs a main menu. Selections A-C will Prompt you for the following information:

— The name of the directory where the program resides (the directory will be created if it does not exist)

— The command that runs the program (e.g., "lotus" for Lotus 1-2-3).

Add Selections A-F one at a time, in any order, as needed. You MUST execute Selection G when the last menu choice has been added.

A. Add WORD PROCESSING Menu Choice

B. Add SPREADSHEET Menu Choice

C. Add DATABASE Menu Choice

D. Add EXIT TO DOS Menu Choice

E. Add HARD DISK MANAGER Menu Choice

F. Add MISCELLANEOUS PROGRAMS Submenu (Directory: \MISC)

G. Install Completed Main Menu

<< Press F1 to Return >>

Figure 4: Main menu/Directory setup utility

1. A menu item can be added to the main menu by entering the letter of the desired item (letters A through F). This step is repeated for each item that is to be placed on the main menu.
2. The last menu choice (letter G, Install Completed Main Menu) is entered after all the desired menu items have been added to the main menu.

These two steps are described in more detail below.

Constructing the menu

In step 1, when selections A, B, C, or F are entered, directories are created for the respective applications. With selections A-C, the user is prompted to supply the name of the directory; in selection F, the directory is automatically called \MISC.

Also, in selections A, B, and C, since these menu selections will activate specific applications programs, the name of the command that calls up that specific program must be entered. For example, if selection A is executed, the user is prompted to enter the command that executes the word processing program. Suppose that program is *MultiMate;* the user must enter the command that calls up the *MultiMate* program, which in this case is wp.

Depending on the speed of ones system, a few minutes may be required each time a menu selection is added to the main menu. During the process, various messages are displayed that provide information about the action being taken. The Menu/Directory Setup screen is redisplayed after a selection has been added. The process is then repeated for another selection. Finally, if there are no further menu additions, the main menu is installed by executing selection G.

Installing the New Menu

The second step in setting up the main menu is the installation. When the Installation routine is started (by entering G from the Setup menu), an information screen is displayed asking the user if the display of the main menu is to be automatic or manual. Manual display means that the menu will be displayed only when the user enters the command MENU after a normal DOS prompt (e.g., the C > prompt).

Instructions

This routine installs your completed menu into your root directory. The Main Menu can be displayed one of two ways:

- AUTOMATICALLY, whenever your system is turned on or a system reset is performed; or,
- MANUALLY, by entering a command (called MENU) whenever you wish to call up the Main Menu.

For automatic menu display, it is necessary to create (or add to) an AUTOEXEC.BAT file. If this file already exists, the necessary commands will be appended to the end of that file.

Enter the command AUTO to have the menu displayed automatically. Enter the command MANUAL to have the menu displayed manually.

<< Press F1 to Return >>

Figure 5: Information screen for installing new menu

The command MANUAL must be entered to set up a manual display of the main menu; AUTO is used for automatic display. When AUTO is entered, the batch file creates an AUTOEXEC.BAT file, if one does not already exist. If this file does exist, then the contents of the file are displayed on the screen.

The user is then asked if additional commands may be added to the end of the file so that the main menu can be displayed. This is done through a confirmation prompt: "Continue (Y/N)?" A Y response adds the necessary commands to the end of the AUTOEXEC.BAT file and completes the installation process. N aborts the AUTO routine and the screen informs the user that the MANUAL option should be used to install the main menu.

When either the MANUAL or AUTO routines are finished, the user is informed that the installation is complete. In both cases, the user is placed in the DOS environment, with the standard DOS prompt (C >). Users who have chosen the AUTO option must reboot their system to see the main menu. If the MANUAL option has been executed, only the command MENU must be entered to see the new menu.

The menu/directory setup program files

The batch files that run the Menu/Directory Setup utility are some of the longer routines contained in *Hard Disk Manager.* The utility begins when selection 1 is entered from the Disk/Directory menu. This activates the 1.BAT file in the \HDU\DISK directory; it contains the following commands:

1. BAT

```
1: echo off
2: cls
3: type setup. scr
4: echo ENTER SELECTION:
5: prompt $e [22;18H
```

The function of this file is to display the Menu/Directory Setup screen.

The files used by this utility can be grouped as follows

1. The letter batch files (A.BAT through F.BAT) in the \HDU\DISK directory; these are used for adding selections to the main menu.
2. The .TXT files, which are used by the letter batch files as input files for EDLIN routines executed in those files; they also are files that are combined with other files.
3. The files in the \HDU\DISK\MP directory, which are used when the Miscellaneous Programs choice is added to the main menu.

4. The G.BAT file and all of the screen and batch files located in the \HDU\DISK\AUTO directory; these files are used during menu installation.

The first three categories relate to the addition of individual menu items to the main menu. The last category involves the installation of the newly completed menu into the system. These are described in detail below.

The program files for adding menu selections

The letter batch files add the individual menu items to the main menu. Although some of these files tend to be quite lengthy (some are over 100 lines), the functions they perform are fairly simple and there is a great deal of repetition.

The A.BAT file and the four files to which it passes control (DOCOPYC1.BAT, WPMORE.BAT, DOCOPYC2.BAT, and WPSTART.BAT) are reproduced. An understanding of the workings of these files will apply to all the other letter files. It should be noted that the program files for selections A, B, and C are more complicated than the other selections because the user is specifying a directory; this is not the case in selections D, E, and F.

Five batch files are executed when A.BAT is selected:

- A.BAT, which calls a subroutine batch file DOCOPYC1.BAT
- A.BAT then calls WPMORE.BAT
- WPMORE.BAT executes WPSTART.BAT
- WPSTART.BAT calls a subroutine batch file, DOCOPYC2.BAT

The subroutine files DOCOPYC1.BAT and DOCOPYC2.BAT are COPY CON routines for: 1) user input of the directory names, and 2) command execution names for the Word Processing program. The same files are also used by the batch files for Selections B and C.

How the program files work

The A.BAT file begins by immediately passing control to the DOCOPYC1.BAT file, where the user is prompted to input the name of the directory containing the word processing program. The first three lines of A.BAT are shown below:

A.BAT (beginning)

1: echo of f

2: cls

3: command /c docopyc1 WORD-PROCESSING wpdir. tmp c:\wp

The call is made to the DOCOPYC1. BAT subroutine batch file in line 3 above.

There are a number of arguments following the command: the name of the batch file (DOCOPYC1), and three replaceable parameters that are used by DOCOPYC1. The breakdown of components in line 3 is as follows:

Component:	Function
command /c	Invokes secondary command processor
docopyc1	This is the batch file subroutine
WORD-PROCESSING	This is the %1 replaceable parameter in the subroutine, indicating the directory name
wpdir. tmp	This is the %2 parameter in the subroutine for a temporary file that holds the user's input
c:\wp	This is the %3 replaceable parameter in the subroutine, which is the text of the example

Note that there is a hyphen in "WORD-PROCESSING." This is because the spaces are interpreted as delimiters between the arguments.

The DOCOPYC1.BAT functions to execute the COPY CON routine for the user input of the directory name. It is structured in a subroutine context so that, should < Ctrl > < Break > be pressed, the user is not left out in DOS somewhere with no menu and no prompt. It contains the following commands:.

```
DOCOPYC1.BAT

1: echo off
2: cls
3: echo    First, you must specify the name of the %1 directory.
4: echo    Use the format shown in the example below. (If you make a
5: echo    mistake, press [Ctrl] [Break], and start over.)
6: echo (Example: %3)
7: echo Please ENTER the directory name, PRESS the F6 key and then PRESS
   Enter
8: copy con: %2
9: exit
```

In line 3, the %1 variable is replaced by "WORD-PROCESSING." The %3 variable in line 6 is replaced by "c:\wp." In line 8, using the COPY CON command, the batch file becomes user-interactive. The %2 variable is replaced by "wpdir.tmp." The COPY CON command takes the user's input (which is the directory name) and stores it in a file called WPDIR. TMP. In line 9, the EXIT command returns control to the file that made the subroutine call, which in this case is A. BAT. Command execution resumes in A. BAT at line 4. The entire contents of A. BAT are listed as follows:

```
A. BAT
1: echo of f
2: cls
3: command /c docopyc1 WORD-PROCESSING wpdir. tmp c:\wp
4: echo of f
5: cls
6: if not exist wpdir. tmp goto ABORT
7: copy wpbegin.txt + wpdir. tmp + cr.txt wpbegin2.txt
8: copy wpstart. txt + wpdir. tmp wpmore. bat
9: del wpdir. tmp
10: wpmore
11: ABORT
12: echo Program has been interrupted. Please retry
13:pause
14:cls
15:type setup. scr
16:echo ENTER SELECTION:
17:prompt $e [22;18H
```

Line 4 turns the echo off again, since DOS turns echo on when control moves from one batch file to another. In line 6, a check is made to determine if the subroutine was concluded without a < Ctrl > < Break >. If this is not the case, control shifts to the ABORT section where an error message shown before the menu is redisplayed.

If WPDIR. TMP has been created without problems, in line 7 a text file is created around the user's directory name input. This file, WPBEGIN2.TXT, will be used later on for the batch file that runs the Word Processing menu choice. In line 8, the directory name input is added to a one-line text file, WPSTART.TXT; the result is the batch file WPMORE. BAT.

The contents of WPMORE. BAT are as follows:

WPMORE. BAT

1: wpstart <directory name as %1 variable>

Line 1 of WPMORE.BAT executes the WPSTART.BAT file, with the user's directory name input as a %1 variable. Thus, if the user specified his or her word processing directory as c:\wp, then line 1 of WPMORE.BAT would be:

wpstart c:\wp

From the WPMORE.BAT file, control is passed to the WPSTART.BAT file. The WPSTART.BAT file begins by displaying a message. Then, six IF commands check for the existence of the numbered batch files (1.BAT through 6.BAT) in the root directory. This is to determine what menu number to give the item that has been selected for addition to the main menu:

1: if not exist 1. bat goto 1 CHOICE

2: if not exist 2. bat goto 2 CHOICE

3: if not exist 3. bat goto 3 CHOICE

4. if not exist 4. bat goto 4 CHOICE

5. if not exist 5. bat goto 5 CHOICE

6. if not exist 6. bat goto 6 CHOICE

If a 1.BAT does not exist, then the new menu item will be number 1; control is then passed to the 1CHOICE section of the batch file. If it does exist, the test for the existence of 2.BAT is performed, and so on. (Note that the maximum number of menu choices that can be automatically added to the menu is 6: If a 6.BAT file is found to exist, the program will display an error message and return to the Setup menu.)

Next come the individual subsections for the installation of the selected menu item onto the specific location of the main menu (1CHOICE, 2CHOICES, etc.). These sections are similar to one another except for certain variables. The 1CHOICE section contains the following commands:

1: :1CHOICE

2 : cd\hdu\disk

3: edlin mainmenu. tmp <1 wpinput. txt

4: cd\

5: md %1

```
6: cd\hdu\disk

7: cls

8: command/c docopyc2 WORD-PROCESSING 1. tmp

9: echo of f

10: cls

11: if not exist 1. tmp goto ABORT

12: copy \hdu\disk\wpbegin2. txt + 1 tmp + \hdu\disk\end.txt \1.bat

13: goto END
```

In line 3 above, the menu item is added to the main menu, using EDLIN to edit the MAINMENU.TMP file. The input for the EDLIN routine comes from the redirected IWPINPUT.TXT file. In line 5, the directory is created, using as the %1 variable the directory name supplied by the user in A.BAT.

In line 8 above, control is passed to another batch file subroutine, DOCOPYC2. BAT. This subroutine batch file is exactly like DOCOPYC1.BAT except for the text of an ECHO command. In DOCOPYC2.BAT, the user supplies the command that executes the Word Processing program.

Control returns from DOCOPYC2.BAT to line 9 above. As in A.BAT, the IF NOT EXIST command in line 11 checks for successful completion of the DOCOPYC2 subroutine. The COPY command in line 12 sets up a batch file that will run the menu selection. The user's input is combined with WPBEGIN2.TXT and END.TXT, forming the 1.BAT file in the root directory.

In the 2CHOICES section, this combined file would be 2.BAT; for 3CHOICES, it is 3.BAT; and so on. If the user's input from the first COPY CON command was c:\wp and the input from the second COPY CON command was wp,

At the end of each subsection (in this case, 1CHOICE), control is then passed to the END section, where the following message is displayed:

Be sure to

- install the menu (selection G) after adding all your menu choices
- copy the Word Processing program files into the c:\wp directory

This message is different when the Spreadsheet, Database, or other menu option has been added. A %l variable is used for the directory name, so the user's directory name input is displayed in the message. The Setup screen is then redisplayed, and the user is ready to add another menu selection or to install the completed menu.

The program files for installing the menu

The batch files that make up the installation process include G.BAT in the \HDU\DISK directory, and all of the files in the \HDU\DISK\AUTO directory. The function of this routine is to copy the just-completed main menu into the root directory, and to create the process that makes this menu accessible. The process begins when a G is entered from the Setup menu. This activates the G.BAT file, which contains the following commands:

```
G. BAT
1:  echo off
2:  cls
3:  cd auto
4:  type instruct.scr
5:  echo ENTER COMMAND:
6:  prompt $e [20;16H
```

After the current directory is changed to the \HDU\DISK\AUTO subdirectory (line 3), an instruction screen is displayed. This instruction screen describes the automatic versus manual option for displaying the main menu.

When the user enters the MANUAL command, the following batch file is activated:

```
MANUAL.BAT
1:  echo of f
2:  cls
3:  echo Copying mainmenu to root directory...
4:  copy \hdu\disk\mainmenu. tmp \mainmenu. scr
5:  copy\hdu\disk\menu.bat
6:  cd \
7:  cls
8:  echo Your menu system has now been installed. To display your
9:  echo menu at any time, simply enter the command MENU.
10: prompt $n$g
```

The above batch file simply copies to the root directory the two files critical to the

Manual process: MAINMENU.SCR and MENU.BAT. The AUTO.BAT file, in contrast, is somewhat more complicated.

AUTO.BAT

```
echo off
cls
echo Copying main menu to root directory...
copy \hdu\disk\mainmenu.tmp\mainmenu.scr
cd \
if not exist autoexec.bat goto NOAUTO
goto AUTO
:NOAUTO
echo Making AUTOEXEC.BAT file
cd \hdu\disk\auto
copy \hdu\dospath.txt + autoexec.tmp \autoexec.bat
Cls
echo Your menu system has now been installed. Reboot your computer
echo (by pressing [Ctrl] [Alt] [Del]) to display the main menu.
prompt $n$g
goto END
:AUTO
cd \hdu\disk\auto
if exist flag.txt goto HAVEDONE
Cls
echo There already is an AUTOEXEC.BAT file in your root directory.
echo It contains the following commands:
type \autoexec.bat
type makeauto.scr
prompt Continue (Y/N)?
```

```
goto END
:HAVEDONE
echo Your new main menu has now been installed. To continue,
pause
cd
cls
type mainmenu.scr
echo ENTER SELECTION?
prompt $e [22;18H
:END
```

Figure 6: Contents of AUTO.BAT for menu installations

The AUTO.BAT file copies the MAINMENU.SCR file to the root directory, and then uses an IF command to determine if the system contains an AUTOEXEC.BAT file. This file is used to automatically display the main menu. If it does not exist, the AUTO.BAT file creates one with the command:

```
copy\hdu\dospath.text + autoexec.tmp \autoexec.bat
```

The path specified by the user when the *Hard Disk Manager* was installed was stored in a file called DOSPATH.TXT This is combined with some other commands to form the AUTOEXEC.BAT file.

If an AUTOEXEC.BAT file already exists, the authors assume that the user may not wish to have the existing one obliterated. A "Continue (Y/N)?" prompt asks permission to append some specific commands to the end of the existing AUTOEXEC.BAT file. The N.BAT file aborts the installation with instructions to install the menu manually. The Y.BAT file is as follows:

Y. BAT

```
echo of f
cls
echo Adding commands to your AUTOEXEC.BAT file...
cd\
copy\autoexec.bat + \hdu\dospath.txt + \hdu\disk\auto\autoexec.tmp
copy \hdu\disk\auto\nureturn.tmp \return.bat
```

```
7: copy \hdu\disk\auto\dospath2.txt \hdu\disk\auto\flag.txt
8: cls
9: echo Your menu system has now been installed. Reboot your computer by
10: echo pressing [Ctrl] [Alt] [Del], to display the mainmenu.
11: prompt $n$g
```

The long COPY command in line 5 above appends the contents of DOSPATH.TXT and AUTOEXEC.TMP to the existing AUTOEXEC.BAT file. Suppose the DOS path specified by the user was C:\DOS and the existing AUTOEXEC.BAT file simply ran the clock program for an AST board (ASTCLOCK).

The COPY command in line 6 places a new RETURN.BAT file in the root directory. This *will* cause the new main menu to be displayed when the < Fl > key is pressed, instead of the Hard *Disk Manager* menu. The COPY command in line 7 creates a file called FLAG.TXT, its existence simply serves to indicate that the necessary commands have been appended to the AUTOEXEC.BAT file. The AUTO.BAT file checks for the presence of this file to prevent the same commands from being added to the AUTOEXEC.BAT file again if a new main menu is installed.

The miscellaneous programs option

When the Miscellaneous Programs selection is installed on the main menu, a submenu is displayed when this menu choice is selected. The first item on this submenu, "Add A Selection To This Menu," does exactly what its description says. All of the files associated with the Miscellaneous Programs submenu are contained in the directory \HDU\DISK\MP.

Program files for the miscellaneous programs option

When selection 1 on the menu is entered, the following batch file is executed:

1. BAT

```
echo of f
cls
type mpinstru.scr
echo Continue (Y/N)?
prompt $e[17;18H
```

If the user responds with N to the "Continue (Y/N)?" prompt, the Miscellaneous Programs menu is redisplayed. The Y.BAT file adds the new menu item to that menu. This is a long batch file similar to the WPSTART.BAT file described earlier. It performs the following operations:

1. Using a subroutine batch File (DOCOPYC3.BAT), the user is prompted to enter the name of the menu item that is to appear on the Miscellaneous Programs menu screen. This file is similar to DOCOPYC1.BAT described earlier. Using a COPY CON command, the user's input is placed in TEMP.TXT.

2. A check is made of the number of menu items that already exist, using the Exist condition of multiple IF commands:

```
cd\misc
if not exist 2.bat goto 2CHOICES
if not exist 3.bat goto 3CHOICES
if not exist 4.bat goto 4CHOICES
if not exist 5.bat goto 5CHOICES
if not exist 6.bat goto 6CHOICES
goto OTHEREND
```

   For example, if a 2.BAT file does not exist, control is passed to 2CHOICES where the new menu item will be labeled "2."

3. In the subsections (2choices, 3choices, etc.), three COPY commands remake the Miscellaneous Programs screen with the new menu pick. The first COPY command adds a menu number to the user's input, and the second COPY command adds this combination to the menu. The last of the three prepares the menu for the next time a selection is added.

```
copy mp2begin.txt + temp.txt temp2.txt
copy mp1.scr + temp2.txt + mp2.scr miscprog.scr
copy mp1.scr + temp2.txt + mpline.scr,
goto CONTINUE
```

4. Control then passes to CONTINUE. A subroutine batch file (DOCOPYC2.BAT) is executed that prompts the user for the name of the command that runs the program. The COPY CON command again is used to make this a user-interactive batch file. COPY CON places the input in TEMP.TXT.

```
echo ENTER the command, PRESS the F6 key, and then PRESS Enter:
copy con:temp.txt
```

Using the same IF command procedure as before, a batch file is written to run the new menu choice. Depending on what numbered batch files already exist, control is passed to 2BAT, 3BAT, 4BAT, etc.

5. In the 2BAT through 6BAT subsections, the TEMP.TXT input is combined into an appropriate numbered batch file. In the 2BAT subsection, for example:

copy mpbegin.txt + temp.txt + mpend.txt 2 bat goto F1 FIRSTEND

6. Control passes to FIRSTEND where completion messages are displayed. After a pause, the Miscellaneous Programs menu is redisplayed, containing the new menu pick.

Instructions

This routine allows you to add menu selections to the MISCELLANEOUS PROGRAMS SUBMENU Screen. As many as five new menu selections may be added to the menu. (If you need more than five, refer to chapter 4 of "Hard Disk Manager.")

You will be prompted for the following input:

The name of the program selection that will appear on the MISCELLANEOUS PROGRAMS SUBMENU Screen. The menu number will be supplied automatically.

The command that executes the menu selection.

<< Press F1 to Return >>

Figure 8: Instruction screen for miscellaneous programs option

Resetting the menu

The Menu/Directory Setup utility allows the user to add up to six menu items automatically. On the seventh try, the following error message is displayed:

A total of six items has already been installed... program ABORTED.

The only time this should happen is if there have been some repetitions, since there are only six choices, A-F. To find out what has gone wrong, the user must do the following:

1. First, examine the temporary main menu. This is done by selecting the Exit To DOS on the *Hard Disk Manager* menu, and then entering the following command:

type \hdu\disk\mainmenu.tmp

2. Decide which of the menu items is superfluous. Unless a menu item has been placed on the menu manually, there should be some duplications. (Proceed to the next step even if the menu looks all right.)

3. Make note of the numbered items that should be on the menu and then enter the following command:

dir\?.bat

This should produce a listing of numbered batch files in the root directory (1.BAT, 2.BAT, and so on).

4. Erase the numbered batch file for every menu item that does not belong. For example, to erase the 4.BAT file, the command is

   erase \4.BAT

6. Return to *Hard Disk Manager* (by entering the command HDU) and run the Disk/Directory Setup routine again for the desired menu item. Be sure to install the menu when done (selection G).

To start a main menu again from scratch, select Exit To DOS, and erase all the numbered batch files (see steps 3 and 4 above). Then, copy the file MAINMENU.TMP from the *Hard Disk Manager* program disk back onto the C drive. This is done by entering the command:

copy a:\hdu\disk\mainmenu.tmp c:\hdu\disk

Now run the Disk/Directory Setup utility from the beginning. When the completed menu is installed, it will replace any existing main menu previously created.

The disk & directory view/print utilities

These routines allow the user to view or print the contents of a disk or directory. When 2 is entered from the Disk/Directory menu, a submenu containing the View/Print options is displayed. The operations performed by the three menu selections are fairly simple.

The view/print contents of a directory utility

To view the contents of a particular directory, the user must enter the command VIEW followed by the directory path. To print a directory, the user must enter the command PRINT, again followed by the directory path.

Disk & Directory View/Print Menu

1. View/Print contents of A Directory
2. View Contents of All Directories
3. Print contents of All Directories

<<Press F1 to Return>>

Figure 9: View/print options menu

Instructions

This routine allows you to view or print the contents of a specific directory.

To view the contents of a directory, enter the command VIEW followed by the path and directory name. There will be a pause between screens if the contents exceed the size of one screen.

To print the contents of a directory, enter the command PRINT followed by the path and directory name.

To print the contents of the \WP directory, the command is entered as

print \wp

<< Press F1 to Return >>

Figure 10: Instruction screen for view/print directory contents

The view/print directory program files

The two program files behind View Directory utility are VIEW.BAT and DOVIEW.BAT. Their contents are as follows:

VIEW. BAT

```
echo off
cls
command /c doview %1
echo of
cls
type view.scr
echo ENTER SELECTION:
prompt $e [22;184
setscrn
```

DOVIEW.BAT

```
echo off
cls
echo Here are the contents of the %1          directory:
dir %\1 /p
echo End of directory listing.
exit
```

In the above batch files, DOVIEW.BAT is a subroutine batch file called by the VIEW.BAT file. In line 3 of VIEW.BAT, the call is made to the DOVIEW.BAT file; the EXIT command at the end of the DOVIEW.BAT file returns control to line 4 in VIEW.BAT. This technique is used to ensure the redisplay of a menu should < Ctrl > <Break > be pressed during program execution. Line 9 of both VIEW.BAT and PRINT.BAT executes the batch file SETSCRN.BAT.

The two program files behind Print Directory utility are PRINT.BAT and DOPRINT.BAT. Their contents are as follows:

PRINT.BAT

```
1:  echo off
2:  cls
3:  command/c doprint %1
4:  echo off
5:  cls
6:  type view.scr
7:  echo ENTER SELECTION:
8:  prompt $e [22;184
9:  setscrn
```

DOPRINT.BAT

```
1:  echo off
2:  cls
3:  echo  PLEASE MAKE SURE THAT
4:  echo  -YOUR PRINTER IS TURNED ON
5:  echo  -AND THAT IT IS "ON-LINE"
6:  pause
7:  dir %1 >prn
8:  exit
```

As in the View Directory utility, the DOPRINT.BAT file is a subroutine of the PRINT.BAT file. Line 3 of PRINT.BAT makes the call to DOPRINT.BAT; control is returned to PRINT.BAT with the EXIT command at the end of DOPRINT.BAT.

In the above batch files, the DIR command is the key component. The directory name specified by the user when the PRINT and VIEW commands are entered is substituted for the %1 replaceable parameter. In the DOPRINT.BAT file, a reminder to turn on the printer is displayed with the ECHO commands. The output of the DIR command is redirected to the printer with the "> prn" specification.

The view contents of all directories utility

The second utility on the Disk & Directory View/Print menu allows the user to get a screen listing of the directory files contained on the hard disk. This is a simple, two-file routine. When the user enters 2, the 2.BAT file in the \HDU\VIEW directory is executed.

The view contents program file

The two program files behind the View Contents of All Directories utility are 2.BAT and DOTREE.BAT. Their contents are as follows:

2.BAT

```
echo of f
cls
command /c dotree2
echo of f
cls
type view. scr
echo ENTER SELECTION
prompt $e [22;18H
setscrn
```

DOTREE2.BAT

```
echo of f
echo The disk contents will be displayed in a few moments...
echo (Press any key to continue when  "More" is displayed in Lower corner.)
tree /f | more
echo End of disk listing.
pause
exit
```

The DOTREE.BAT file functions as a subroutine of 2.BAT. Line 3 in 2.BAT makes the call to DOTREE.BAT. In line 7 of DOTREE2.BAT, the EXIT command returns control to 2.BAT.

The central command in the above batch files is the TREE command, with the /F option (line 4 of DOTREE2.BAT). This command displays a listing of all directories on a disk; the /F option includes the files in each directory. The I more specification causes the scrolling to pause after each screen of information.

The View/Print submenu is redisplayed when the listing is completed. Line 9 in 2.BAT executes the SETSCRN batch file.

The print contents of all directories utility

The third utility on the Disk & Directory View/Print menu permits the user to generate a printout of all the directories and files on the hard disk. It is executed when the user enters 3 from the Disk & Directory View/Print menu.

The print contents program file

There are only two files associated with this utility: 3.BAT and DOTREE3.BAT. The contents of these files are as follows:

3. BAT

```
echo off
cls
command /c dotree3
echo of f
cls
type view.scr
echo ENTER SELECTION:
prompt $e [22;18H
setscrn
```

DOTREE3.BAT

```
echo off
cls
echo  PLEASE MAKE SURE THAT
echo  -YOUR PRINTER IS TURNED ON
```

```
5:  echo  -AND THAT IT IS "ON-LINE"
6:  pause
7:  echo Printing will begin in a few moments...
8:  tree /f >prn
9:  exit
```

The call is made to the DOTREE3.BAT subroutine in line 3 of 3.BAT. As before, this technique is used to ensure that a menu is redisplayed in the event the user presses <Ctrl > < Break > during program execution.

Like the 2.BAT file, the key command is the TREE command, with the /F option (line 8 of DOTREE3.BAT). The " >prn" specification redirects the output of the command to the printer.

The format utilities

There are two reasons for the presence of these utilities in this package. The first reason is security. It really requires very little effort for an inexperienced user to enter the command FORMAT and inadvertently obliterate everything on a hard disk. Since the hard disk is rarely formatted, these utilities are set up to format floppy disks only. The second reason for the format utilities is convenience. Particularly when high-capacity or system disks are being formatted, it is easy to forget the various switches that must be used with the FORMAT command.

The format a data disk utility

The first of the format utilities, Format a Floppy (Data Disk), will format a 360-KB or high-capacity floppy disk for normal usage as a data disk. When a 3 is entered from the Disk/Directory menu, the 3.BAT file in the \HDU\DISK is activated.

The format a data disk program file

The Format a Floppy (Data Disk) utility consists of two program files: 3.BAT and DOFORM3.BAT. The second batch file is a subroutine that is called by 3.BAT. By placing the FORMAT command in the subroutine, a menu will be displayed should the user press < Ctrl > < Break > before the utility is completed.

The contents of these batch files are as follows:

```
    3. BAT
1:  echo of f
2:  cls
3:  command /c doform3
```

```
4:  echo of f
5:  cls
6:  type diskmenu. scr
7:  echo ENTER SELECTION:
8:  prompt $e [22;18H
9:  setscrn
```

DOFORM3.BAT

```
1:  echo of f
2:  cls
3:  echo This prepares 360 KB or High-Capacity floppies for use as data disks.
4:  format a:/v
5:  exit
```

The DOFORM3.BAT file is called as a subroutine in line 3 of the 3.BAT file. Note that the FORMAT command in line 4 in DOFORM3.BAT is written to format a disk in drive A. The /V switch will cause DOS to prompt the user for a volume label. The EXIT command at the end of DOFORM3.BAT returns control to line 4 of the 3.BAT file. The Disk/Directory menu is then redisplayed. Line 9 executes the batch file SETSCRN.BAT.

The format a system disk utility

The second format utility, Format a Floppy (System Disk), performs the same operation as the first, except that the disk can be used as a boot (system) disk. This means the computer can be started using this disk because all of the operating system files required for a system start-up will be copied onto the disk during formatting.

The format a system disk program file

Two program files are executed when the user selects this menu pick: 4.BAT and DOFORM3.BAT The difference in these batch files and the 3.BAT and DOFORM3.BAT files described above is only the message that is displayed and the use of an additional switch in the FORMAT command. The message indicates a system disk is being formatted; the FORMAT command includes the /S option:

```
format a:/s/v
```

The /S switch indicates to DOS that the disk is to be formatted as a system disk. It should be noted that a disk should not be formatted in this way unless it really will be used as a boot disk. This is because an unnecessary amount of disk space will be occupied by the system files.

The format a 360-KB/high-capacity disk utility

The third format utility on the Disk/Directory menu is useful only if the user's system includes a high-capacity disk drive. This utility allows a user to format a 360 KB floppy disk in the high-capacity drive. This disk can then be used by that drive. (In certain situations, the reliability of these disks may be an issue; the reader should refer to "The Compatibility of Storage Media") When the user enters 5 from the Disk/ Directory menu, the 5.BAT file in \HDU\DISK is executed.

The format a 360-KB/high-capacity disk program file

Like the two other Format utilities, there are two program files associated with this menu choice: 5.BAT and DOFORM5.BAT. The commands in the 5.BAT and DOFORM5.BAT files are the same as the commands in the above utilities, with two exceptions: The message that is displayed refers to the high-capacity drive, and the format command is written as

```
format a:/v /4
```

The /4 option puts the high-capacity drive into the 360-KB formatting mode.

Modifying the disk/directory utilities

Although the Disk/Directory utilities cover many aspects of disk and directory management, the authors believe that many users will have requirements that will not be met by a generic package such as this. There are some operations that were intentionally not included. For example, there is no provision for use of the MD (Make Directory) or RD (Remove Directory). These commands are fairly easy operations for DOS. Experienced users will probably find it easier to execute these commands outside a menu or batch-file environment. The "Exit to DOS" menu choice can be useful for such situations.

However, if the system is to used by PC novices, it may be necessary or desirable to totally structure all aspects of disk and directory management. This section describes how to add, delete, or modify the Disk/Directory utilities.

Here are a few general suggestions and reminders for commands and operations that may be involved in modifying or creating disk organization utilities. Most of these tricks were used in the Disk/Directory utilities.

1. The COPY CON command can be used in a batch file as a way of obtaining user input without interrupting the execution of the batch file. The command is preceded by instructions, and the user presses < F6 > and < Enter > when finished. The input is stored in the filename that follows the COPY CON command.
2. User input obtained with the COPY CON technique can be combined into batch files or menu screens using the COPY command to append files to one another.

3. Using the EDLIN program with a redirected input file is a technique for automatically remaking a menu screen in a batch file. The input file must contain all the commands and data that would be entered if EDLIN were used manually for the same editing process.
4. The EXIST and NOT EXIST conditions of the IF command are useful for checking the validity of filename parameters entered by the user. Pathnames cannot be used in this command for DOS versions earlier than 3.0; it is necessary to change the directory to the current directory containing the file before the IF command is executed.
5. The MORE command is a useful way of controlling the scrolling of the screen displays exceeding the size of one screen. Piping is used to pass the output of a command through MORE, as in:

   type info.scr | more
6. In circumstances where it is possible that the user may press < Ctrl > < Break > before a utility is completed, it may be useful to call the main body of the batch-file program as a subroutine batch file. This is done through the use of the command

COMMAND /C <batch filename>

If the commands following COMMAND redisplay a menu, these commands will be executed if the user presses < Ctrl > < Break> while the subroutine is executed.

Adding and deleting menu items

Adding or deleting menu items in the Disk/Directory menu will not present many difficulties. The only area where the task may be a bit more complicated is in the Menu/Directory Setup utility, mainly because of the number of files involved.

Some possible modifications and enhancements

There are any number of changes and modifications in the Disk/Directory utilities that can be made. The user may modify, delete or add menu selections to the existing routines.

This section describes these procedures and provides some suggestions for possible modifications and new additions. These are utilities that use DOS features or commands not covered in the existing utilities. The descriptions basically cover only the actual program files.

A directory sort utility

This is an easy utility to add to the Disk & Directory View/Print menu. It allows the user to see or print directory listings sorted by date, size, or filename. It uses the

VIEW.BAT and DOVIEW.BAT files from the View/Print Directory Contents utility, almost intact. Here are the two original files:

VIEW.BAT

```
1:   echo of f
2:   cls
3:   command /c doview %1
4:   echo of f
5:   cls
6:   type view.scr
7:   echo ENTER SELECTION:
8:   prompt $e [22;18H
9:   setscrn
```

DOVIEW.BAT

```
1:   echo of f
2:   cls
3:   echo Here are the contents of the %1 directory
4:   dir %1 /p
5:   echo End of di rectory Listing.
6:   pause
7:   exit
```

The files could perhaps be renamed DIRSORT.BAT and DOSORT.BAT. (The filename in line 3 of VIEW.BAT would have to be changed to whatever filename replaces DOVIEW.BAT.)

The DIR command (line 4) in the DOVIEW.BAT file is the key component that must be modified. First, the SORT command is added to the end of the DIR command:

```
dir %1 /p | sort
```

This allows the user to alphabetize the directory listing by passing the directory information through the SORT filter in the above command.

To sort directory listings by date or file size, the /+n switch is added to the end of the SORT command. (The "n" represents the screen column number that is to be the primary sort key; the default is column 1.) For example, to sort by file size, the switch would be set as / + 14:

dir %1 /p | sort /+14

For a sort by date, one has to choose between a sort by month, day, or year, since only one column number can be entered. To sort by month, for example, the switch setting is / + 24.

It should be noted that the use of the SORT command in the above examples does not permanently alter the order of the directory listing. Subsequent issuance of the DIR command alone would produce an unsorted directory listing.

A remove directory utility

This utility is for users who wish to structure the removal of directories in a batch-file and menu environment. The RD command requires that a directory be empty of any files or subdirectories before it is removed. Thus, before a specified directory can be removed, it may be necessary to erase files or remove any subdirectories.

Before executing the RD command, it would probably be a good idea to precede the operation with some instructions indicating that an empty directory will have files listed. Suppose the specified directory was TEST. The listing for that directory would appear as follows:

```
Directory of C:\test
.      <DIR>      8-30-86    2:14p
..     <DIR>      8-30-86    2:14p
       2 File(s)  1052672 bytes free
```

4
Database Management Systems

Database Management Systems (DBMS) exist in a variety of forms to overcome the inherent limitations in the traditional file processing approach the business use of the computer. They utilize different storage organisations to accomplish flexible data structuring. They can describe data bases with multiple entry points to the data and processing paths through the data from an entry point. This chapter is an overview of some desirable DBMS properties and functions. Since data base terminology is not standardized, new terms are often introduced, with alternatives.

Figure 1 illustrates a DBMS. The user with an application program requirement is separated from the data base by the DBMS. The DBMS sits between the user and the data base. This diagram is important because it emphasizes the role of the DBMS as intermediary between the user and the data base.

Figure 1: Diagram of DBMS interfacing with an operating system

Most computers operate today under control of an operating system. The operating system supports different devices and access methods to data stored on those devices. Examples of devices are magnetic disk and drum as well as magnetic tape. Some access methods are sequential, indexed sequential, random, and direct. The operating system performs necessary functions in controlling the computer operations-managing storage in a variety of ways. A second diagram of a DBMS that uses the operating system of the computer is shown in Figure 2. Again, the DBMS sits between the user and the data base. No longer do user application programs utilize directly the storage and access facilities of the operating system. The DBMS calls upon the operating system hardware and programming modules to provide data storage and access services.

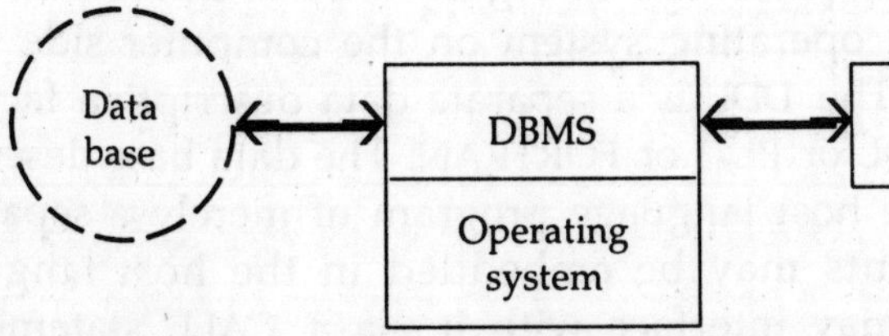

Figure 2: Diagram of DBMS interfacing with an operating system

In Figure 1 and 2, the DBMS is treated as a black box. This black box needs some more analysis. One major component of a DBMS is the data base manager (DBM). The DBM is that part of the DBMS that actually controls the data base storage and access. Note that the DBM is not a person. It is a combination of hardware devices and programming systems. The term is often confusing because the word "manager" popularly connotes an individual who manages something. That individual in the data base environment is the DBA, the data base administrator.

The DBM is the computer side of the DBMS. It organizes and provides physical access to data bases stored on physical devices. Said in another way, the DBM controls the data base organization, formats the storage devices, and provides storage and retrieval access to the data base. The DBM may call upon and utilize the computer operating system in carrying out these functions at the computer level. Specific DBMS utilize different names for it (for example, DMR for data management routines), but the DBM function must be a part of the DBMS software.

The user sits at the other side of the DBMS, as shown in both Figures 1 and 2. The DBMS must look out to the user as well as to the computer and the data base. A more complete view of a DBMS is shown in Figure 3. This figure incorporates the operating system (OS), the data base manager (DBM), a data description language (DDL), and a data manipulation language (DML). A complete and self-contained DBMS includes all of them. By definition, the DBMS must have the DBM module. It may also have its own DDL and DML. As shown in Figure 3, it uses the facilities of the operating system, but is complete with DBM, DDL, and DML. It might also operate as a stand-alone system fully utilizing the computer without any interface to an operating system by providing all of the storage and access functions through its own DBM, but this is rarer than an operating system environment.

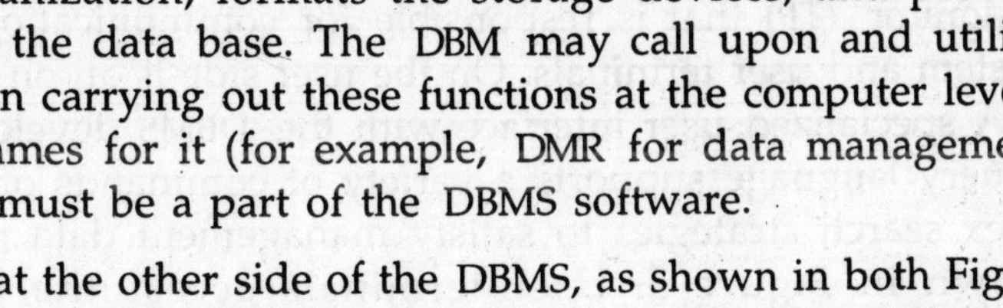

Figure 3: Move detailed view of DBMS with own DDL and DML

Still another philosophy is represented in Figure 4 by a DBMS that provides a nucleus DBM interface with the operating system on the computer side and with a host language on the user side. The DDL is a separate data description facility related to a host language such as COBOL or PL/I or FORTRAN. The data base description may be completely separate from the host language program of merely a separate section of program. The DML statements may be embedded in the host language as an extension to that language or may interface with it via a CALL statement. A user program now consists of some mix of host language, DDL and DML statements.

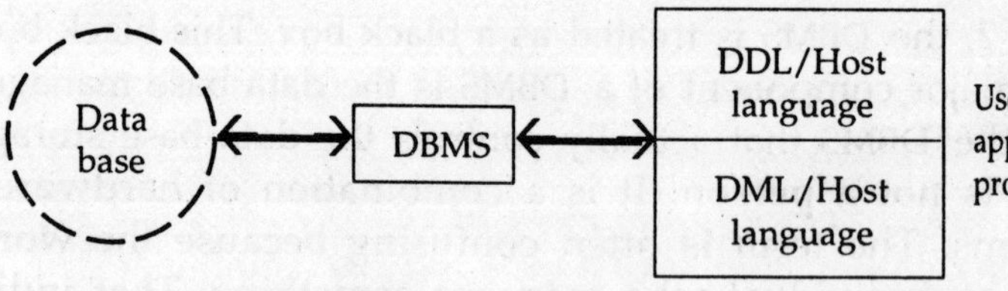

Figure 4: DBMS with a host language interface

Access to the data base by a variety of users with different data needs, coupled with improved communications systems attached on-line to the computer system, gives rise to still further components of a DBMS. On the computer side is a Teleprocessing Monitor (TP) that is responsible for communications control between the computer system and user terminals. On the user side is an on-line and interactive inquiry facility. A specialized user interface with the DBMS develops around a query language. The query language supports a variety of commands of searching the data base and complex search strategies to satisfy management data needs. A functional diagram is shown in Figure 5. User terminals access the data base via the teleprocessing system. Application programs may access the data base via the teleprocessing monitor for on-line activity of the DBMS directly for batch processing.

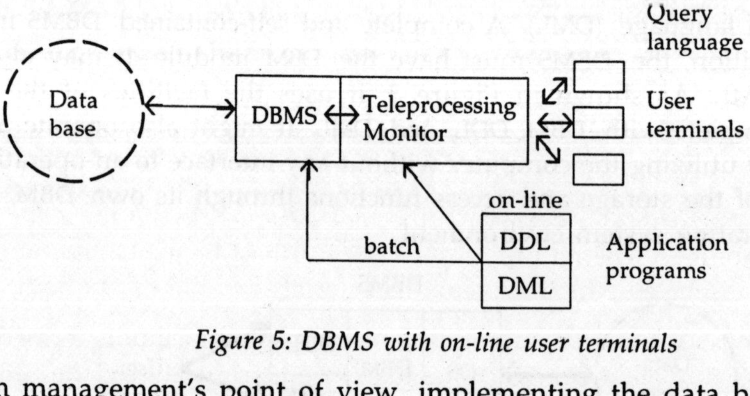

Figure 5: DBMS with on-line user terminals

From management's point of view, implementing the data base approach need not imply a single self-contained system. The complete system may actually be constructed from different program products. Setting aside the computer storage and operating system, one needs modules for the DBM to manage the data storage and access, the DDL and DML for a application programs, the teleprocessing monitor for on-line access to the data base, and the user query facility. These modules can easily represent different program products implemented and marketed by different vendors. The variety of approaches that are represented by program products and vendors is part of the confusion that often surrounds the whole subject of data base management systems.

The point is that DBMS may and, in fact, have evolved in different ways. Each has its own group of supporters and each group feels that this approach is in some sense best. The variety of currently available products reflects individual judgments about the DBMS marketplace. Some of the systems are directly competitive because they perform the same functions. Others are supportive in the sense that they perform only some of the DBMS functions and are used in conjunction with other products to complete a full range of services. All are illustrative of separate developments by different organisations without any apparent common denominator.

The data base management system

The fundamental theme of the data base concept is centralization. A DATA BASE is a collection of related data placed in the custody of a central authority-the DATA BASE ADMINISTRATOR (DBA).

It is essential to clarify the concept of "custody" at this point. The data contained in the data base is neither owned nor used by the DBA. The owner of an item of data is usually the department or group which creates or assigns values to the item in the data base. It is this group which has given the DBA custody and defined the policies which he must enforce. The END USERS of an item of data are those departments, groups or individuals which have been authorized to access the data by the DBA following the policies established by the owner. Indeed, the end user and the owner can be one and the same. The situation is roughly analogous to the custodian of a building who was hired by the owner to maintain and control the use of the facility.

As custodian, the DBA is faced with the task of safe-guarding the data while at the same time making it readily available to authorized end users. Since it must be assumed that the data base is in a constant state of evolution, the DBA has the added responsibility to control and direct this evolution.

The DATA BASE MANAGER (DBM) is the tool designed to aid the DBA in carrying out these responsibilities. The nature of the DBM can best be explained by considering the two distinct languages which serve as its interfaces.

The first of these is a data base definition facility. This facility is termed the DATA BASE DESCRIPTIVE LANGUAGE (DBDL) and is used primarily by the DBA. Via the DBDL, the DBA defines the content and form of the data base and the policies governing its accessibility to end users and APPLICATION PROGRAMMERS collectively termed REQUESTORS. This definition is referenced by the DBM as it carries out its activities of data storage and retrieval.

The second facility of the DBM is termed the DATA BASE COMMAND LANGUAGE (DBCL). This language serves as the means of communication between the application programmer and the DBM to convey requests for storage and retrieval of data. It is important to note that this document assumes that the end user always communicates with the DBM via an application program. No distinction is made between specific and general application programs. Thus the subject of generalized information storage and retrieval languages or systems is subsumed under the heading of application programs. Consideration has been given in the requirements to ensure that the facilities required to support such "generalized application programs" are included.

To further define the DBM the following paragraphs describes its relationship to the other elements of the data processing system.

Almost all modern data processing facilities include an operating system. The operating system is primarily responsible for scheduling of jobs and allocation of resources. Neither of these functions are included in the DBM except that the DBM is responsible for allocating external storage space to the various portions of the data base. This would in general be a sub allocation of space previously assigned to the DBM by the operating system.

Another common element of today's systems is the teleprocessing monitor. These monitors are typically responsible for communications control, scheduling of message processing programs and in some cases control of data access by concurrently executing programs. The DBM, as described here, affects the teleprocessing monitor only in the fact that the DBM assumes responsibility for controlling all access to the data base.

All other elements of the data processing system are viewed as application programs wishing to store or retrieve data in the data base.

The DATA BASE MANAGEMENT SYSTEM (DBMS) consists of three basic elements.

1. the REQUESTOR—the end user of the data or an application programmer acting as his agent.
2. the DATA BASE ADMINISTRATOR—the custodian of the data
3. the DATA BASE MANAGER—the software/hardware facility which controls:

   a. data base access;

   b. two languages:

   (1) the DATA BASE DESCRIPTIVE LANGUAGE used by the DBA to define the content of, and policies governing the data base;

(2) the DATA BASE COMMAND LANGUAGE used by the application programmer to store and retrieve data;

(i) utility programs invokable by the DBA.

The following sub-sections describe the basic concepts underlying in DBDL and the DBCL.

The data base descriptive language (DBDL)

The DBDL is the language used by the DBA to describe the data base and its usage. The primary user of this descriptions is the DBM which must have this information to satisfy the storage and enforce the policies governing such commands. It should be noted that this description also serves as the documentation of the data base and thus will be used as a means of communication between the DBA and the requestor.

The DBDL includes the facility to describe four facets of the data base:

1. Content—an enumeration of the data types and their relationships to be contained in the data base.
2. Physical Representation—a description of the way that the content will be stored.
3. Logical Representation—a description of the way that the content will appear in the application program.
4. Integrity and Security—a description of the policies which govern the maintenance and usage of the data.

The first three of these items correspond to the levels of the DBDL discussed in these requirements. The three levels of description are given the names ENTITY, PHYSICAL and LOGICAL. The following discussion treats the three levels in that order in which a DBA would typically develop them.

The ENTITY LEVEL consists of an enumeration of the content of the data base. The term ENTITY derives from the concept that each ENTITY RECORD TYPE corresponds to some real world entity about which data is to be recorded. The ENTITY FIELD TYPES represent the specific characteristics which may be recorded for each entity.

Entity Relationships are to define the relationships which are to be recorded between or among the defined entities. Once such relationships have been defined, it is often useful to treat them as new entities about which data is to be recorded. The tern ENTITY CONSTRUCT is used to refer to these new entities constructed from existing entities and their relationships. It should be emphasized that the entity level of the DBDL serves to enumerate the content and relationships to be recorded but contains no information regarding the way in which this data is to be represented in the data base. The remaining two levels of the DBDL are concerned almost exclusively with representation.

Assuming that the DBA has now described the content of his data base at the entity level, he would typically proceed to the PHYSICAL LEVEL. This portion of the DBDL is used to define the way in which the data base is to be represented on external storage. The basic unit at the physical level is the STORED RECORD which is analogous to a physical block or a portion of a physical block. Each stored record is composed of DATA ELEMENTS. Stored records are grouped into DATA SETS which consist of SPACE EXTENTS and usually discontiguous FORM EXTENTS. A space extent is a physically contiguous portion of external storage. A form extent is a portion a data set containing occurrences of a single stored record type.

Having now defined the content and physical representation of the data base, the DBA can prepare the logical file descriptions. The term, LOGICAL FILE, represents a subset of the data base as it is to be presented to an application program. Each logical file is a collection of LOGICAL RECORDS which are in turn composed of related DATA ITEMS. In general, a data item is defined by indicating the entity field type to which it corresponds.

The three levels of the DBDL are used by the DBA to express the content physical representation, and several possible application oriented representations. There remains the need to specify the policies governing the integrity and security of the data base. The term INTEGRITY covers validation of data entering the data base and backup/recovery facilities to protect the data base from accidental loss or destruction. SECURITY includes protection against unauthorized access to the data base and against intentional destruction or invalidation of the data base. The specification of these policies can be performed by the DBA at each of the three levels of the DBDL.

The data base command language (DBCL)

The DBCL is the language used within an application program to access the contents of the data base. The requirements stated in the succeeding sections treat this language as a set of six primitive *commands*. Although the requirements intentionally leave these commands unnamed to avoid any specification of language syntax, in this discussion they will be given the names *Open*, *Retrieve*, *Replace*, *Add*, *Delete*, and *Close*.

The DBCL is not a complete programming language, and hence is always used in the context of an existing programming language referred to as the *Host Language*. The requirements do not necessitate extensions to existing languages under the assumption that the subroutine linkage facilities of most language could be used as the interface. At the same time they do not preclude the extension of such languages to include specific statements which invoke the DBCL commands.

The DBCL deals strictly with the logical level description of the data base. This is essential to permit restructuring of the physical data base representation without affecting existing application programs. The following paragraphs describe briefly the function of each of the primitive commands.

The *Open* command identifies the logical files which will be referenced by succeeding commands. In addition it may supply information regarding the use of the file such as security codes, processing intent and exclusive control requirements.

The *Retrieve* command identifies a logical record which is to be retrieved from the data base and presented to the application program. The record to be retrieved can be identified by its relative position in the file, by its identifies or by qualifiers based on the content of the record. The command can also indicate that exclusive control is required.

The *Replace* command identifies a logical record which is to be returned to the data base. The record to be replaced must have been previously retrieved with exclusive control indicated.

The *Add* command is used to add a newly created logical record to the existing logical file.

The *Delete* command is used to delete an existing logical record. As with the *Replace* command, the record involved must have been previously retrieved with exclusive control indicated.

The *Close* command is used to inform the DBM that the logical files are no longer needed by the application program. If exclusive control was requested in the corresponding *Open* command it is terminated as the files is closed.

As was stated earlier, these commands deal strictly with the logical level data base description. The DBM bears complete responsibility for transforming the effect of these commands, specified at the logical level, into the necessary actions required at the physical level.

Comment on the guide report

The following comments are sufficient to place the *guide* report in perspective for the purpose of this chapter.

1. A new position is defined for a data base administrator (DBA). His role is that of custodian of the data base as distinguished from its owner.
2. The data base manager (DBM) manages the data on the computer side of the system. It interfaces with the operating system and also the teleprocessing system that are part of the overall computer environment.
3. The DBA has the responsibility to define the data base, and he is provided a facility to do this in the form of a data base descriptive language (DBDL).
4. The end user is a requestor who accesses the data base through an application program, most likely via a programmer who uses a data base command language (DBCL).

5. The DBDL describe three levels data: entity, physical, and logical. Application programs deal with the logical data. The data base consists of stored records at the physical level. Entity data are the vehicle for "materializing" logical data from physical data. Entity data are a middle level between the logical and physical. This level provides an indirection that defines data independence between logical and physical data.

   The entity descriptors describe the mapping between physical data occurrences and logical data occurrences. The conception of entity data is both independent of the application's use of the data and the way the data are physically stored. The descriptors relate logical data requests of application programs to the physical data.

   The value of a third level of a trichotomy as opposed to the more conventional dichtomy of logical and physical data is the subject of some debate.

6. The DBCL always interfaces with a "host" language. It need not, however, be an extension to the host language. It can be implemented via *call* statements. The commands recommended by the Report appear to be "end user"—oriented and deal strictly with logical data.

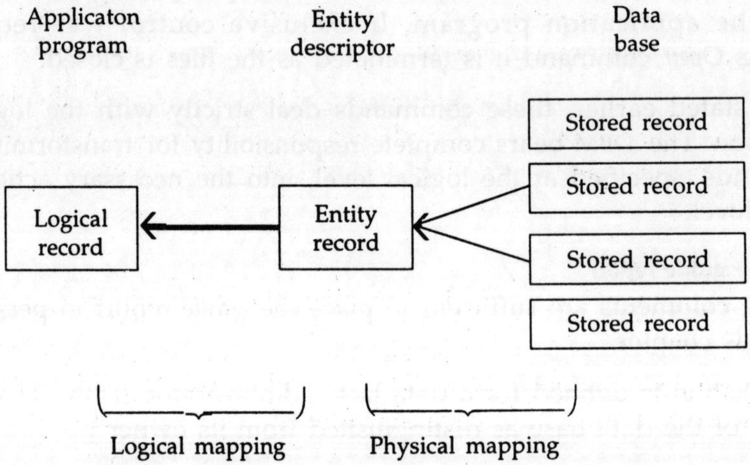

Figure 6: Three levels of GUIDE-recommended data

7. The DBDL includes also facilities to describe the policies that govern the integrity and the security of the data base. The Report is clearly written at a conceptual level without any regard to implementation. The concepts are an aid in understanding the complex subject of data base management systems.

Excerpts from the CODASYL 1971 data base task group report

The Data Description Language and the Data Manipulation language

The data description language (DDL's)

The DDL's are the languages used for describing a DATABASE, or that part of a data base known to a program. These descriptions are in terms of the names and characteristics of the DATA-ITEMS, DATA-AGGREGATES, RECORDS, AREAS, and SETS included in the database, and the relationships that exist and must be maintained between occurrences of those elements in the database.

A DATA-ITEM is the smallest unit of named data. An occurrence of a data-item is a representation of a value.

A DATA-AGGREGATE is a named collection of data-items within a record. There are two types: vectors and repeating groups. A vector is a one-dimensional, ordered collection of data-items, all of which have identical characteristics. A repeating group is a collection of data that occurs an arbitrary number of times within a record occurrence. The collection may consist of data-items, vectors, and repeating groups.

A *record* is a named collection of zero, one, or more data-items or data-aggregates. There may be an arbitrary number of occurrences in the database of each record type specified in the schema for that database. For example, there would be one occurrence of the record type *payroll-record* for each employee. This distinction between the actual occurrences of a record and the type of the records is an important one.

A *set* is a named collection of record types. As such, it establishes the characteristics of an arbitrary number of occurrences of the named set. Each set type specified in the schema must have one record type declared as its *owner* and one more record types declared as its *member* records. Each occurrence of a set must contain one occurrence of its owner record and may contain an arbitrary number of occurrence of each of its member record types.

An *area* is a named sub-division of the addressable storage space in the database and may contain occurrences of records and sets or parts of sets of various types.

A DATABASE consists of all the record occurrences, set occurrences and areas which are controlled by a specific schema. If an installation has multiple databases, there must be a separate schema for each database. Furthermore the content of different data bases is assumed to be disjoint.

A SCHEMA consists of DDL entries and is a complete description of a database. It includes the names and descriptions of all of the areas, set occurrences, record occurrences and associated data-items and data aggregates as they exist in the database....

A SUB-SCHEMA also consists of DDL entries. It, however, need not describe the entire database but only those areas, sets, records, data-items and data-aggregates which are known to one or more specific programs. Further, it describes them in the form in which they are known to those specific programs and it may also rename them....

The data manipulation language (DML)

The DML is the language which the programmer uses to cause data to be transferred between his program and the database.

The DML is not a complete language by itself. It relies on a host language to provide a framework for it and to provide the procedural capabilities required to manipulate data.

Relationship between DDL and DML

The relationship between DDL and DML is the relationship between declarations and procedure. The declarations impose a discipline over the executable code and are to a large extent substitutes for procedures written in the DML and the host language; that it, they are implicit procedure which may be invoked by the execution of DML commands.

Relationship between DDL/DML and The Data Base Management System (DBMS)

Though this report is not a complete specification for a Data Base Management System, it may be helpful to an understanding of the DDL/DML to conceptualize a complete system.

The numbered arrows in Diagram 1 trace a call for data by user program 1, and are explained in the following. Calls for data by other user programs are handled concurrently by the Data Base Management System (DBMS), but this is not shown in the diagram.

'1' a call for data by a user program to the DBMS. All calls for the services of the DBMS are made in the DML.

'2' the DBMS analyses the call and supplements the arguments provided in the call itself with information contained in the object version of the schema for the database, and in the object version of the sub-schema invoked by the user program originating the call. The schema describes the data base in terms of the characteristics of the data and the implicit relationship between data items. The sub-schema is a subset of the schema. It describes the data known to the program invoking it in the form in which the DBMS makes it available, and expects to find it, in that program's USER WORKING AREA (UWA). In this conceptual system it is assumed that the object version of the sub-schema contains only the differences from the schema and is not complete in itself. The source form of the schema is written in the Schema DDL, and the source form of the sub-schema is written in the Sub-Schema DDL.

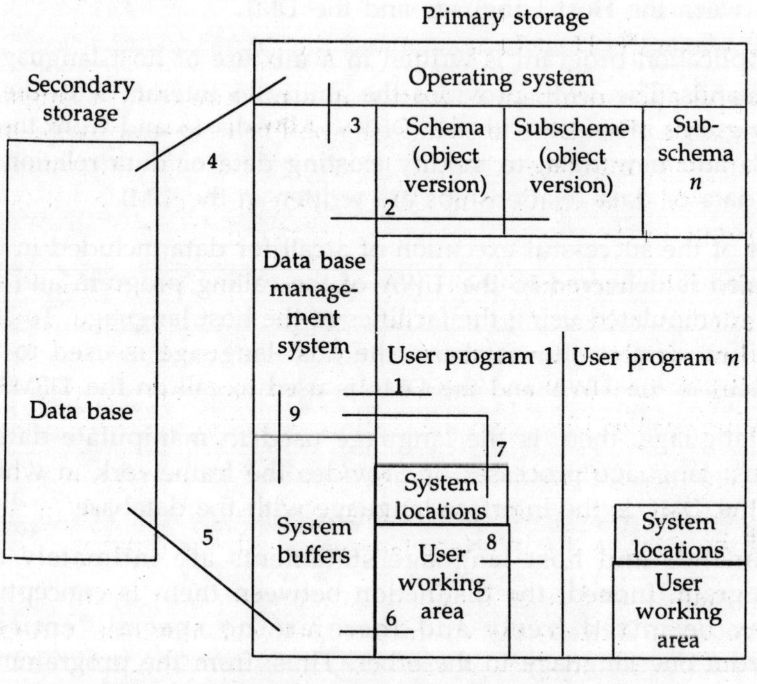

Figure 7: Conceptual data base management system

'3' on the basis of the call for its services and information obtained from the object versions of the schema and sub-schema, the DBMS requests physical I/O Operations, as required to execute the call, from the Operating System.

'4' the Operating System interacts with secondary storage.

'5' the Operating System transfers data beween secondary storage and the System Buffers.

'6' the DBMS transfers data, as required to fulfill the call, between the System originating the call. Any required data transformations between the representation of the data as its appears in a program's UWA, are handled by the DBMS.

'7' the DBMS provides status information to the calling program on the outcome of its call. The information provided is: currency status information, Error Status Condition Codes, area-name and record-name.

'8' data in a program's UWA may be manipulated as required, using the facilities of the host language.

'9' the DBMS administers the System Buffers. The System Buffers are shared by all programs serviced by the DBMS. User programs interact with the System Buffers entirely through the DBMS.

Relationship between the Host Language and the DML

A users application program is written in a mixture of host language statements and DML commands. The DML provides the ability to interact with the database in that it is the language interface with the DBMS. All calls to and from the database to retrieve data, to add new data, to modify existing data or data relationships and to delete existing data or data relationships are written in the DML.

As a result of the successful execution of a call for data included in the database, the data requested is delivered to the UWA of the calling program and may then be referenced and manipulated using the facilities of the host language. To add new data or return modified data to the database, the host language is used to initialize the appropriate values in the UWA and the DML is used to call on the DBMS's services.

The host language, then, is the language used to manipulate data in primary storage. The host language processes or provides the framework in which the DML functions, and the DML is the interface language with the database.

DML commands and host language statements are intimately mixed in an application program. Indeed, the distinction between them is conceptual. The two languages may be mixed freely and there are no special "entire" or "exit" requirements from one language to the other. Thus, from the programmer's point of view, he is using a single language—a language which has the combined capabilities of the host language and DML.

The schema and the sub-schema

Concept of schema and sub-schema

The concept of separate schema and sub-schema allows the separation of the description of the entire database from the description of portions of the database known to individual programs. The concept is significant from several points of view:

An individual programmer need not be concerned with the universe of the entire database but only with those portions of the database which are relevant to the program he is writing. Since the database may contain data which is relevant to, and shared by, multiple applications, this may be important to ease the writing, debugging and maintaining of programs.

A program is limited to the subset of the schema that is known to it via its sub-schema. To a large extent, this automatically ensures the privacy and integrity of the rest of the database from that program.

A measure of data independence is provided for programs in that certain changes may be made to the schema for the database-and the database adjusted accordingly-without affecting existing programs using that data. This is possible because the sub-schema may vary in certain important aspects from the schema of which it is a subset.

It allows a common language to be specified for defining a data base while allowing that part of the database known to a program to be described in a manner which is oriented towards the conventions of the language in which that program is written.

Application programs, the user working area (UWA), and system communications locations

Conceptually, the UWA is a loading and unloading zone where all data provided by the DBMS in response to a call for data is delivered and where all data to be picked up by the DBMS must be placed. Each program has its won UWA. The data in the UWA of a program is not disturbed except in response to the execution of a DML command or by the user program's host language procedures. There is no implication that UWA locations are contiguous....

System support functions

In addition to the DDL's and the DML, the specifications for a complete DBMS should include descriptions and language specification for:

The Utility or Service routines which are required to support a database in day to day operations. Examples of such routines are:

a. Dump, Edit, and Print routines

b. Load routines

c. Preconditioning routines

d. Garbage collection routines

e. Statistical gathering and analysis routines

f. Compare routines

The data base Recovery System including activity logging, checkpoint and rollback.

A language which permits modification of a schema or sub-schema and causes the changes to be reflected in the database itself. Without such a language, changes to the schema can only be made by developing an entirely new schema and restructuring the database in accordance with the new schema.

The assignment of areas to devices and media space, and specifying and controlling buffering, paging, and overflow. The term Device/Media Control Language (DMCL) was coined by the DBTG for these aspects of a DBMS.

The data administrator function

In an environment where a database includes data which is shared by many user programs, it becomes necessary for the schema and perhaps the sub-schemes to be developed certainly. In such an environment a database is, in a sense, a compromise between the needs of the various user programs. The database will therefore require a means of mediating conflicting needs.

Organizing During this phase the Data administrator builds the schema and perhaps the sub-sachems. The schema is always in the domain of the Data Administrator.

He will:

Employ a data structure(s) that models the business or problem. This is provided in the Schema DDL in terms of areas, records, sets, data-items, and data-aggregates.

Assign names in such a manner as to assure their uniqueness.

Select search strategies based on the needs of the various users of the data base.

Assign PRIVACY LOCKS and issue PRIVACY KEYS at various levels to the users of the database, based on need to utilize those portions of the database affected by the PRIVACY LOCKS.

Assign areas to devices/media based on time/space requirements.

Load the database.

Monitoring it is the Data Administrator's responsibility to monitor the database for usage, response, privacy breach, and potential reorganization. He may use various longing facilities or sampling techniques to gather statistics.

Reorganising As a result of information gained through his monitoring, or because of new information required in the database, the Data Administrator may have to reorganise the database. He may:

Reassign areas to different devices/media.

Change the schema and/or attributes of elements of the schema.

Change the database to reflect the changes in the schema

Remove "dead" records and compact space,...

Accessing of Records

Though this report is not a proposal for DBMS as such, the Schema DDL provides language to specify the access methods required at the record level and at the set level; and the DML provides commands which allow advantageous interaction with such specifications and with any relationships which have been declared.

The following items are important to an understanding of the approach taken in the accessing of records:

The DML provides for the selection of individual records.

Depending on the entry in the schema for a record, a record occurrence may be accessed on the basis of any of the data-items values in the record, or on the basis of a concatenation of such data-items values.

The DML is not an inquiry language and does not provide for selection criteria in the form of Boolean expressions.

A record may always be accessed through any of the sets in which it participates as a member.

A record may always be accessed by a complete scan of an area...

Record-selection-expressions based on identifiers All record occurrences in the database can retrieved on the basis of their DBMS assigned unique identifiers... In addition, if the declared LOCATION MODE for a record type is CALC, any record of that type may be retrieved by specifying its record name and the value of the data-item specified as the CALC key.

Positional-record-selection-expressions Positional record-selection-expressions are all relative to the current record of set-name, or the current record of that setname,

The member records to be retrieved in the logical order declared for that set, either in the *next* direction from the current record of the set.

The *owner, the first,* the *last,* or the "n"th record of these to be retrieved...

Location mode

The Schema DDL provides for the following access methods to be specified in the *location mode* clause for each record entry appearing in the schema...

b. Calculation. Retrieval is based on the values supplied by the run-unit for the data-names which are contained in the sought record and which have been declared as CALC Keys. The DBMS transforms the values provides into a unique identification and retrieves the record on the basis of that identifier.

c. VIA set-name. Retrieval depends on the relationships which have been established for the sought record by the DBMS on the basis of set declarations in the schema.

Sets

Characteristics of sets

The following is relevant to an understanding of the concept of a set:

A set is a named collection of record types.

An arbitrary number of sets may be declared in a schema.

Each set must be named and must have one owner record type and one or more member records declared for it in the schema.

Each set must have a *set order* specified for it in the schema.

Any record type may be declared in the schema as the owner type of one or more sets.

Any record may be specified as both an owner record in one or more sets and a member record in one or more different sets.

The capability for a record to participate as both owner and member in the same set is not supported by the language herein defined.

A record occurrence cannot appear in more than one occurrence of the same set.

A set occurrence is a collection of one or more logically related record occurrences.

Each occurrence of a set includes one occurrence of its owner record. In fact, the existence of the owner record in the database is a condition of the existence of the set occurrence and distinguishes that set occurrence from all other occurrences of that set-name.

A set occurrence which contains only an occurrence of its owner record is known as an empty set.

In addition to the occurrence which contains only an occurrence may have an arbitrary number of occurrences of each of the member records declared for it in the schema.

A special type of set which has exactly one occurrence and for which the DBMS is the owner may be declared. For convenience, this is known as a singular set.

Ordering of sets

Each set named in the schema must have a *set order* specified for it. The effect of this is to cause the DBMS to control in accordance with the set order specified, the logical order of the member record occurrences within each set occurrence. The logical order of the number records of a set is completely independent of the physical placement of the records themselves. Thus, the same member record occurrences could participates in occurrences of two different sets and be ordered differently in each of those sets.

The member records of each occurrence of a given set may be ordered in one of several ways:

Sorted in ascending or descending sequence based on the values of specified keys. The keys specified may be data-items in each of the member records, the member records' names or their unique identifiers, or any combination of these.

In order resulting from inserting new member record occurrences into the set:

a. *First*, that is, as the immediate successor to the owner record occurrence.

b. *Last*, that is, as the immediate predecessor to the owner record occurrence.

c. *Next, Prior*, that is, after or before another record occurrence which is selected by the user program storing or inserting the record in the set.

Set mode

Sets declared as chains For each occurrence of a set declared to have a mode of *chain*, a chain of pointers is created which can be followed and which provides for serial access to all records in the set occurrence. The pointers may or may not be embedded in the records themselves....represents a set occurrence with two-member records. The owner record of the set occurrence contains a pointer to the first member record in the set which in turn contains a pointer to the second member... If a non-embedded approach were taken the data content of the records would be separated from the pointers. Of course records may be members in multiple sets. To the extent that the mode of such sets is *chain* there would then be multiple chains passing through these records or, associated with them. As a result, when any given record is accessed, a pointer for each chain in which the record participates is available and may be followed.

A chain them may have embedded or non-embedded pointers. The essential aspect of a chain however is that there are pointers, directly or indirectly linking one record in the chain, to the next record in the chain.

Chains are always processable in either direction from any given record in the chain. However, the linkage provided between the records in a chain is only in the *next* direction unless the optional clause *linked to prior* is used. When this clause is used, additional links in the reverse direction are also provided...

In addition, the occurrences of any of the member record types specified for a set may be declared to be *linked to prior* This causes the owner record of the set occurrence to be accessible directly from each of the member record occurrences...

The unique identifies assigned by the DBMS for every record occurrence in the database are used as pointers. Space for a minimum of one pointer is required for each record and must be assigned by the DBMS for each chain in which a record participates as owner or member. Additional pointers and space are required if the chain is declared to be *linked to prior* or its members are declared to be *linked to owner*.

The unique identifiers mentioned here are known as DATABASE-KEYS...

Sets declared as pointer arrays A pointer array is the functional equivalent of a chain.

In sets declared as pointer arrays, member record occurrences do not contain pointers to each other nor are member record occurrences normally associated with pointers which are explicitly chained to other pointers. Member records, however, may contain pointers to their owner record occurrences and each owner record occurrence is associated with a list of its member record occurrences. In effect, the *next* pointers contained in or associated with the member records of a chain are collected together in a list in which *next*is normally determined not by following a pointer but by contiguity. Since this list of pointers may be ordered, any *set order* declared for a set is equally applicable to chains and pointer arrays...

The list of member record occurrences developed for pointer arrays allows some logical operations to be performed procedurally on the member records listed, without the necessity of accessing the records themselves. Thus, for example, where membership in a set has a known meaning, logical *and* and *or* operations can be performed on the members of two or more sets or set occurrences without accessing any of the member records themselves. This is also true to some extent of chains implemented with non-embedded pointers.

Maintenance of set relationships

The establishment and maintenance of relationships between records specified by means of declaring sets in the schema, is a responsibility of the DBMS

Such maintenance is required whenever:

A record which has been declared as an owner or member in one or more sets is added to deleted from the database.

A record is explicitly inserted or removed from a set.

A record is modified in a way which changes its logical position in the set.

A record is modified in a way which changes the set occurrence in which it participates.

Programmers are not involved in the mechanics of this process but must initialize with appropriate values those data-items which are required by the DBMS to perform its functions. Such data-items are declared in the schema. Programmers must also ensure that all areas containing any record occurrences affected by maintenance operations are open for update...

Representation of data structures

Introduction

As stated...one of the objectives of the Data Base Task Group is "to allow data to be structured in the manner most suitable to each application...without requiring data redundancy." To achieve this it must be possible to represent relationships by methods other than physical juxtaposition of records.

The Schema DDL...provides the facility to declare structures through the medium of the set. The set is, in effect, a building block which allows various data structures to be built...

In addition, the absence of structure may be represented by declaring records in the schema which do not participate in sets.

Sequential data structures

A sequential data structure is one in which each element in the structure, except the first and last, is related to the element preceding it and the element following it. A list is an example of a sequential data structure...a list may be a one-way list, where each element points only to the next, a two-way list or a circular list.

And single set occurrence is, in fact, a representation of a sequential data structure or list whose elements are record occurrences. It may be specified as a one-way or two-way list...

In a diagram of a set:

The arrow points from the owner record type to the member record type.

There may be "n" occurrences of the owner record type.

There is a "one-to-n" relationship between the owner records and the member records. Thus, for each occurrence of the owner record, there may be "n" occurrences of the member record

Trees

A tree structure is a hierarchical structure in which each element may be related to "n" elements at any level below it, but to only one element above it in the hierarchy. However, the highest level element is known as the root of the tree and only has dependents...Each node in the tree has one branch or edge entering into it, but may have zero, one or more branches out of it...

Since every set may have an arbitrary number of record types specified as its members and an arbitrary number of member record occurrences of each of the types specified; and since an arbitrary number of levels of sets is permitted, a tree of any breadth and depth can be represented.

Networks

A network is the most general form of data structure. In a network any given element may be related to any other. It differs from a tree in that the restriction on the number of branches entering a node does not apply... Thus, the fact that a record may participate as a member in more than one set, and therefore may have more than one owner, allows networks to be built.

In using sets to represent networks, it must be remembered that each set represents a collection of one-to-many relationships. Where there is a many-to-many relationship it can be represented by two sets, the owners of which are the records involved in the relationship. The members of both sets are a third record type, each occurrence of which represents one association between two occurrences of the owner records. Since it is often desirable to store information about the associations themselves these records may be useful apart from their role in the representation of many-to-many relationships.

Data and information

A survey confirmed by stating that only 34 MIS chiefs of the 500 companies considered themselves as Chief Information Officers (CIO) and only half of those reported to the Chief Operating Officer of above. What most organisations have is a data processing manager who is not even close to the executive suite and whose boss is almost as far away. The title of data processing manager is also deceiving; it sounds like one who manages the processing of data and thereby manages the data. What most data processing managers manage are people, People who operate the computers, people who maintain the complex system software for today's sophisticated computers, and people who program and maintain the application software that processes the data.

So, what is data? Data is the plural of datum. Collins defines datum "as a fact of figure from which conclusions can be inferred." Datum in the computer world is 00001010 or any other string of zeros and ones. Digital computers are binary creatures that only know if a bit is off or on. All the marvellous things that computers can accomplish are done by manipulating those zeros and ones. Does 00001010 mean anything to you? 00001010 is 10 in binary notation. Does 10 means anything to you? Ten dollars, 10 apples, 10 desks, or possibly Bo Derek. A datum, even if translated from zeros and ones to human language, does not mean anything by itself. It must be combined with at least one other datum to form data which must be processed by specific procedures which apply relevant meanings and facts to produce information. Information is the form in which data becomes useful. Usually a programmer translates a user procedure into a set of instructions understandable to the computer to process the data. The program transmits the information to the human on a screen (CRT) and/or in a printed report.

Information has value and can be acted upon. Data on the other hand, must be processed or analysed for meaningful management input. In this context information has both a recognisable format and a content. Information does not necessarily deal with a specific fact but rather a collection of related facts which are interrelated in a meaningful way. Information must also incorporate comparability and consistency. In other words, information must have the same value and the same meaning when utilised across various organisational entities. Comparability implies that information will have the same meaning and context throughout the organisation.

How much information does your organisation have? Four hundred pieces of data can be combined in to an almost unlimited number of combinations. The actual equation is 400! which has been calculated to be 10 power. This number is large but finite. Many organisations claim to have more than 50,000 data items. 50000! exceeds the capabilities of contemporary computers. Some body must tell the computer what the relevant information is.

Imagine those millions of business professionals trying to base their organisational decisions on "inconsistent, untimely, inflexible, inaccessible" data that is "unaligned with current business needs."

Below are a few of the many reasons most data is in such a mess.

- Each user function request may be programmed separately, specifying its own data requirements. "The information is derived from data files that were designed and developed on an application by application basis for transaction processing and are not organised to provide access as needed for management planning and control."
- Programmes may be allowed to call each datum whatever they want to.
- Up-to-date program documentation does not exist.

Data redundancy

One result of the above is data fragmentation which is usually called data redundancy. Data redundancy means that a single datum is stored more than one. For instance, each employee's home address might be stored in

- the payroll file
- the insurance file to maintain information about each employee's current insurance, claim history, and the like,
- the subsidiary insurance file to maintain the same insurance information about the employee's dependents.
- personnel file which contains all the information about an employee except,
- the skills file which contains all the skills that each employee has including a proficiency rating, and
- the employee performance file which contains all of the employee's performance ratings.

Conservation is usually an annual cry; costs must be cut. Yet data redundancy remains unchallenged; and data redundancy is costly.

Assume that the same datum is stored in ten places. Assume also that the datum must be changed. The costs to the organisation can include

- additional salary, fringe benefits, and overhead for entering the same and
- additional salary for someone to verify or correct the additional nine entries.

When the system was initially established, data redundancy caused the following types of expenses:

- additional programmer salary and computer charges to create an additional nine files,
- additional programmer salary and computer charges to program an additional nine access methods, telling the computer how to retrieve and change the datum,
- additional programmer salary and computer charges to test and debug the additional nine access methods,
- additional analyst and programmer salaries and computer charges to create information from the data, and
- additional computer charges to store the additional nine files.

Correlation of various statistics indicate that the accumulated cost of data redundancy for just storage in the 1980s could be between four hundred billion and two trillion dollars.

Perhaps even worse than the cost is the fact that all the updates will rarely be done and that some users will get wrong information. If your DP organisation is smart enough to update all instances, it is physically impossible to update all instances simultaneously, thereby creating the situation that some user could get the wrong information; and wrong information can be costly.

Automated information

Our ability to develop true decision support and strategic planning systems will hinge on our ability to automate the analysis of the external and internal data to provide strategic information.

Truly this represents a quantum leap. Yet without this leap, the costs of producing the information will, in many cases, exceed the value of the resulting *information*.

As information increases and access to it becomes easier, one must upgrade the lax security that permits a hacker to penetrate computer files and make unauthorised, and often undetected, changes to valuable information. Of course, the lax security allows a competitor to pirate your confidential information. The following communication between a computer operator and a hacker demonstrates the laxity of computer security.

"Well we could post our information about your system on a few bulletin

> boards. Then a few hundred less talents would try to log on. I'll bet a crasher would have fun with this VAX or that beautiful DEC-20 in Detroit. And there's always the possibility that another large car company would let us use their system in exchange for data we have. You can never tell about these things."

The GUIDE statistics are revealing. Forty per cent of the respondents do not have a security program even though when asked "if the information within your installation's data processing or communication facility were wrongfully modified, destroyed, or disclosed, of what magnitude would the consequences be?"

19% said catastrophic,

42% said severe, and

21% said considerable,

that is, 82% predicted that bad things would happen.

Computer "viruses" planted by saboteurs to attack computer files and functions can knock out computing systems and the vital operations they control for days.....The "virus" can multiply inside computer programs, 'infect' other programs, and be passed from one program to another wreak whatever havoc their creators desire....

The telephone system is run by computers, the power grid is controlled by computers, inter bank transfers are controlled by computer. In other words, global collapse of our technological infrastructure is the worst case.

Survey respondents also rated the consequences of lax security:

23% said internal disruption of operations.

20% said direct dollar loss,

19% said loss of customer confidence,

17% said legal or regulatory sanctions,

14% said loss of public confidence, and 7% said loss of physical assets.

> "...estimates that thieves collectively take as much as three billion dollars from industry every year."

These problems affect the bottom line, often substantially. Managing data can add substantial amounts to your return per share. Sometimes it can make the difference between red ink and black ink; sometimes it can mean survival.

A Wall Street analyst stated in his research report that the system "had in effect added $1.50 to the value of the shares."

Data is valuable; data is precious; data is the lifeline. Manage and protect or vanish!

Information planning

The basis of the information technology culture is a plan or sometimes many plans. These plans are presumably the cornerstone of successful organisations because they define what to do under any and all conditions. These contingency plans are useless, however, if, they are not supported by the correct information. To cite an absolutely dreadful example of multiple contingency plans that failed because the right information was not available to the right person at the right time is the Challenger space shuttle catastrophe.

Many organisations do not have contingency plans; GUIDE reports that 61% of its responding members do not have a planning organisation for information services.

The leading advocate of information planning is the world's acknowledged leader in computers, IBM. IBM has also been *Fortune* magazine's most admired American company in its annual surveys until 1987 when it dropped to seventh place. IBM developed its information planning system, formally known as Business System Planning (BSP), for its own internal use in the late 1960s.

Until the control and planning department was established, IBM had little overall direction in the internal use of computers. In fact, little coordination took place between divisions; most data processing activities were confined to locations and units within divisions. Consequently, each manufacturing plant and marketing region developed and operated its own system. Although the individual systems carried out similar functions, they differed in design and performance; they could not be used interchangeably and could not communicate with each other.

The result was redundancy of data and excessive use of the data processing resources required to develop and maintain such systems. Even with this large expenditure of resources by each division, the systems were mainly satisfying the local department needs of the business, rather than doing an overall data processing job. The business was not getting the return on investment from data processing that is could have because the information needs of the business, and particularly those of the general manager responsible for the business, were not being accommodated.

BSP

IBM decided that BSP was a worthwhile concept in its own right and decided to spread the word. Whatever IBM decides is right usually becomes the *de facto* if not the *de jure* standard. In *Business Systems Planning*, IBM stated that hundreds of BSP studies had been completed by 1978. That means that thousands have probably been completed by 1988. GUIDE reports that 18% of its responding members who have planning organisations use BSP.

It is probable then that almost all of the Fortune 500 companies have had a BSP or similar study. Yet *Fortune's* most admired American company survey indicates a rather dismal rating for many of America's most prestigious companies, a rating provided by other CEOs in the same industry classification. This implies that although a BSP or similar study may have been done, many have not been implemented or have been implemented poorly. Another indication is the lack of success stories of organisations that use data to win. There are about thirty success stories described in various publications. Thirty out of thousands is a bad ratio.

R. Umbaugh, vice president of Southern California Edison, "believes data processing managers should not speak 'computerese' but address management in terms familiar to them return on investment, contributions to objectives, effect on the bottom line, improvement in productivity and direct support of the company's goals.

The standard output of BSP includes information architecture, business processes, data classes, current system support, application portfolios, architecture priorities, and information resource management. Do any of those terms really mean anytning to the CEO? Can a CEO determine what the ROI is, or what the contribution to objectives is, or the effect on the bottom line? BSPs may be done, but implementation is often delayed or forgotten because there is no provable and/or measurable ROI for the millions of dollars of investment that most implementations require. The BSP is intended to

- Provide a formal, objective method for management to establish information systems priorities without regard to provincial interests
- Provide for the development of systems that have a long life, protecting the systems investment, because these systems are based upon the business processes that are generally unaffected by organisational changes
- Provide that the data processing resources are managed for the most efficient and effective support of the business goals
- Increase executive confidence that high-return, major information systems will be produced
- Improve relationships between the information systems department and users by providing systems that are responsive to user requirements and priorities
- Identify data as a corporate resource that should be planned, managed, and controlled in order to be used effectively by everyone.

These are the laudable BSP objectives. A formal objective method for management to establish information system priorities is laudable but what is its ROI.

- Provide for the development of the systems that have a long life and protect the system investment is laudable but how does that contribute to enterprise objectives.

- Provide that dp resources are managed efficiently and effectively is laudable but how does that effect the bottom line.
- Improve relationships between dp and users is definitely laudable but how does that improve productivity.
- Identify data as a corporate resource is extremely laudable but how does that directly support the company's goals.

Management-DP communication

CEOs and financial officers are not interested whether or not their information technologies are state-of-the-art unless the answer can be linked to *improved financial performance* of the enterprise. Justification of information technology applications *must* be linked to either 1) improving the performance of the already existing organisation, or 2) improving the chances of success for new business opportunities and strategies.

The CEO is not comfortable with the current set of tools/techniques used to justify the investment in information technology. They lack the crispness in definition and results expected by the CEO.

It is obvious that a major problem is the lack of communication. DP people and senior management do not speak the same language which erodes the latter's confidences in DP. Senior management, on the other hand, often fails to communicate its needs and desires to DP people, This is a problem both groups must strive to overcome if data is to be used effectively.

Manifesto for senior management:

Understand how your organisation ought to change as it becomes a fully electronic enterprise. Electronics are changing products, services, fabrication techniques, selling techniques, decision making, flows of information, mechanisms of control and management structures.

One of Martin's recommendations is the development of an entity relationship (ER) model. An ER model shows what an organisation needs to maintain independent data about and how those things relate to each other. ER models are essential in developing subject data bases. These are entity types that have a high affinity between themselves, so that access to information about them can be optimised to reduce computer response times, requests that are currently plaguing data processing departments.

Does your organisation have an ER model? If you do not know, either it does not have one, or it has an incorrect model; otherwise you, the CEO, should have provided input. A nonexistent or incorrect ER model will provide incorrect subject databases. Incorrect subject databases will probably cause more problems and increase the user backlog.

It is also advantageous to adopt a sensible data resource management plan because it can help in establishing the real cost of data processing and in making realistic allocation to functional organisations. Such a plan is also helpful in developing new information systems in the proper sequence based on the needs of the organisation.

Priority setting is described as 'the squeaky wheel theory,' an overtly 'political process' or a total 'mystery.' In addition, user management often believes that if you do not like the priorities-wait a week and they likely will change.

In our discussion with executive management and user management we have asked their perceptions of the planning and priority setting mechanisms for the data processing function. As to planning, the response most frequently encountered is that data processing appears to have a different view of the future. However, they also state that data processing management does not participate in strategic business planning.

The proper sequencing should be based upon

business related impacts and priorities,

ROI or IRACIS or IRACISACSR, and government regulations.

"Computers and Information Technology will significantly benefit the enterprise if chosen and applied properly. A key to the decision is a financial justification that reflects value-added for strategic support and intangible benefit opportunities."

There are other ways in which DP departments can work to reduce the communication gap between DP personnel and management and/or users. Relationships between users and DP departments can be enhanced by

- developing information systems within organisational priorities instead of DP priorities,
- developing information systems that fulfill users' requirements within reasonable timeframes, and
- permitting users to access the data with user friendly inquiry languages, expert systems, or executive information systems.

"Also, with marked technological advances being made in the field of communication, the efficient processing of information which connects Toyota with its domestic dealers in indispensable. Taking these factors into account, Toyota and the dealers are carrying out joint research and development of the effective utilisation of information and of online technology."

Furthermore, management can be provided with

- an awareness of the data processing function,
- a solid planning base for determining the need for data processing resources and establishing the appropriate budget,
- confidence that data processing is doing the right things with the right amount of resources, and
- an open, two-way channel with information systems management.

EIS

By building an EIS that highlights a company's critical success factors in a way that is accessible to senior management-as opposed to delivering pounds of computer printouts-MIS can position itself as a vital, responsive, involved participant in the running of the corporation.

The same article quotes Ronald Neese, data administrator for Browning Ferris Industries, as saying, "The EIS gave us an entree in to the executive suite that we didn't have. Now we are involved in the decision making process in a way we never were before."

EIS provides information systems management with

- a significant personnel time savings, since they will not need to negotiate between the various user functional groups about which information system is developed next.
- a reduction of friction between DP personnel and users,
- a significant reduction of the current backlog because unworthy information systems will be eliminated
- users will be using 4GLs, 5GLs, or expert systems, and
- increased speed in information system development.

Finally, treating data and the information it generates as a valuable corporate resource results in

- having all the required data when it is needed.
- being able to locate and effectively use all the required data
- reduced costs for acquiring and maintaining the data.
- controlling and increasing the quality of the data, and
- reducing the cost of storing the data by eliminating redundant data.

Better management of all resources requires information. The information to make these decisions must be readily available. Without doubt, there is an abundance of data. *Information* is scarce. The use of data a purposeful knowledge is context dependent. One of the main tasks of information management is to bring the necessary information to the decision maker at the right time and in the right format.

Pragmatically, the importance of information becomes clear whether we consider information as a generic resource or as a scarce commodity. Adequate treatment of information is always very important for enterprises.

Financial advantages and ROI

The actual dollar savings generated by treating data as a valuable corporate resource will pay for sensible data resource management plan many times over. Then why don't more companies implement a sensible data resource management plan? Many different answers are given by various organisations. Three of the more common ones are noted below.

- Nobody has been able to convince the CEO that there really is a significant ROI.
- The CEO does not believe in all these new-tangled gadgets.
- The study takes too long and is out of date before it is published.

Timely solutions are required. IBM has blamed its recent lacklustre financial performance on its failure to provide its customers with solutions. John Akers, chairman of IBM, says that the company "got out of touch with its customers. It persisted in trying to sell them products when what they wanted was solutions-help in getting their thousands of computers to talk to each other, help in wringing both productivity gains and competitive advantage out of their investments in data-processing equipment."

IBM has since discovered that providing solutions is lucrative in its own right and does sell more hardware and software. It "is bursting into the potentially lucrative business of systems integration-analysing a customer's business and then installing the proper mix of hardware and software, be it IBM's or not, to make the customer most productive-all for a fat fee."

DP growth

But I sincerely believe that Richard Nolan's article on the six stages of data processing profiles has really pinpointed the major cause. Until an organisation has reached at least the middle of stage 3, it is neither practical nor possible for an organisation to do a sensible data resource management plan, much less implement it. If this conclusion is correct, most organisations are still in the data dark ages and will suffer the consequences of being overrun by enlightened enterprises. The GUIDE statistics cited earlier affirm the validity of this conclusion.

However, *Data Resources Management Planning Methodology* points out that it is important not to rush into data resource management planning (DRMP) too soon. An attempt to implement it "before the prerequisite environment is in place is likely to fail conspicuously, waste resources, and jeopardise future attempts to implement DRMP." It also states that the prerequisite environment should include.

- integrated database technology for retrofitting existing applications;
- senior management who understand the benefits of DRMP and communicate their enthusiasm to the functional management level;
- senior management who provide an arbitration system to resolve political differences that could jeopardise DRMP;
- a corporate data resource policy that includes
    - a statement of the objectives,
    - a statement of the data resources included,
    - a statement that the enterprise owns the data and that business functions are given custodial responsibilities, not ownership,
    - guidelines for collecting and documenting the data,
    - a statement fixing the responsibility of implementing and monitoring the policy,
    - guidelines for cost accounting of and resources with the default access being no access,
    - guidelines for accessing the corporate data resource with the default access being no access,
    - guidelines for security and protection including sanctions for improper use,
    - guidelines for protecting individual privacy, and
    - knowledge of data sources and structures; and
- a data resource team that
    - can communicate upward and downward within the enterprise,
    - has sufficient political astuteness to minimise antagonism,
    - has thorough understanding of the enterprise and its objectives,
    - can analyse the enterprise's industry position and make recommendations to improve its IRACIS,
    - can translate user requirements into programming specifications,

- can recommend software techniques to fulfill data needs,
- can make the data resource both accessible and sharable, and
- can recommend hardware including networks.

Companies which redefine the factors of competition with information technology will obtain a strategic advantage over those employing the computer to the traditional factors of competition.

Another problem facing senior management is the ever increasing cost of data processing and the apparently decreasing user satisfaction and service levels. Disenchantment has reduced spending for new equipment.

Costs and budgets

In the early days of data processing when the overall budget and cost of data processing was relatively insignificant in relation to the corporate budget, it was normal to treat DP costs as general administrative overhead. It became apparent that some users were taking advantage of data processing because the services were free to the user. At this point, user charge back systems were developed to allocate actual DP resource costs to each user based on use. The charge back reports are complex and include charges for items like

- actual CPU seconds used for processing the user application,
- clock or overall elapsed time that the user applications required,
- connect time
- the user assigned priority, where the user pays a premium for express service and receives discount for slow service,
- the number of input and output operations,
- the quantity of storage assigned to the user, and
- the number of lines or pages printed by the user.

Most users could not actually verify the details of the DP invoice. Questions or complaints were usually answered by DP personnel saying that the computer made up the bill, and therefore it must be right. In such a case, DP is usually in the same quandary as the user because most invoices are computed by vendor supplied software which relies on detailed knowledge of the internal computer architecture to perform the computations. DP cannot verify the invoice any better than the user!

Regardless of such problems, the charging systems were generally fair and performed an adequate analysis of resources consumed by each user when each user and individual files, runs, reports, and the like. Life has become more difficult with the introduction of database managements systems. A working definition of a DBMS is that it permits multiple users from multiple functional organisations to have concurrent access to a single occurrence of organisational data.

Multiple problems immediately suggest themselves.

- Who pays the more than $1,000,000, required to install the DBMS when multiple users are sharing data in unequal proportions?
- Should manufacturing be charged for entering and maintaining data that is only of interest to marketing?
- Who pays for the acquisition of and the use of user inquiry languages? A further refinement of this question is who pays for the user information center?
- Who pays for the executive information systems or decision support systems or expert language or artificial intelligence language that are installed specifically to assist all levels of management in making better decisions?
- Who is credited with the profits generated by a data processing implementation of a marketing suggestion?

This last question is very important because the amount of the profits can be great. Airline reservation systems provide one example of just how great those profits can be.

Per dollar spent airlines make more money on reservation systems than they do on flying passengers. Edward Stockman, an airline analyst at Paine Webber, says that in a good quarter the airlines have an 8 to 10 per cent profit margin overall, while computer reservation systems make as much as 20 percent profit.

Max D.Hopper, Senior Vice President of AMR Information Systems, is quoted in the same source as saying

> Although our revenue were substantial, we are coming down to lower margins is looking at 20% but even a 20% margin is good.

And, Robert L.Crandell, chairman of AMR, "once said that if he were faced with the choice of losing Sabre or eliminating aircraft, he would sacrifice the planes." American reported 190 million dollars profit on 490 million dollars Sabre revenues in 1985.

Related to cost is the DP budget. One of Nolan's first level benchmarks in determining the DP stage of any organisation is to compare the rate of growth of the DP budget to the rate of growth in the company's sales. A higher budget rate indicate that DP is expanding rapidly. This expansion may be good or bad, but senior management does not know unless they have a benchmark long range plan.

The DP long range plan cannot be developed unless

- a current application inventory exists

- a desired future application inventory exists,
- a senior management priority and delivery date has been applied to the future application inventory and
- a current capacity plan exists.

A current capacity plan is concerned with the resources the organisation has now and the additional resources needed to install future applications in the priority and date sequence specified by senior management. When the above conditions are met, a DP budget can be established and all DP requests for additional resources can be measured against the DP long range plan and budget.

> Senior management, however, take a broader view of data processing. The data processing function represents a large and probably growing investment in service. And senior management are primarily concerned with maximising the return on this investment. They therefore expect data processing resources to be allocated where they give maximum benefit to the company, and the data processing organisation to operate economically and control its costs.
>
> Application that are selected for automation must give an adequate return on investment and support overall corporate objectives.
>
> Therefore, if a proposal for a data processing application is to be accepted by the company and its intended users, it must represent a good investment. Moreover, the expected return must be such that the proposal stands high enough on the list of investment alternatives to be attractive and receive attention.

Data processing managers are in a hideous quandary. They are usually far removed from the executive suite and have no easy access to senior management. More often than not, they report to a functional manager, often an accounting manager, since DP usually began developing accounting applications.

Thirty years ago DP had a relatively small net budget, since almost all new developed applications were based on the ROI that the application cost would be more than offset by direct labor reductions. Most of the first applications were in accounting because it was easy to determine the number of accounting clerks that could be replaced by a payroll application or an accounts receivable application. The fact that most of these direct labor savings did not occur did not seem to deter data processing from getting larger and larger budgets or senior management from agreeing to those budgets. Because most applications were accounting, it seemed natural to place data processing under some level accounting manager. This meant that accounting projects often continued to be top priority and only if any DP resources were left over did work for other users get done. Whereas this practice may have been beneficial for accounting departments, it was not good for the enterprise as a whole. Accounting applications should only be approved if they have the best IRACIS of all competing requests. The only priority that should be considered above IRACIS is government mandate.

Probably the highest priority application within any organisation is to satisfy the various decrees issued by the many governmental units that all organisations must interface with.

Other than government mandate, investments in new DP applications should be treated as any other organisation investment. The ROI should be acceptable and the resources should exist to implement the application. Only senior management can and should make those decisions.

This process can be made easier with careful planning.

Enterprise-wide Information Management (EWIM) is planning organisation, implementation, and control of information resources to meet current and future strategic goals. EWIM is a set of concepts and tools that enable a manager to determine, for his/her enterprise, what can and should be done with Information Technology.

The IBM Los Angeles Scientific Center has been investigating and developing a new approach to information technology. They have been reviewing the numerous plans, methodologies, tools, software, books, and seminars on enterprise modelling and are attempting to classify them within their Enterprise-Wide Information Management (EWIM) framework. The Analyst Workbench made a survey of the then existing tools and classified them by their family ancestors. There are four major families and one combination. The original and probably most used tool is IBM's BSP. IBM's BSP guide defines BSP as "a structured approach to help an organisation establish an information systems plan that can satisfy its near and long term information needs."

BSP products

BSP's basic method is to interview senior management to determine what information they want and need, including time frame, granularity enterprise value, and security.

BSP's output includes

- business processes
- data classes
- subject databases
- application portfolio and
- action plan for implementation.

BSP's major advantages are a detailed action plan and IBM support. Its major disadvantage are that it is manual, time consuming, and costly, which is true of anything manual that requires many calendar months of many people's effort.

BSP has spawned additional products each of which attempts to enhance BSP. STRADIS (McAuto) enhanced BSP by adding Gane/Sarson dataflow diagrams and functional decomposition of business processes.

McAuto justifies STRADIS on many factors including

- decreasing the risk of losing money on system development,
- saving project time because a standard approach is used, and
- providing senior management with a formal assessment procedure.

Information granularity by area of decision

GUIDE'S DB/DC Extensibility automated the Gane/Sarson dataflow diagrams and uses a data dictionary for control. A data dictionary is an automated facility for recording relationships, definitions, current usage and other information about the enterprise data resource.

> Many users involved in integrated system development efforts believe that use of a dictionary is *the* most effective method of co-ordinating the definition and use of the data for the system and is particularly important if a large system is involved.

In BSPI, IBM added graphic techniques to convert the BSP matrices into more understandable diagrams. GUIDE's ISP added data administration guidelines and states "historically, the handling of information has been less than adequate."

This is an amazing statement since it was made by the largest user group of the largest computer vendor world wide (IBM). These GUIDE reports are produced by GUIDE committees and this committee membership included

- Dominion Textile Limited,
- Wisconsin Department of Transportation,
- Peat, Marwick, Mitchell & Company,
- Boeing Computer Services,
- IBM,
- Cities Services Oil Company,
- Rohm and Haas Company,
- University of Illinois,

- Johns-Manville Service Corporation,
- Merrill Lynch, Pierce, Fenner & Smith, Inc.,
- Joseph Schlitz Brewing Company,
- Owens-Illinois, Inc.,
- Deere & Company,
- Pepsico, Inc.,
- AMOCO Production Company, and
- Northwestern Mutual Life Insurance.

The traditional GUIDE method for producing committee reports is to have a general overall consensus from all committee members and their respective enterprises. This means that

- the largest computer manufacturer in the world (IBM),
- the largest stockbroker in the world (Merrill Lynch),
- one of the Big Three accounting and consulting firms
- two of the largest oil companies in the world
- a university in the forefront of advanced computer technology
- one of the world's largest computer consulting companies
- a large American state
- two large American consumer goods companies and
- six other U.S and Canadian Fortune 500 companies

have all agreed that "the handling of information has been less than adequate."

Program requirements analysis

Systematically derived, requirements analysis data serve as a basis for planning and establishing resource needs. The analysis data formulate the program as a *paper model* (described later) that can serve as a basis for management. A well-conceived and disciplined analysis activity for a new program, such as a data management program, will bring good results regardless of size. Small organisations can very appropriately gather key talents in brainstorming session to analyse requirements and debate the issues of how to satisfy them. In large organisations, program requirements analyses should stem from an engineering activity at a management level equivalent to product design or manufacturing. It can be wisely allied with an overall data management activity. Through such an alliance, the basic program criteria, plans, and directives can be maintained consistently and effectively.

The brainstorming approach to analysis can take in total groups if they are small. All interests are thus represented, and being invited to contribute in basic planning is motivating. But, as bigger groups are concerned, this becomes impractical. A systematic approach will tap as wide a range of intelligence as feasible. All of the areas that will ultimately be needed to satisfy the requirements formulated by the analysis should be represented. Typically, product design and development engineers are supported by specialists of safety, human engineering, reliability, maintainability, value engineering, training, provisioning and procurement, manufacturing, testing, packaging, operational engineering, training and publications, and marketing. The effort to coordinate, schedule and maintain an efficient, timely, and effective analysis is exceedingly difficult, yet critical, to program success.

A number of techniques for conducting and recording results of requirements analysis have been attempted with varying degrees of success. A simple approach that has been used in described later. But, new and improved methods are continually tried, primarily to reduce complexities and delays of assimilating and using the vast amounts of analysis data involved in large programs. It is important that the techniques applied be tailored to particular requirements at hand.

Common pitfalls and problems in requirements analysis programs

- Lack of program understanding/appreciation of benefits
- Lack of leadership
- Distrust of disciplines involved
- Inadequate funds and time
- Difficult scheduling-interactive update requirements foster untimelines
- Too much or too little in content of data records, depth of coverage, and formats
- Coordination and cooperation requirements
- Continuous conflicts to resolve issues
- Prototype testing out of context with analysis data
- Update and related data incompatibilities
- Cultism

Combined with development and deployment operations, the process of requirements analysis have been allied with system engineering management. The constituents of system engineering management in terms of analysis requirements as defined in one standard used. The standard first requires preparation of a SEMP, the abbreviation for System Engineering Management Plan. The three parts of the plan and all subject areas to be considered for comprehensive analyses as covered by the plan.

The architect of a data system will heed well the ingredients of proper requirements analysis because the products are data-records that serve as basis for program evolution. Using forms (data management tools), a 10 point procedure can document the required elements concerned in an analysis as a desired program baseline plan on "as planned" model: (1) define the program objectives in terms of functions that must be satisfied by the program (the program could be a system such as a data management system) and in terms of applicable criteria for achieving the desired performance, schedules, and costs within prescribed limitations; (2) show relationships between sequential functions that must occur to satisfy program objectives and criteria; (3) define the technical requirements imposed by each function; (4) define synthesized solutions that will satisfy the collective technical requirements most advantageously using equipment, computer software, personnel, and data; (5) analyze and compare alternate solution and then select those to be tested or used; (6) show computed quantity requirements (including test equipment, tools, spare parts and personnel); (7) define the required facilities to house selected items in accordance with program objectives and criteria; (8) break down completed estimated costs of selected design solutions, and show their probable total effectiveness and worth; (9) describe optimum routines for acquiring and deploying selected requirements; and (10) provide means for keeping the analysis data up to date as a baseline to future progress.

The requirements analysis process is interactive in formulating optimum approach so special mention is due the requirements analysis sustaining effort. As with most concept, requirements data will be found lacking as time and test reveals misconception or new innovations are discovered. The task of keeping the baseline data current is not small, but is small when compared to solving problems that result if program deviations from the as planned model are allowed without rebaselining. Once the baseline is lost, product definition and change control may be in jeopardy.

Simplifying records of requirements analysis

To make the records of requirements analysis effective, the architecture of the data management system will tailor them to enterprise conditions. Using the 10 step procedure outlined for program requirements analysis, records for different past programs have ranged from tons to only a handful. Depending upon program size, complexity, time and dollar constraints, and criticalities imposed such as high reliability and low risk requirements, forms to record results of analysis that were observed varied from dozens containing more than a hundred columns to two containing only three columns. In the latter case, the forms were used to rapidly formulate program requirements for a new item distribution system, and the system serves as an example of how data management can simplify record keeping.

First, using program criteria objectives, each function necessary to accomplish the mission requirements was listed. The list was then cut and pasted, one function at a time, on magnetic blocks. The blocks were then arranged sequentially across a magnetic blackboard in the order necessary to accomplish objectives—some, of course, one above the other signifying the need for parallel actions. Lines were then drawn between blocks to show functional relationships as well as timing. Translated to a roll of wrapping paper, this simple diagram served as basis for analysis summary records consisting of a form with only three columns.

The center column of the analysis record sequentially listed the functions extracted from the wrapping paper diagram. Left and right columns on each side proved for design solution allocations of subsystem, activity, and data requirements established from analysis of each function. Scrap paper and blackboard notes were used to sketch out alternatives, compute costs, and list problems. Selected solutions were then entered on the form. A further recapitulation of allocated requirements on a second form then served as requirement specifications for the subsystems, activity and data requirements. The following sample portrays an analysis record as extracted from the initial entries of this simple distribution program/system analysis record.

Allocated Solution	Input Item Distribution Function/Activity Requirements	Allocated Output Solution
Subsystems docking	1. Receiving and inspection. Unload carrier at dock, receive and inspect goods, initiate or annotate documentation as required/applicable.	Subsystems over, short, damaged return.
Activities receiving inspection		Activities receiving inspection
Data waybill bill of lading packing list customers return documents		Data warehouse receipt receiving report inspection checklist inventory sattus change release
Subsystems locator	2. Location designation. Indicate the exit position where goods are to be moved and stored.	Subsystems locator
Activities receiving inspection		Activities location designation

Data	Data
packing list	bin card
warehouse	
receiving report	

Subprogram requirements analysis

Using the overall program baseline, detailed plans for each major functional requirements are needed to formulate working routines. Detail plans show how all of the elements of the program analysis are to be satisfied in operations such as manufacturing, test, training, and logistics. Additional needs for equipment, personnel, facilities, and operational data may result, but it is desirable to derive means of satisfying these requirements using items previously approved. The techniques of supportive subprogram analysis are similar to the basic program analysis, but they may be made simpler or more thorough depending upon technical complexities, prescribed schedules, and available resources.

Developing program models

Paper models (data that define ideal) are being widely used as analytical/managerial tools in mathematical and physical sciences, and in sociology, economics, psychology, and the behavioural sciences. Using the requirements data from program and subprogram analysis and aftermath detail design data, a theoretical management systems model (ideal) for program accomplishment can be developed. Thereafter, additional analysis can provide a practical management assessment model that systematically derives the best utilisation of resources for program accomplishment and measurement of actual results. Using projection techniques, analysis of predicted outcomes can be used to establish trends. Means to measure and alter routines according to potential risks and trends can be built into an assessment submodel. Finally, an integrated theoretical/practical data system model completes an integrated program model.

The integrated program model can serve as a management control tool. By checking program status and trends in progress, variances to the "as planned" can be readily detected and actions judiciously undertaken to correct undesirable trends and to rewards, as appropriate, outstanding performance. Again, however, the model must be current to be effective. Outdated data will usually greatly offset costs of model update.

Supporting resources for data management programs

The intricate architecture of a data system for an enterprise will consist of many resources, and the most important of all will be the human beings that it seeks to support. With the well being and innermost feelings of want and need of all individuals involved, the data system architect will strategically structure resources to fit overall requirements.

Equipment and material, automation and audiovisual aids

Many tools are employed to help us manage data. Common tools that everyone will use include the dictionary, telephone books, memoranda, and desk files. Gadgetry and automation aids extend from mechanical desk calendars to huge electronic complexes of computers and communication networks. Technology is continually developing and implementing improved devices supported by automation and audiovisual aids for storing, retrieving, processing, handling, or otherwise developing and transferring data and displaying them. Improvements in these media will probably always be needed to cope with growth in data volume and with increasing demands for a more adequate supply of data to speed up technological and social achievement.

Control data for program control

Control data are sensors and measuring tools that identify abnormal situations and flag the for action. The data focus management's attention on problem sources, sometimes indicate probable cause, and, in some cases, the best remedy. Control data are used in the assessment model when modeling is applied.

Data for program control consist of overall program plans and parts broken down in terms of both requirements and responsibilities: (1) meaningful and measurable discrete tasks and events that are programmed; (2) data that indicate the relationships of (1), (2) and (3). The latter data are vital to management in showing where programs are ahead or behind schedule, whether desired performance is being achieved, if costs overruns or cost underruns prevail, and in showing corrective action requirements based on predetermined model standards.

Control room media

Programs revolve about an authority, usually a manager, for here is where key decisions are rendered. A program control room often serves as the visibility headquarters, if not a working center, for this authority. It can often be conveniently combined with, or placed adjacent to, a data center.

Data from charts and data from models and displays in a control room should be complete enough to show both future plans and the current status of programmed activities and events. In back of master charts or displays, charts of secondary data are usually made available. These data serve as back up to the master charts and permit the authority to explore areas in more depth when problems or unusual successes may be evidenced. The resources of visibility data in the control room should show requirements and key responsibilities under an integrated data scheme.

General Application (GA)

Check lists, general
Commercial teletypewriter services
Deficiency notices
Film and card stock

Forms, all types
Guides and standards
Paper stock
Policy and procedures
Pricing/cost records
Production status reports
QA check lists
Standing operating procedures
Telephone/intercommunication equipment
  production stock
"Tickler" files

Determining Data Requirements

Approved data list(s)
Check lists
Criteria lists
Forms
Requirements analysis data

Writing

Markers
Outlines, lists of illustration and tables
Recorder-playback equipment
Shorthand machines
Typewriters

Illustrating

Air brush equipment
Art supplies (prints, markers, etc.)
Drafting equipment//machines
Lettering machines
Rub-on or stick-on transfers

Quality Assurance

Check lists
Editing forms
Engineering review
Review forms
Validation
Verification forms

Subcontracting for data program resources

Management should carefully consider the pros and cons of directly acquiring resources for their data programs or contracting with outside firms to furnish them. Assessment of these make or buy pros and cons, should incorporate all aspects of impacts on costs, schedule, and performance, and should reveal the most appropriate approach. Both long and short time applications should be assessed according to specific program urgencies, availabilities, money interest rates, competition, growth expectations, and any other aspect that might influence decisions.

Capital outlays for resources can be greatly reduced by using leased equipment, facilities, services, and personnel. Both short and long term agreements can prove advantageous in expanding available resources at comparatively low costs. The most common lease is that for equipment. Items of all types and values can be leased. Similarly, services may be leased such as typing, illustrating, computing or processing, data handling, production and distribution, microfilming, and storage and retrieval of data. Skilled personnel and required material are also commonly leased under "time and materials" agreement documents.

Computer implications for management

Some implications, of course, have been suggested in previous chapters. For examples, the ability of a manager to access online files in search of answers to queries carries definite planning and control overtones. In this chapter we shall first briefly summarize the functions of management. We shall then gain an overall perspective on the remaining chapters of this text by looking at the impact which the introduction and use of computers can have in the areas of planning and making decisions, organizing, staffing, and controlling. Economic implications also be considered.

Management functions

What is management? For our purpose, *management* is defined as the process of achieving organizational objectives through the efforts of other people. Three important points of this definition may be emphasized. The first point is that management is a *process*-i. e., *management consists of a number of interrelated steps or function which,* when satisfactorily performed, lead to the achievement of goals. The second point is that without the establishment of specific impossible. The third point is that the successful practice of management involves people working together in harmony to achieve desired results. The availability of quality information is, of course, a requirement for a smoothly functioning operation.

The business manager is a practitioner of the art and science of management. It is his job to carry out the basic management functions necessary to attain company goals. Of course, the objectives pursued vary according to the manager's mission; however, the functions of *planning, organizing, staffing, and controlling* are performed by all managers.

Planning

The planning function looks to the future; to plan is to decide in advance a future course of action. Thus, *planning* involves making decisions with regard to (1) the selection of both short-run and long-run business strategies and goals; (2) the development of policies and procedure which will help accomplish objectives or counter threats; (3) the establishment of operating standards which serve as the basis for control; and (4) the revision of earlier plans in the light of changing conditions. The steps followed in *planning and in arriving at rational decisions are:*

1. *Identifying the problem or opportunity.* Meaningful planning may begin when a manager understands and has correctly defined the problem or opportunity which he faces. Information is needed to bring about awareness.
2. *Gathering and analyzing relevant facts.* To plan and made decisions, managers must have information.
3. *Determining suitable alternatives.* The manager must seek out the most attractive possible course of action. The appropriateness of the options selected is determined by the manager's skill by the quality of his information.
4. *Evaluating and selecting the most appropriate alternative.* The manager must weigh the options in light of established goals and then arrive at the plan or decision which best meets the company needs. Again, the correctness of this choice depends upon managerial skill and information quality.
5. *Following up on decision.* Broad plans may require supporting supplementary plans. For example, if the result of thee above steps is a decision to acquire a computer, then additional plans must be made (a) to locate the new computer department in the organization, and (b) to staff it with operating personnel.

Organizing

The organizing function involves the grouping of work teams into logical and efficient units in order to carry out plans and achieve goals. In a manufacturing company, employees may be grouped formally into production, marketing, and finance divisions. In each of these divisions, workers may be further organized into smaller units. The marketing division, for example, might consist of advertising, direct selling, and marketing research departments. Salesmen might be further organized by territory, by products sold, and by type of customer contacted. Managers at each organizational level receive formal authority to assign goal-directed tasks; they then must motivate and coordinate employee efforts if goals are to be achieved. To sum up, *organizing* is "the grouping of activities necessary to accomplish goals and plans, the assignment of these activities to appropriate departments, and the provision for authority delegation and coordination."

Staffing

One aspect of the *staffing* consists of selecting people to fill the positions which exist in the organizational structure of the business. The staffing activity also includes (1) the training of employees to meet their job requirements, (2) the preparation of employees for promotion to positions of greater responsibility, and (3) the reassignment or removal of employees when such action is required.

Controlling

Unlike planning, which looks to the future, the *control* function looks at the past and the present. It is a follow-up to planning; it is the check on past and current performance to see if planned goals are being achieved. The *steps in the control function are:*

1. *Setting standards.* Proper control requires that predetermined goals be established by planners. These standards may be expressed in *physical terms* or in *monetary terms.* The setting of a realistic standards requires quality information.
2. *Measuring actual performance.* Timely and accurate performance information is essential to control.
3. *Comparing actual performance with standards.* Comparison is action oriented. Computer can provide this information to managers on an *exception basis only* when performance variations are outside certain specified limits.
4. *Taking appropriate control action.* If actual performance is not up to the standard, it may be because the standard is unrealistic. Therefore, replanning may be necessary to revise the standard. Unfavourable performance may have to be corrected by reorganizing work groups or by adding more employees. Thus, the control actions taken may require further planning, organizing, and staffing activities. If outstanding performance is noted, the appropriate action may be to reward the individuals or groups responsible.

The process of management is a continuing one. The *order* of the four managerial functions presented here is a logical one and we shall use this order as the basis for the presentation of the material in the next four chapters. In practice, however, managers carry out these functions simultaneously. "Plans beget subordinate plans, old plans require modifications, and new plans develop while old ones are in effect. Thus, it is impractical to insist on a special time sequence for the various functions.

Managerial implications of computers

We saw that quality information could support good decisions; good decisions should lead to effective performance of managerial functions; and effective functional performance should lead to the attainment of organizational goals. It is not surprising, therefore, that the acquisition and use of a computer may have important managerial implications.

Planning and decision-making implications

We can consider this broad topic from at least three viewpoints. *First,* it is possible to look at the implications involved in *planning for computers. Second,* we can look at the impact of *planning with computers.* Finally, we can look at the computer-oriented *decision -making techniques* which are now gaining acceptance.

Planning for computers

In light of the importance of information in the decision-making process, it would be logical to assume that top executives have always actively participated in the planning and implementation of new systems which would influence their future decisions. Alas, such leadership has often been lacking! A study conducted a few years ago by the management consulting firm of McKinsey & Company concluded that no company achieved above-average results without the active participation of top executives. The study further pointed out that 18 of 27 of the nation's *largest* computer users obtained results which, at best, could only be described as marginal. Other studies conducted in the past have arrived at similar conclusions.

In short, many executive apparently felt that the introduction of a computer was primarily a technical problem. They were content to define the goals of the new system vaguely and then to turn the entire project over to data-processing specialists. Such abdication ignored the far-reaching personnel and organizational implications of the undertaking. Without precisely defined managerial information needs and without the backing at the top echelons which is often required to secure cooperation and overcome resistance to procedural and organizational change, the specialists could be excused if their efforts resulted in marginal results.

Top managers should realize that their serious involvement in planning for computers is perhaps the most important single factor determining the success or failure of a computer installation. They should also be aware of the magnitude of the problems which will have to be overcome. Firms which have been successful in making computers pay off have been through in the initial planning stages. A careful *feasibility study* is required to answer such questions as:

1. What data-processing improvements are needed-i.e., what are the data-processing objectives of the firm?
2. Has proper attention been given to systems review and redesign?
3. Is a computer usage the best way to achieve all of the objectives? Have noncomputer alternatives been evaluated?
4. Have all computer alternatives been considered?
5. If an in-house installation is justified, have all feasible machines and vendors been considered?
6. Have different acquisition methods been studied?

If, as a result of careful study and planning , a decision is made to order a computer, then the following additional plans must be developed:

1. *Technical Preparation plans* Prior to the delivery of hardware, the computer site must be laid out and prepared; initial programs must be written and tested.
2. *Organizing plans* It is important that adequate attention be given to the composition and location of the computer department.

3. *Personnel preparation plans* Staffing plans should be made to fill the new jobs which will be created. For example, the selection and training of programmers should take place without delay so that they may begin preparing the initial programs. Plans should also be made to alleviate the hardships brought about by the elimination of jobs.
4. *Control plans* The quality of the information produced must be controlled. The accuracy of input data must be considered. And internal controls should be created to minimize error and disclose fraud when and if it occurs.

Planning with Computers. Information played an important part in he successful completion of each of the steps in the planning procedure which was presented earlier. Generally speaking, computer usage can improve planning by providing effective information which (1) leads to problem awareness, (2) supports problem analysis and selection of alternatives, (3) influences the choice of the most appropriate option, and (4) permits feedback on the implementation of decisions. More specifically, *the use of computers can have an impact on the planning function by:*

1. *Causing faster awareness of problems and opportunities* Computers can quickly signal out-of-control conditions requiring corrective action when actual performance deviates from what was planned. Masses of current and historical internal and external data can be analyzed by the use of statistical methods including trends analyses and correlation techniques in order to detect opportunities and challenges. Planning data stored online may permit managers to probe and query files and receive quick replies to their questions.
2. *Enabling managers to devote more time to planning* Use of the computer can free the manager of clerical data-gathering tasks and permit him to concentrate more attention on analytical and intellectual matters. The computer is an intelligence amplifier which broadens man's time dimension.
3. *Permitting managers to give timely consideration to more complex relationships* The computer gives the manager the ability to evaluate more possible alternatives. It makes it possible for managers to do a better job of identifying and assessing the probable economic and social effects of different courses of action. Awareness of such effects, of course, influences the ultimate decision. In the past, oversimplified assumptions would have to be made if resulting decisions were to be timely. More complex relationships can now be considered and scheduled. In addition to broadening man's time dimension, the computer can furnish him with planning information which could not have been produced at all a few years ago, or which could not have been produced in time to be of any value.
4. *Assisting in decision implementation* When decisions have been made, the computer can assist in the necessary development of subordinate plans which will be needed to implement these decisions. Computer-based techniques to schedule project

activities have been developed and are now widely used. Through the use of such techniques, business resources can be utilized and controlled effectively.

Computer usage can certainly improve the effectiveness of managerial planning. But before leaving the subject of planning with computers, it should be emphasized that computers *do not* "make decisions." Rather, they follow program decisions made earlier by managers and programmers. Although experiments are being conducted by extremely able researchers attempting to improve the machines' ability to solve ill-structured problems, it is man who defines problems, selects strategies to follow, and formulates hypotheses and hunches. *Heuristic* is a word which means "serving to discover." Much of planning is judgmental or heuristic in nature, and man is far superior to machine in the heuristic area of intellectual work.

Decion-making techniques

A number of quantitative managerial aids have been introduced which utilize computers to provide the framework for decision-producing analyses. These techniques can be used to (1) speed up problem or opportunity awareness, (2) permit more timely consideration of increasingly complex relationships, and (3) assist in decision implementation. In particular, the computer-based techniques of *network analyses, mathematical programming, and simulation* have managerial implications.

Network Analysis

Both PERT are network models which are used to plan, schedule, and control complex projects. The basic concepts of PERT and CPM are similar. The following procedure is used to set up a network model:

1. *All* the individuals *activities* to be performed in the project must be identified.
2. The sequence of each activity must be determined—i.e., it must be known what elements have to be completed prior to the start of a particular activity and what tasks cannot commence until after its completion.
3. The *time interval* required to complete each activity must be estimated.
4. The *longest sequence* of events in the project must be identified. The sum of the individual activity times in this sequence becomes the total project time, and this sequence of activities is known as the *critical path.*

Network models have gained widespread acceptance. The Department of Defense requires that they be used on all major defense contracts, and major construction projects employ them. They have proven quite effective in helping manage the transition to computer data-processing systems. The use of PERT and CPM improves the *planning* function because it forces managers to identify *all of the project activities which must be performed. Control* is also improved because attention can be focused on the sequence of activities in the critical path. Managers quickly become aware of potential problems. If a critical activity begins to slip behind schedule, steps can be quickly taken to correct the situation. By trading project cost against project time, several alternative paths can initially be computed to help in planning. By a greater commitment of resources, managers can often reduce the time required to complete certain activities in the critical path. The effect of a greater resource commitment, however, is often higher project cost. Network models can simulate the effects on time and cost of a varying resource mix. Computations for small networks can be produced manually, but a computer is needed with networks of any significant size. Most computer manufacturers have PERT and CPM packaged programs available.

Mathematical programming

The purpose of mathematical programming is to find the best strategy from among a large number of options. Most mathematical programming work involves the use of *linear programming*. Not to be confused with computer programming models are used to find the *best combination* of limited resources to achieve a specified objective. One important class of linear-programming applications is in blending operations, where the objective is often to minimize the cost involved in the production of a given amount of blended product. For example, cattle feed may be mixture of minerals, grains, and fish and meat products. The prices of these ingredients are subject to change, so the least expansive blend required to achieve specified nutritional requirements is subject to variation. Linear programming can help managers quickly determine the correct blend to use to minimize cost while meeting product specifications.

In addition to blending, linear programming is being used for such diverse purposes as scheduling manpower, selecting media for advertising purposes, determining minimum transportation costs from given supply points to specified points of delivery and determining the most profitable product mix that may be manufactured in a given plant with given equipment. Practically all linear-programming applications require the use of a computer. As a powerful *planning* tool, linear programming enables a manager to select the most appropriate alternative from a large number of options. It is also a technique which may aid the manager in carrying out his other functions. Its use in scheduling manpower, for example, has definite staffing implications.

Simulation

In the physical sciences, experiments may be performed in a laboratory using small models of a process or an operation. Many complex variations may be possible in these tests, and the results show the scientist what happens under certain controlled conditions. Simulation is similar to scientific experimentation in that managers may evaluate proposed strategies by constructing business models. They can then determine what happens to these models when certain conditions are given. Stimulation is thus a trial-and-error problem-solving *approach*; it is also a *planning* aid which may be of considerable value to executives.

Simulation models have helped managers decide, for example, whether or not to expand operations by acquiring a new plant. Among he dozens of complicating variables which would have to be incorporated into such models are facts and assumptions about (1) present and potential size of the total market, (2) present and potential company share of this total market, (3) product selling prices, and (4) investment required to achieve various production levels.

Simulation models are also used to improve inventory management. The problem of managing inventories is complicated because there are conflicting desires among organizational units, and what is best for one department may not be best for the entire firm. To illustrate, the purchasing department may prefer to buy large quantities of supplies and raw materials in order to get lower prices; the production department also likes to have large inventories on hand to eliminate shortages and to make possible long—and efficient—production runs; and the sales department prefers large finished-goods inventories so that sales will not be lost because of out-of-stock conditions. The finance department, on the other hand, views with concern large inventory levels since storage expense is increased, risk of spoilage and deterioration is increased, and funds are tied up for longer periods of time. Through the use of simulated inventory amounts and for longer periods of time. Through the use of simulated inventory amounts and simulated assumptions about such factors as reorder lead times and cost of being out of stock, managers can experiment with various approaches to arrive at more profitable inventory levels.

In short, we see from this brief summary of simulation that it can aid in planning by permitting managers to give timely consideration to complex relationships. Of course, in many respects there is nothing new about simulation.

As Franklin Lindsay points out:

> A corporate planner who sets forth half a dozen alternative investment schemes, together with the costs and expected return from each, is simulating each alternative so that his board of directors can judge their relative merits. But the new mathematical tools, together with high-speed computers, extend tremendously the capabilities of simulation processes.

Organizational implications

The organizational framework of a business is structured on the work to be done and on the human and physical resources to be committed. With the introduction of a computer, however, significant changes are likely to be made in data-processing activities and thus in those departments which are engaged in informational activities. When this happens, it is often desirable to restructure the organization in the interests of greater efficiency. Work groups may be realigned; tasks formerly assigned to a number of departments may be eliminated or consolidated in a single new computer department; and existing departments may be eliminated or the scope of their operations may be sharply curtailed. Basic changes of this nature require the attention of top executives.

We have seen earlier that broader information systems are now being designed and implemented. Related to this trend is an organizational issue of fundamental importance. The issue to be decided is to what extent the new systems should concentrate or *centralize* authority and control in the hands of the top-level managers. With a computer, a greater degree of centralized control *can* be supported in a business because top managers can be furnished with information from outlying divisions in time to decide on appropriate action. Without computers, such action must be determined by a a lower-level manager because of time, distance, and familiarity factors. But although greater centralized control *can be supported* with a computer, it is *not necessarily a requirement*. The defree of centralized authority and control which *should* exist in the new system is determined by managerial philosophy and judgment and not by computer usage. The impact of the path chosen on future organizational structure, basic company philosophy and policies, and managerial authority of managers below the top echelons will be great. Certainly, decisions of this magnitude require the serious consideration of top executives; they are just too fundamental to be left to data-processing specialists of lower-level managers. We shall look more closely at the questions of computer department organization and the centralization of decision-making authority.

Staffing implications

Data-processing changes often bring about organizational stress. The introduction of computer also requires employee adjustments. Staffing decisions are necessary (1) to select and train workers for new jobs and (2) to deal with employees whose jobs have been eliminated or reduced in content or appeal. REsistance may be expected from employees and managers because of significant changes occurring in the alignment of work groups, in the content of individual jobs, and in the methods of performing data-processing tasks. Proper planning and leadership can reduce this resistance.

In addition to considering the implications of filling new jobs and of coping with resistance to change top executives should also realize that it does no good to attempt to install sophisticated system if company managers at all levels are usable to (1) define their information needs, (2) develop analytical planning, decision-making, and control procedures, (3) state specifically these analytical procedures, and (4) interpret and make use of the output of the sophisticated systems. If the machines are to be effectively utilized, it will generally be necessary to undertake an educational effort to acquaint managers with computer capabilities and with the analytical tools which will make use of those capabilities.

Control implications

Several ways in which computer usage can affect the control function have already been pointed out, so we need not dwell long on the subject here. The *control implications of computer usage* include the facts that:

1. Computers can quickly signal out-of-control conditions, thus bringing about faster awareness of problems. Going a step further, programmed analyses may be carried out by the computer to present recommended courses of action to managers.
2. Triggered control reports, based on the *principle of exception*, may be prepared only when actual performance varies from planned standards. Managers are thus relieved of much routine paper shuffling and are freed to concentrate on more important personnel and environmental matters.
3. Computer-based techniques such as PERT and CPM may permit more effective control of business resources.
4. Computer systems make it possible to centralize authority and control previously delegated to lower echelons because of time, distance, and familiarity factors.
5. Internal control and auditing techniques will generally have to be revised to accommodate computer systems.

Economic implications

From an economic standpoint, the acquisition of a computer cannot be taken lightly. An investment decision involving many thousands of dollars must be made. It is the duty of top executives to determine if a computer can be justified economically. A computer *can* improve the firm's economic position by reducing ratio of expenses to revenues in tangible and intangible ways. But there is no guarantee that profits *will* be improved merely because a computer is installed. On the contrary, many firms have invested large sums in computers and have received returns of *less* than a dollar for each dollar spent.

Computer acquisition is a difficult capital-investment decision; it must be recognized as such by the top officers in the company. They must also be aware that the level of expenditures initially required is *frequently underestimated* and that this level will probably continue to increase in the years after acquisition. Finally, they must consider the possible economic implications of *not keeping pace with competitors* in the development and use of new information systems.

Control and the computer

Of course, if managers are to perform this function of the management process satisfactorily, the information upon which control decisions are based must be of high quality. Therefore, the *second* major consideration in this chapter will be the examination of the *controls which are applied to processing techniques and procedures* in order to produce a high-quality information output. More specifically, the topics covered in connection with this second consideration are *internal control, administrative controls*, and data controls.

Managerial control: A synopsis

The control function of the management process is a follow-up to planning activities-i.e., it is the check on current performance to determine if planned goals are being achieved. Thus, control activities are involved in the day-to-day administration of a business. You will recall that the general control procedure consists of several steps: (1) the establishment of predetermined goals or standards; (2) the measurement of performance; (3) the comparison of actual performance with the standards; and (4) the making of appropriate control decisions.

The information output of the computer can help the manager carry out this procedure in many ways. First of all, better information about such things as the effectiveness of the firm's sales and distribution efforts, the quality and cost of the firm's products and services, and the strengths and weaknesses of the company's financial position can lead to better planning and to the creation of *more realistic standards.* Computer simulation can assist managers in setting goals by showing them the effects of various alternate decision when certain conditions are assumed; and computer-based network models such as PERT and CPM can improve planning (and therefore control) by forcing managers to identify all project activities which must be performed.

Computer processing systems can also help managers control by gathering, classifying calculating and summarising *actual performance data* promptly and accurately. Once performance data are read into the computer, it is possible for the machine to *compare* the actual performance with the established standards. Periodic reports showing this comparison can be prepared; in some systems, triggered reports may be furnished to the m manager only when variations are outside certain specified limits.

It is also possible to program the computer so that it signals when *predetermined decisions* should be carried out. For example, a program may specify that when the inventory of a certain basic part falls below a given level, an output message signals the need to reorder and indicates the reorder quantity. But thus relieving man of many of the routine operational control tasks, the computer frees him to devote more time (1) to planning future business moves and (2) to leading the all-important human resources of the organisation. Such a man-machine relationship, in other words, makes it possible for man to concentrate more of his attention on the heuristic area of intellectual work-an area in which he is far superior to the machine-while the machine is permitted to take over the well-structured control tasks. Of course, an assumption underlying everything said in the above paragraphs is that the *information produced* by the computer system *is of high quality*. If it is, total business operations may be well controlled; if it isn't, inadequate managerial performance may be expected. Internal control arrangements are therefore needed to assure managers that accurate and proper information is being produced by the computer.

Internal control

Internal control is the total of all the control arrangements adopted within an organisation to (1) check on and maintain the accuracy of business data; (2) safeguard the company assets against fraud and other irregularities; (3) promote operating efficiency; and (4) encourage compliance with existing company policies and procedures.

Need for internal control

In computer systems the data-processing activities are typically separated into several departments with a number of employees being responsible for some portion of the total activity. For example, in the processing of a customer order, credit approval may come from one location, control of the inventory of ordered items may reside in another department, customer billing may be handled by a third department, and receipt of payment for items shipped may be in a fourth location. Thus, the organisational structure separates those who authorise and initiate the order from those who record and carry out the transaction. And both of these groups are separated from those who receive payment for the order. Such a division of data-processing activities makes it difficult for fraud to go undetected, since several people from different departments would have to be party to any deception. Also, personnel in each organisational unit can check on the accuracy of others in the course of their routine operations.

The tendency is for data-processing *activities to be centralised* as a result of computer usage. Centralisation of activities, along with greater integration of processing steps, may make it possible for a single department to perform all the steps required to process a customer order. In the past, internal control has been achieved by the reviews and cross-checks made by personnel at separate points in the organisational structure. In other words, *internal control was employee oriented*. With fewer departments involved, however, and with the likelihood that fewer people are cross-checking data, it *may appear* that, even though source documents originate outside the computer department, the use of computer systems results in a reduction of internal control.

Such a reduction *can occur* in inadequately controlled centralised computer department. But there is no reason why a company *should* have less internal control because of computer usage. On the contrary, there is no reason why *systems-oriented controls*, in the form of computer programs, cannot be substituted for employee-oriented controls; and there is no reason why the separation of duties and responsibilities cannot be maintained *within* the computer department to safeguard the integrity of the systems-oriented controls. In fact, there is no reason why a firm cannot achieve better control because of (1) the computer's ability to follow policies and execute processing procedures uniformly, (2) the difficulty of changing and manipulating, without detection, proper programmed systems controls, and (3) the computer's inherent accuracy advantage when given correct input data.

Organisation and internal control

Separation of activities *within* the computer department can help maintain the integrity of systems-oriented controls. One important control principle is that there should be an organisational separation between those who design and prepare the new systems and those who prepare the input data and operate the equipment. In other words, analysts and programmers would design, maintain, and make necessary changes on programs, but they *should not* be involved with day-to-day production runs; equipment operators, on the other hand, should not have unrestricted access to completed computer programs, nor should they be involved with making changes in data or programs. Completed programs and their supporting documents should be kept and controlled by a librarian who is not engaged either in planning or maintaining programs or in operating processing equipment. These programs and documents should be issued to interested parties only proper authorisation.

Auditing and internal control

Business information systems undergo periodic examinations or *audits* by *internal auditors* and by *external auditors*. The evaluation of internal control arrangements is the point of departure in auditing. Although no exact audit procedure is used, the auditors seek to determine, by observation, inquiry, and review of charts and manuals (1) whether a proper organisational separation of duties has been made and (2) whether adequate controls have been created to maintain accuracy, safeguard assets, etc.

During the course of the examination, attention is turned to the *audit trail* to determine if controls are effective and if reported procedures and policies are being followed. The audit trail begins with the recording of a transaction, winds through the processing steps and through any intermediate records which may exist and be affected, and ends with the production of output reports and records. By selecting a representative sample of previously processed source documents and by following the audit trail, the auditor can trace these documents through the data-processing systems to their final report or record destinations as a means of testing the adequacy of systems procedures and controls. In a manual system, original transaction may be recorded in one or more books of original entry; from there they may be connected to the final output by means of ledgers, documents, and summary totals. A visual and readily traceable trail is thus created.

With the introduction of computer systems, however, the *form* of the to rail has changed. Of course, *it cannot be eliminated* because of the desire for good internal control and because of tax and legal requirements. The Internal Revenue Service, in a report on the use of EDP equipment, said that "...the audit trail or the ability to trace a transaction from the general ledger back to its source document must not be eliminated." Nevertheless, intermediate steps in the information systems which were previously visible *have seemed to vanish* into reels of magnetic tape, into magnetic disks, and into magnetic cards and strips. To those auditors not familiar with computer systems, a portion of the audit trail "disappeared" at the entrance to the computer site. Since a "lost: audit trail is naturally a serious control matter, accounting literature is full of articles on this subject.

Nor will the audit trail become more visible in the future. The increased use of online direct-access storage devices to hold intermediate data and the substitution of online processing techniques for batch processing will result in an even greater decrease in the visible portion or the trail. For example, source documents may be replaced by machine-language recordings made with transaction recording equipment; input data will originate from widely dispersed locations through the use of remote terminals (again, to paper documents need be involved); and a reorder message for a basic part may be transmitted by the computer to the supplier through the use of data-communications facilities with no paper documents being prepared. In examining such systems, the auditor must be satisfied that adequate controls are incorporated to prevent unintentional or deliberate damage to "invisible" files and records stored in an erasable medium.

In a majority of the past electronic systems audits which have been made, the "around-the-computer" approach has used. In this approach, the assumption is that if the input data to the computer are correct and if the output is properly handled, then the intermediate processing must be correct. This approach owes much of its popularity to its simplicity and familiarity to the auditor. An alternative is the "through-the-computer" approach, where the auditor verifies (1) that the input data are correct and (2) that internal processing is properly conducted. He then assumes that output is correct. The around-the-computer approach may be suitable for audits made during the initial phases of a computer changeover and for some low-volume, uncomplicated systems; the through-the-computer method is frequently preferable for larger, more sophisticated procedures. Many auditing authorities recommend that a combination of approaches be employed.

The *function* of the auditor will probably not change in the future; but his *techniques* will certainly be subject to revision as a result of computer usage. One of the greatest challenges facing the systems designer and the auditor will be to devise ways of preserving an audit trail which (although it may seem to be nearly invisible) must be readily retraceable. Furthermore, this trail must be kept as simple as possible, and it must not require great masses of supporting printed detail. To perform their function properly, auditors will need to understand computer systems.

On the basis of the definition of internal control given earlier, we can separate the *types of controls which should be developed* into two categories. In the first category are administrative controls designed (1) to comply with existing company policies and procedures. In the second category are *data or procedural controls* which are created to check and maintain the accuracy of business data. Prevention of fraud and other irregularities is controlled by organisational separation of duties and by administrative and data controls. In the remaining pages of this chapter we shall briefly survey some of the computer-related administrative and data controls which the auditor may look for during his examination.

Administrative controls

In checking operational efficiency and procedural consistency, the auditor is interested in techniques which have a direct bearing on *systems design, programming, and computer operation.*

Systems-design controls

We see that systems and program *documentation* is needed to provide a means of recording, analysing and communicating information. Good documentation promotes operating efficiency; it also *provides the basis for the evaluation and control of new and existing computer systems.* New system specifications should be designed with audit and control considerations in mind. Without good supporting documents and flowcharts on existing systems, managers and auditors will probably not know if and when systems changes have been made. In short, poor documentation represents a basic internal control weakness. Therefore, one of the most important controls which can be exercised over systems design is to assign authority to one or more individuals to make sure that systems and program flowcharts, decisions tables, etc., are correctly prepared and maintained. Specifically written control procedures should be established for this purpose, and, standardised charting symbols and methods should be used.

Programming controls

A detailed explanation of the purpose of each program together with copies of all related documents should be kept in a *program file.* A manual containing *standard programming procedures* should also be prepared and kept up to date. The operating policies and approaches which are to be followed by personnel should be specified. Among the topics to be covered are program documentation methods and standards, program testing and modification procedures, magnetic tape labeling and retention policies, and the use of standardised symbolic names to describe company data. Such specified procedures promote consistency, reduce program maintenance problems, and make it easier for others to take over the work of a program who decides to leave the company.

A definite procedure should be formulated to handle *program changes.* Changes should be made only after written approval is given by someone in a position of authority, e. g., the manager of the affected department. It is sometimes a good policy to postpone making a number of minor changes until the end of an accounting cycle so that data handling remains consistent throughout the accounting period. Changes in programs should be made by programmers and not by computer-operating personnel. All changes should be charted and explained in writing; when completed, they should be reviewed and cleared by someone other than a maintenance programmer. All documents related to the change should be made a part of the permanent program file.

Computer-operation controls

Computer-operation controls may be maintained in the following ways:

1. *By the use of appropriate manuals*: A standard *operating manual* should include an explanation of the procedures established to deal with such things as the issuance and return of program and data tapes and cards and the means of scheduling and keeping records of equipment operating time. A manual of *program operating instructions* should be available to tell the operator how each program should be run. These instructions can specify the peripheral equipment to use, the console-switch settings to make, the action to take on all program halts, the exceptions to standard procedures and routines which may be needed, the input data to use, and the disposition of the output information obtained.
2. By *the creation of a data-security program.* Definite controls should be established to safeguard programs and data from fire and water damage of destruction. Duplicate program and master file tapes may have to be kept at a location away from the computer site. A fireproof storage vault at the computer site is a wise precaution. The importance of proper identification of, and control over, library tapes, cards, disks, and blank forms cannot be overemphasised. Adequate insurance protection should be provided.
3. *By control over console intervention.* It is possible for the computer operator to bypass program controls. He has the ability to interrupt a program run and introduce data manually into the processor through the console keyboard. With organisational separation of program preparation and computer operation, it is unlikely that the operator will have enough knowledge of the program details to manipulate them successfully for improper purposes. But the possibility of unauthorised intervention should be reduced in a number of ways. Since, for example, the console typewriter may be used to print out a manual intervention, the paper sheets in the typewriter can be prenumbered and periodically checked. Other approached using locked recording devices may be employed. Additional control techniques include rotating the duties of computer operators and having them account for operating time (manual intervention is slow; manipulation can thus result in processing times that are longer than necessary for affected runs).

Data controls

Data controls are concerned with the accuracy and propriety of the data flowing through a processing system; therefore, let us consider these controls at the *input*, *processing*, and *output* stages.

Input controls

The purpose of input controls is to make sure that (1) *all authorised* input transactions are identified, (2) these transaction are *accurately recorded* in a machine-usable form at the *right time*, and (3) *all* these transactions are then sent to the processing station. Among the control techniques which may be adopted are:

1. *The use of prenumbered forms.* Whenever possible, simple and effective control is to use serially numbered forms so that documents my be counted for A missing number in the sequence signals a missing document.
2. *The use cf control totals.* When batch processing is used, certain totals can be computed for each batch of source documents. For example, the total dollar-sales figure may be computed on a batch of sales invoices prior to, perhaps, key punching. The same calculation can be made after key punching to see if the figures compare. Control totals do not have to be expressed in dollars. They can be the totals obtained from adding figures in a data field which is included in all source documents being considered. A simple count of documents, cards, and other records is an effective control total. For example, the number of cards processed in the computer-operating department can be compared with the count of the number of cards which are delivered for processing. Similar comparisons between records on magnetic tape and the number of inputs source documents may be possible. Of course, with control totals as with other data controls, the volume of transactions and the importance of the data should determine the degree of control and the amount of money which is spend to maintain that control.
3. *The use of transcription methods.* One means of controlling data transcription is to have knowledgeable clerks conduct a pre-audit of source documents prior to recording the transactions in a machine-usable form. If input is by means of punched cards, the card verifier can be used. Transaction recording devices are available which can reduce errors caused by recopying, by key punching, by illegible records, and by loss of documents.
4. *The use of programmed checks on input.* Program instructions can be written to check on the reasonableness and propriety of data as they enter the processing operation. For example, program checks can be written to determine (1) if certain specified limits are exceeded, (2) if the input is complete, and (3) if a transaction code or identification number is active and reasonable. When online processing is used, lockwords or passwords may be required from remote stations before certain files can be accessed.

Processing controls

Processing controls established (1) to determine when data are lost or not processed and (2) to check on the accuracy of arithmetic calculations. These controls may be classified into hardware *and* software categories. Important hardware controls include parity checks (i. e., checks that test whether the number of digits in an array is odd or even) and the use of dual reading and writing heads in input/output equipment. Although not a built-in hardware control, a definite program of preventive maintenance can pay big dividends by reducing the number of machine malfunctions.

Software or programmed controls include the input checks mentioned above. The number of possible programmed controls which may be used is limited only by the programmer's imagination. Some of the possibilities include:

1. *The use of record count.* As a check against a predetermined total, the computer can be instructed to count the number of records which it handles in a program run.
2. *The use of tape labels.* The external labeling of magnetic tapes should be carefully controlled. These outside labels may give those interested such information as the tape contents, the program identification number and the length of time the contents should be retained. Internal header and trailer controls labels may also be recorded on the tapes themselves. The first (or header) record written on the tape gives the program identification number and other information. Before actual processing begins, then, a programmed comparison check may be made to make sure that the correct tape reel is being used. Since information on a master file will be erased if the file should accidentally be written upon, this is an important precaution. The last (or trailer) record contains a count of the number of other records on the tape.
3. *The use of sequence check.* In batch processing, the records are in some kind of sequence, e. g., by employee number or by stock number. Programmed checks to detect out-of-sequence and missing cards and records prevent a file from being processed in an incorrect order.
4. *The use of structural checks.* A test of the transactions to be processed can be made to determine whether the debits and credits called for represent acceptable combinations. Transactions with unacceptable debit and credit combinations are rejected.

Output controls

Output controls are established as final checks on the accuracy and propriety of the processed information. Among the output control methods which may be employed are:

1. *The use of control totals* How do the control totals of processed information compare with the input control totals? For example, is there agreement between the number of records which were delivered for processing and the number of records which were actually processed? A basic output control technique is to obtain satisfactory answers to such questions.

2. *The review of interested parties* Feedback on a regular basis from input-initiating and output-using departments points out errors which slip through in spite of all precautions. Follow-up action must be taken to correct any file inaccuracies which may be revealed.

3. *The use of systematic sampling* Internal auditors can check on output by tracing randomly selected transactions from source documents through the processing system to the output destination. This should be done on a regular and systematic basic.

4. *The use of prenumbered forms* Certain output forms should be prenumbered and accounted for in the same manner as input documents. Blank payroll-check forms, for example, should be closely guarded.

The relational approach to data base management is of fundamental importance and is having a profound influence on the development of other approaches. Paradoxically the relational approach is not widely used at the time of writing, but that is because it has taken a very long time to bring a comprehensive relational system on the market. While the relational approach is simple in principle, in practice it is difficult to implement well. However, the difficulties are expected to disappear as time goes on, and it is expected that the relational approach will be commonly used in business by the second half of the 1980s. Accordingly, the student of business needs to be acquainted with the approach.

Some currently available relational systems are ORACLE from Relational Systems and MULTICS Relational Data Store from Honeywell. The most important system is probably System R from IBM; a prototype of this system has been constructed and tested, although performance problems have delayed its release. The language used for manipulating the data base with these three systems is SQL mentioned in the previous chapter.

We begin by examining the schemas used to define a relational data base. Relational data base systems are three-level systems, so that we have a conceptual schema, storage schema, and external schema. Following a description of the schemas we shall see how a relational data base is manipulated using SQL.

We attempt to illustrate the basic principles of the relational approach in this chapter, avoiding peripheral implementation details where possible.

The relational schemas

We shall look at the conceptual schema in some detail, since an understanding of the principles behind it is crucial to an understanding of the relational approach. In contrast there is nothing special in the storage schema definition, as it involves the usual pointers, storage files, inversions, and indexes. Indeed the details of the storage schema will be quite specific to the particular implementation, so that from a business standpoint our coverage need only be minimal. In contrast again, the relational external schema can involve some additional principles found only in the relational approach at the time of writing. However, these additional principles can be deferred until after we have studied SQL.

The relational conceptual schema

The great characteristic of the relational conceptual schema is its simplicity. Essentially it contains only a specification of each of the relations that occur in the data base. We gave a definition of a relation, but it is worth repeating:

> Definition of a relation. A relation is a conceptual file in which (1) each conceptual record is unique and (2) each conceptual record has the same number and types of fields, that is, the relation contains only fixed format, fixed length conceptual records.

Thus the simple conceptual files in which we used in a CODASYL data base in the previous chapter, are in fact relations. This may well puzzle or even disappoint the leader who may well be eager to understand the new features of the relational conceptual schema. The truth is that the relational conceptual schema is distinguished not by the features it contains but by the features it does not contain. If we compare with a CODASYL conceptual schema, the essential differences are:

1. In a conceptual CODASYL data base the conceptual files may be relations, or they may not for example, a conceptual life may contain duplicate records. Nevertheless it is good practice to use relations as CODASYL conceptual files.
2. In a CODASYL conceptual data base the 1:n relationships between conceptual files are specified in the conceptual schema by means of owner-coupled sets. In a relational data base relationships between relations are not explicitly specified in the conceptual schema. They are implicitly specified, however, because of the specification of the connection fields supporting the relationships.

WHNUMB	CITY	WH-AREA
WH1	DALLAS	37,000
WH2	NEW YORK	50,000
WH3	CHICAGO	20,000

WAREHOUSE

WHNUMB	EMPNUMB	SALARY
WH2	E1	22,000
WH1	E3	21,000
WH2	E4	25,000
WH3	E6	23,000
WH1	E7	25,000

EMPLOYEE

Fig.: Some conceptual records of the relations Warehouse and Employee. The child connection field (or foreign key) is shown in color.

As an example of a relational conceptual schema, we give one for the conceptual database the conceptual schema definition language is the one used with IBM's System R:

```
CREATE TABLE  WAREHOUSE  (WHNUMB    (CHAR(5),   NONULL),
                          CITY      (CHAR(20),
                          WH-AREA   (INTEGER)
CREATE TABLE  EMPLOYEE   (WHNUMB    (CHAR(5),   NONULL),
                          EMPNUMB   (CHAR(5),   NONULL),
                          SALARY    (INTEGER)
```

System R permits the definition of a conceptual schema interactively at a terminal, by means of a CREATE TABLE command issued for each relation to be specified as shown above. With System R a relation at the conceptual level is often called a *base table.*

The simplicity of the schema definition above is apparent. We specify only the relations and their fields. Normally we would also specify the primary keys in the conceptual schema. However with System R we specify primary keys in the internal schema. However with System R we specify primary keys in the internal schema. Nevertheless we do specify that primary key and connection field values not be null (NONULL).

It was mentioned above that relationships are only implicitly specified by means of the connection fields. This is quite sufficient. Both the parent connection field WHNUMB in WAREHOUSE and the child connection field WHNUMB are specified as having up to five characters of data. This means that a WHNUMB value in EMPLOYEE can be tested for equality with a WHNUMB value in WAREHOUSE, and this is the principal means by which a relationship is specified in relational data manipulation languages.

For example, suppose we wish to retrieve all the child EMPLOYEE records of a given WAREHOUSE record. The necessary relational data manipulation language command would essentially request those EMPLOYEE records for which the WHNUMB value is equal to the WHNUMB value of the given WAREHOUSE. In this way an explicity declaration of the 1:n relationship between WAREHOUSE and EMPLOYEE in the relational conceptual schema is avoided.

Relational terminology

The relational approach has its roots in the mathematical theory of relations. While we have explained the concept of a relation in terms of conceptual files, it may also be defined in terms of mathematical sets, a mathematical set being a collection of unique entities. The mathematical influence is also apparent in the absence of specifications of relationships in the conceptual schema. The specification of the supporting connection fields in all that is necessary and is quite sufficient. Again, to specify children of a parent record or vice versa in a data manipulation language statement, it is only necessary to specify equality of connection field values, this begin quite sufficient and all that is necessary.

As a result of this mathematical foundation, the literature foundation, the literature on relational data bases is full of mathematical terms. These terms are usually precisely defined but are often meaningless to readers whose background is business or data processing. Fortunately there is usually a corresponding term in data processing, and we give a list of the most important relational terms of reference purposes. Furthermore, as relational data base techniques begin to penetrate the commercial market, the trend has been for vendors to use terminology that is either close to that used in conventional data processing or is simple and obvious.

Relation. A restricted conceptual file as explained earlier. With System R the term base table is often used. The term relational conceptual file or relational file is also sometimes used. A relation can also be defined as a mathematical set of tuples.

Tuple. A conceptual record of a relation s a tuple of relation WAREHOUSE. With System R the term row is often used.

```
WH2-NEW  YORK  50,000
```

Degree of a relation. The number of fields in a conceptual record.

Attribute of a relation. A complete column of a relation when looked upon as a table. The term is not used in conventional data processing. The nearest equivalent is field type.

Domain of a relation. A domain is a universal list of values from which a column in a relation is derived. For example, the domain D-CITY could contain a list of all the cities in the world, so that the column under the field CITY in WAREHOUSE is derived from this domain. For every field in a relational data base there is an underlying domain. In some relational systems, when a field type is specified in the conceptual schema, the name of the underlying domain must also be specified.

```
RELATION WAREHOUSE   WHNUMB CHAR(5)     DOMAIN D WHNUMB
                     CITY CHAR(20)      DOMAIN D-CITY
                     WH-AREA  INTEGER   DOMAIN D-WH-AREA

RELATION EMPLOYEE    WHNUMB CHAR(5)     DOMAIN D-WHNUMB
                     EMPNUMB  CHAR(5)   DOMAIN D-EMPNUMB
                     SALARY  INTEGER    DOMAIN D-SALARY
```

The idea is that if two fields from different relations are derived from the same domain, then they can be tested for equality, as can be WHNUMB values from WAREHOUSE and EMPLOYEE records. In the specification above this is another implicit method of specifying that the WHNUMB field is a connection field supporting a one-to-many relationship. System R does not use the domain concept.

Foreign Key. Child connection field.

Use of relations with other approaches to data base management

The advantage of the concept of a relation is its simplicity. In fact the concept has an even greater inherent simplicity than has so far has explained. A full explanation of the other properties of a relation, however, is best given later. Thus if we are willing to accept that a relation is the ideal conceptual file, we might ask why other approaches do not also adopt the relation as the basic conceptual file. The answer is the historical development of these approaches. They originated before the concept of a relation was even heard of in data processing, and it was natural for these approaches do not also adopt the relation as the basic conceptual file. The answer is the historical development of these approaches. They originated before the concept of a relation was even heard of in data processing, and it was natural for these approaches to use the data base equivalent of the records that were common in data processing, and these records included variable length records. Many existing CODASYL, hierarchical, and hybrid data bases contain varying length records, so that even new three-level releases of the corresponding data base systems have to be able to handle these older data bases. As is well known, when a facility is placed in a computer language, if later developments show that the facility is no longer useful, it cannot be removed because of the existing investment in applications making use of it.

Nevertheless it is sensible to make use of relations in the design of new data bases using CODASYL, hierarchical, and other approaches. As mentioned earlier, we used relations for the conceptual files with CODASYL material. The observant reader will also have noticed that we employed only relations in the descriptions of relationships between conceptual files and elementary data base design methods.

The relational storage schema

The relational storage schema is no different in principle from storage schemas with other approaches to data base management. There is at least one storage file corresponding to each conceptual file, and there are typically primacy indexes for direct access on the basis of primary keys, secondary indexes for access via secondary keys, and pointer systems to connect parent records in one storage file to child records in another storage file to child records in another storage file.

These facilities exist in System R. Indexes for primary and secondary key access are provided, the word UNIQUE distinguishing between the two types. Thus to specify a primary key index called WHNUMB-INDEX for the primary key WHNUMB in WAREHOUSE, and a secondary key index CITY-INDEX for the secondary key CITY in WAREHOUSE, we can interactively issue the terminal commands.

```
CREATE UNIQUE INDEX WHNUMB-INDEX WAREHOUSE
CREATE INDEX CITY-INDEX ON WAREHOUSE
```

The word UNIQUE indicates that the elements pointed to by the lowest level of the index are unique. System R was developed under both the interactive operating system VM/CMS and the batch operating system OS/MVS, so that as the reader will probably have guessed, the System R storage schema indexed are really VSAM indexes.

The external relational schema

We can distinguish two types of external schemas for relational data bases, we shall refer to these types as elementary and advanced.

In an elementary external relational schema, we merely define a number of relations, each of which is derived from a relation defined in the conceptual schema. In an elementary external relational schema, a derived relation is either identical to a relation of the conceptual schema, or it is a conceptual schema relation with one or more columns removed and any resulting duplicate external records removed as well.

WHNUMB	EMPNUMB	SALARY	WHNUMB	SALARY	WHNUMB	SALARY
WH15	E50	28,000	WH15	28,000	WH15	28,000
WH13	E55	27,000	WH13	27,000	WH13	27,000
WH15	E59	28,000	WH15	28,000	WH18	27,000
WH18	E62	27,000	WH18	27,000		
WH13	E64	27,000	WH13	27,000		VIEW1
	EMPLOYEE		Two columns from EMPLOYEE			
	(a)		(b)		(c)	

Fig.: The derivation of the external relation or view VIEW1 from the conceptual schema relation EMPLOYEE. VIEW1 is to contain the fields WHNUMB and SALARY, and the first step is the removal of the WHNUMB and SALARY columns (b) is not a relation since it contains duplicate records. To form VIEW1 in (c), these duplicates are removed. Note that VIEW1 is not a particularly useful relation, and it is doubtful that anyone would ever want to define it. The process of extracting columns and removing duplicate records is called projection..

This last point about removal of duplicate records. As explained several times, a relation does not have duplicate records by definition. However, if we remove one or more columns, the result is not necessarily a relation since there may be duplicate rows present. To make it into a relation, these duplicate rows have to be removed. Thus an external conceptual file in the relational approach is also a relation.

With System R an external conceptual file or relation is called a *view*. Thus if we issue the interactive command:

```
DEFINE VIEW VIEW1 (EMPNUMB, SALARY)
AS SELECT EMPNUMB, SALARY FROM EMPLOYEE
```

we have defined an external relation called VIEW1 containing the fields EMPNUMB and SALARY from the relation EMPLOYEE defined in the conceptual schema.

Overview of system R in an interactive environment

Before going on to examine SQL, we give an overview of System R. The User-Friendly System is the terminal control system, which accepts the CREATIVE TABLE, CREATE INDEX, DEFINE VIEW commands for specifying the schemas; it also accepts SQL retrieval expressions and many other commands.

The RD System places conceptual and external schemas in the System R data dictionary following the relevant schema definition commands; however, execution of commands defining a storage schemas causes the storage schema definition to be placed in a data directory. The RD System also accepts SQL data base manipulation commands passed from the UF System; the RD System translates these commands into what are known as access routines that call up the services of the Research Storage System.

The Research Storage System is responsible for arranging for each access of the storage data base. Many accesses may be required for a response to a single SQL command. The RS System does not itself access the data base, however; it issues CALLs to the underlying access methods that are responsible for reading and writing records on storage files.

Structured query language

SQL is easily the most important relational data base manipulation language at the time of writing and is provided for by practically all relational data base systems that have been developed or are currently under development. However, that does not mean that SQL is cast in stone, for it was designed some 10 years ago and contains features that could certainly be improved upon, and no doubt will be in the course of time. We saw that SQL/N is a candidate extension of SQL that permits the use of natural quantifiers

SQL with System R can be used either directly from a terminal as a query and updating language, or it can be *embedded* in a host language such as COBOL or PL/1. There are a fair number of unpleasant details involved with the use of embedded SQL, and so we concentrate on a discussion of SQL as it would be used at a terminal. Embedded SQL is essentially the same except for the additional technicalities, and is described in the chapter supplement. We shall first introduce the elementary structure of SQL, followed by some examples of SQL expressions. More advanced SQL structures and expressions then follow. Our aim is the provision of sufficient material for the reader to actually learn SQL, such as its importance. SQL is an example of a nonprocedural database manipulation language.

Structure of SQL

An SQL expression is constructed from what are called SELECT-FROM-WHERE blocks. A simple SQL statement would be a single SELECT-FROM-WHERE block. In a more complex expression one SELECT-FROM-WHERE block can be nested within another such block. A SELECT-FROM-WHERE block has the structure:

SELECT fieldname, fieldname ...

FROM relation, relation ...

WHERE logical-expression AND/OR logical-expression AND/OR...

At first glance the basic structure looks very close to the SQL/N structure described in the previous chapter. However, there are two important differences. First, the expression retrieves at once the fields specified from all the records of the relation specified, provided that the contents of the record satisfy the conditions specified in the WHERE clause. Thus a conceptual file of records is retrieved; we recall that with SQL/N we could retrieve one record at a time if desired. Second, no quantifiers are needed in the logical expressions.

SQL retrievals with a single SELECT-FROM-WHERE block

The following retrievals all refer to the data base. For convenience we assume that the user's external schema is identical to the conceptual schema.

Retrieval-1: No WHERE clause

Retrieve all the SALARY values from the EMPLOYEE relation.

```
SELECT SALARY
FROM EMPLOYEE
```

The result is,

```
22,000
21,000
25,000
23,000
25,000
```

We see that the list contains duplicates, as does the SALARY column in the EMPLOYEE relation. In the relational approach to data base management all nonstorage files, that is, conceptual files, external files, and retrieval files, are supposed to be relations, at least in theory. However, with SQL that restriction is relaxed as far as retrievals are concerned, and duplicate rows are not removed unless we specifically request it.

If we wanted to retrieve a relation in response to the above request, we would specify.:

```
SELECT UNIQUE SALARY
FROM EMPLOYEE
```

UNIQUE causes duplicates to be removed.

Retrieval-2: Retrieval of complete records

Retrieve all the records in WAREHOUSE

```
SELECT
FROM WAREHOUSE
```

The response is:

```
WH1   DALLAS   37,000
```

```
WH2   NEW YORK 50,000
WH3   CHICAGO   20,000
```

The asterisk is the top line signifies that we want all the fields in the records. Of course we could replace the above expression with:

```
SELECT WHNUMB,  CITY,  WH-AREA
FROM WAREHOUSE
```

Retrieval-3: Simple WHERE clause

Retrieve the employee numbers of employees earning more than $23,000.

```
SELECT  EMPNUMB

FROM  EMPLOYEE

WHERE  (SALARY  >  23000)
```

The response is:

```
E4
E7
```

Retrieval-4: Elimination of duplicates

In what warehouses are there employees earning more than $21,000?

```
SELECT  UNIQUE  WHNUMB
FROM  EMPLOYEE
WHERE  (SALARY>21000)
```

The response is:

```
WH2
WH3
WH1
```

In this case we are clearly interested in a list of unique warehouse numbers. In the case of Retrieval-1 we were clearly interested in all salaries whether duplicates or not. The decision whether or not to have duplicates eliminated is an important one in SQL and often has a significant effect on the processing of the data retrieved. Going back to Retrieval-1 again, had we been interested in the average salary of employees listed in EMPLOYEE, then use of the relation obtained by inserting UNIQUE into the retrieval expression would clearly lead to an incorrect average calculated. We shall return to this point again when we come to computational retrievals.

Retrieval-5: More complex WHERE clause

Give the employee numbers of employees that work in warehouse 'WH1' or 'WH2' and makes less than $25,000.

```
SELECT  EMPNUMB
```

```
FROM  EMPLOYEE
WHERE  (SALARY  <  25000)
AND  ((WHNUMB  =  'WH1')  OR  (WHNUMB  =  'WH2'))
```

The response would be:

```
E1
E2
```

Care has to be taken with more complex logical expression. The EMPNUMB value is selected from an EMPLOYEE record only if the expression is true and either is also true.

The SQL retrieval mechanism

The system uses sophisticated procedures to carry out a retrieval request specified in an SQL expression.

Assuming that there is only one relation specified after FROM then the system can be imagined as checking each record of the relation in turn in ascending primary key sequence. If the record currently under investigation satisfies what is specified in the WHERE clause, then it is selected, and the values in the fields specified after SELECT are displayed.

A slight variation of this visualization may be employed by the user when fields from more than one relation are to be retrieved. We now look at such a retrieval.

Retrieval-6: Retrieval data in two relations

Find the employee numbers for employees earning more than $22,000, and the cities in which these employees work.

```
SELECT  EMPNUMB,  CITY
FROM  EMPLOYEE,  WAREHOUSE
WHERE  (SALARY  >  23000)  AND                              (EMPLOYEE.WHNUMB  =
WAREHOUSE.WHNUMB)
```

The response is:

```
E4  NEW  YORK
E7  DALLAS
```

There are two ways to look at the retrieval procedure here. In the first way of looking at it, if there are two relations following FROM in the retrieval expression, then these two relations have to have a relationship between the otherwise the expression would make no sense. We know that in this case there is a one-to-many relationship between the relations WAREHOUSE and EMPLOYEE. In such case we can visualize the system checking through each record of the child relation, in this case the EMPLOYEE relation, to see if it is acceptable. Acceptability depends on whether the fields in the child record and the fields of its parent record satisfy the logical expressions following

WHERE. If a child record is acceptable, then the specified field from this record together with the specified field from its parent record, is displayed.

The other way of looking at it is much more in the spirit of the relational approach. We imagine that a new relation. Anyway, the effect of natural join is to generate a new relation where each record describes an employee and the warehouse he or she works in. The system can now scan through this relation, record by record, extracting the fields from those records that satisfy the condition that follow WHERE. We emphasize that this is only a way for the user to visualize the retrieval process; in practice it is unlikely that a system would do it in exactly this manner, as it would involve far two many disk accesses and thus be far too slow.

We give one further example involving retrieval of information from two relations.

Retrieval-7. Retrieval data in two relations

Find the employee numbers of employees who work in warehouse bigger than 40,000 units, and find also the cities in which these employees work.

```
SELECT  EMPNUMB,  CITY
FROM EMPLOYEE, WAREHOUSE
WHERE  (WH-AREA > 40000) AND
(EMPLOYEE.WHNUMB  =  WAREHOUSE.WHNUMB)
```

The response is:

```
E1
E4
```

As with the previous retrieval we can imagine that the system scans through the EMPLOYEE relation examining each record in turn for compliance with the WHERE condition in the expression. However, to determine if the WHERE condition is satisfied, the system must check the parent WAREHOUSE record of the EMPLOYEE record under consideration. Alternatively, we can imagine that the system scans through the retrieved WAREHOUSE-EMPLOYEE in Figure 4. Note that either way we must equate the connection fields in the expression.

Structure of SQL expression with nested SELECT-FROM-WHERE blocks

We shall examine first the case where we have a SELECT-FROM-WHERE block containing a second or nested SELECT-FROM-WHERE block. We saw earlier that a SELECT-FROM-WHERE block has the structure.

SELECT field name, field name,...
FROM relation, relation,...
WHERE logical-expression AND/OR logical-expression AND/OR,...

and it is clear that everything that follows WHERE is a condition that is either true or false. Indeed we have had a WHERE clause involving AND and OR in Retrieval-5. The WHERE clause in that case was

```
WHERE (SALARY 25000) AND (WHNUMB = 'WH1')
OR (WHNUMB = 'WH2')
```

and each of the logical expressions so far inserted into SQL expressions involved field values from records belonging to the relations specified after FROM, that is, from the records being considered for possible retrieval.

However, when the condition for retrieval of a record in the relation X depends on the value of fields in records of a related relation Y, the records of which are not being retrieved, then we use a nested SELECT-FROM-WHERE block within a logical expression. The complete structure of an SQL expression can therefore be given as:

SELECT fieldname, fieldname,...
FROM relation
WHERE logical-expression-1 AND/OR logical-expression-1 AND/OR....
AND/OR logical-expression-2 AND/OR logical-expression-2 AND/OR...

Thus we have two types of logical expression, namely, logical-expression-1, which is what we have had in Retrieval-1 through Retrieval-7, and logical-expression-2, which is an expression containing a further SELECT-FROM WHERE block.

There is more than one way to construct logical-expression-2, and we start with the two constructs that are the easiest to use:

1. field IS IN SELECT-FROM-WHERE block, or
   field IS NOT IN SELECT-FROM-WHERE block.
2. EXISTS SELECT-FROM-WHERE block or
   NOT EXISTS SELECT-FROM-WHERE block.

We shall given an additional construct later. Note that since an SQL expression and a SELECT-FROM-WHERE block have exactly the same structure, not only can a logical expression in an SQL expression contain a nested SELECT-FROM-WHERE block, but that nested SELECT-FROM-WHERE block can in turn contain a logical expression that contains a SELECT-FROM-WHERE block, and so on. Thus, quite complex SQL expressions can be generated.

We begin with some examples involving a single-nested SELECT-FROM-WHERE block.

Retrieve-8: Use of IS IN

In what cities is there at least one warehouse employee making $25,000?

```
SELECT CITY
FROM WAREHOUSE
```

```
WHERE WHNUMB IS IN (SELECT WHNUMB FROM EMPLOYEE WHERE
(SALARY = 25000))
```

The response is:

```
DALLAS
NEW YORK
```

We see that the expression contains two SELECT-FROM-WHERE blocks, namely, an outer block and an inner block. To understand the expression, it is best to start by looking at the inner block as a complete SQL expression and so evaluate what it would retrieve if it were. This would be the following list of WHNUMB values:

```
WH2
WH1
```

which are the warehouse numbers for warehouses with an employee earning $25,000. So the expression above is really the same as:

```
SELECT CITY
FROM WAREHOUSE
WHERE WHNUMB IS IN ('WH2','WH1')
```

Incidently this is also a valid SQL expression; it is requesting the CITY value from each WAREHOUSE record with a WHNUMB value in the list that is, with a WHNUMB value in that list of WHNUMB values from warehouse with an employee earning $25,000.

The method of expressing a relationship in a retrieval expression using IS IN followed by a SELECT-FROM-WHERE block does not come naturally to most users. However, it does bring out the essence of the relational approach. Relationships are not explicitly specified in a relational conceptual schema, but instead are specified in manipulation language expressions by equating the parent and child connection field values for each one-to-many relationship used in the expression. However, it can be argued that the method is not all that awkward for the average user. For example, we could rewrite the retrieval request as:

Retrieve each city with a warehouse that is among those warehouses with at least one employee earning $25,000.

and the structure of this sentence corresponds fairly closely to the structure of the SQL expression using IS IN. Perhaps IS IN should be changed to IS AMONG!.

Retrieval-9: Use of IS NOT IN

What is the floor area of those warehouses in which the employees all make more than $21,000?

Before trying to write the SQL expression, we should point out that the request can be rewritten:

What is floor area of those warehouses in which there is no employee making $21,000 or less?

We can do this because of the interplay between the natural quantifier "for all," or "for each," and the natural quantifier "there is not," or "there is no" or "there does not exist," and so on. If we state that for each dollar bill the color is green, that is the same as saying that there is no dollar bill for which the color is not green.

We can further rewrite the above request to more closely mirror the structure of an SQL expression using IS NOT IN:

Retrieve each floor area for a warehouse that is not among those warehouses with employees making $21,000 or less.

The SQL expression is:

```
SELECT WH-AREA
FROM WAREHOUSE
WHERE WHNUMB IS NOT IN (SELECT WHNUMB FROM          EMPLOYEE WHERE
(SALARY > = 21000))
```

and the response is:

```
50,000
20,000
```

The inner SELECT-FROM-WHERE block specifies the set of WHNUMB values for warehouses that have an employee earning $21,000 or less, and this set contains the sole element 'WH1'. We then retrieve from WAREHOUSE the WH-AREA value from each record whose WHNUMB value is not in this set.

Thus the retrieval appears to be reasonably straightforward. However, there is a fundamental subtlety that shows up in this retrieval, and which is quite common in SQL expressions of this type. If the user is not aware of this subtlety wrong information can be retrieved.

It should always be remembered that big data base in larger enterprises can contain data that is important for the welfare of individuals, organizations, and in times of national emergency even nations. The possibility that a decision maker could easily retrieve incorrect information must therefore be investigated seriously.

WHNUMB	CITY	WH-AREA
WH1	DALLAS	37,000
WH2	NEW YORK	50,000
WH3	CHICAGO	37,000
WH5	DENNER	13,000

WAREHOUSE

WHNUMB	EMPNUMB	SALARY
WH2	E1	22,000
WH1	E3	21,000
WH2	E4	25,000
WH3	E6	23,000
WH1	E7	25,000

EMPLOYEE

To understand what could go wrong with the above retrieval, let us suppose that there has been inserted an additional record in the WAREHOUSE relation. The new record describes a warehouse in Denver. For this record there are as yet no employees, so that there are no EMPLOYEE records with the child connection key value 'WH5'. If the above SQL expression is applied to the data base, the response will be:

```
50,000
20,000
13,000
```

so that after the floor area of our new warehouse is retrieved, even though it has no employees at all.

To see how this comes about, must examine the logic of the SQL expression carefully. We must also remember that SQL has its roots in the theory of mathematical sets, to which the strict rules of logic apply. Looking at the inner SELECT-FROM-WHERE block, we see that it still specifies the set of WHNUMB values, giving the warehouses whose employees do not all make more than $21,000. Accordingly, when the SQL expression specifies retrieval of the WH-AREA values in each WAREHOUSE record whose WHNUMB values IS NOT IN this set of WHNUMB values, we are in effect specifying that it is acceptable to retrieve WH-AREA value from a WAREHOUSE record, provided the warehouse does not have employees who earn $21,000 or less. Thus it is acceptable for a warehouse to have no employees at all-there simply must not be employees earning $21,000 or less.

Thus the retrieval request specified by the SQL expression is really:

What is the floor are of warehouses whose employees all earn more than $21,000?

and this will in many cases not be what was intended by the original request. What would probably have been intended is:

what is the floor area of each warehouse that has one or more employees, who all earn more than $21,000.

With this request we are quite clearly specifying that we are not interest in warehouses that have no employees. There is no problem about SQL's capability of expressing this more exact request. SQL is very powerful. Unfortunately the required expression is more complex and involves two different nested SELECT-FROM-WHERE blocks. Referring back to the structure of an SQL expression, we need an expression with the following structure:

SELECT field
FROM relation
WHERE logical-expression-1 AND logical- expression-2

The necessary SQL expression is:

```
SELECT WH-AREA
FROM WAREHOUSE
WHERE WHNUMB IS IN (SELECT WHNUMB FROM     EMPLOYEE)
AND WHNUMB  IS  NOT  IN  (SELECT  WHNUMB  FROM        EMPLOYEE  WHERE
(SALARY  <  =  21000)
```

if the expression were applied to the data base, the response would be:

```
50,000
20,000
```

By means of the first inner SELECT-FROM-WHERE block, we are stating that a WAREHOUSE record is acceptable only if its WHNUMB value occurs in the EMPLOYEE relation, that is, if the warehouse described has employees listed in the EMPLOYEE relation. By means of the second inner SELECT-FROM-WHERE block, we are stating that a warehouse record is acceptable if in addition it has a WHNUMB value that is not in the set of WHNUMB values for warehouses with employees earning $21,000 or less.

It should thus be clear that SQL is not all that easy to use with more sophisticated retrievals. Readers who have studies SQL/N will probably be able to see that one of the difficulties is that SQL does not have the broad range of quantifiers available in SQL/N and English. It is these quantifiers that the writer of precise english sentences uses to avoid theological difficulties encountered with Retrieval-9.

Use of SQL/N with Retrieval-0

As we have seen, there are two ways in which the retrieval could be interpreted, and we shall give the SQL/N expression for each interpretation.

FIRST INTERPRETATION. what is the floor area of warehouses whose employees all earn more than $21,000?

```
SELECT WH-AREA
FROM WAREHOUSE
WHERE (FOR EACH IF ANY EMPLOYEE MEMBER        RECORD   (SALARY >
21000)
```

The quantifier FOR EACH or FOR ALL in SQL/N is the same as FOR EACH IF ANY or FOR ALL IF ANY, meaning the logical expression is to be tested as true only if there are any EMPLOYEE member records.

The response for the data base is:

```
50,000
20,000
13,000
```

SECOND INTERPRETATION. What is the floor area of warehouses that each have one or more employees, all of whom earn more than $21,000?

```
    SELECT WH-AREA
    FROM WAREHOUSE
WHERE (FOR ONE AND ALL EMPLOYEE MEMBER RECORDS (SALARY > 21000
```

Here we are stating that we wish to retrieve a WAREHOUSE parent record, provided there is one EMPLOYEE child with SALARY greater than $21,000, and provided all child EMPLOYEE records have a SALARY greater than $21,000. This can be concisely specified using the natural quantifier FOR ONE AND ALL.

The response for the data base is

```
50,000
20,000
```

At risk of tiring the reader with the ins and outs of Retrieval-9, the SQL quantifier EXISTS can be used to replace IS IN, as indicated earlier in the structure of logical-expression-2.

Retrieval-10: Use of quantifier EXISTS with Retrieval-9

We shall make use of the quantifier EXISTS with the two interpretations of Retrieval-9.

FIRST INTERPRETATION. What is the floor area of warehouses whose employees all earn more than $21,000?

```
SELECT WH-AREA
FROM WAREHOUSE
WHERE NOT EXISTS (SELECT
                  FROM EMPLOYEE
                  WHERE (SALARY<= 21,00)
                  AND (EMPLOYEE.WHNUMB
                  = WAREHOUSE.WHNUMB)
```

Referring to the data base, the response is:

```
50,000
20,000
13,000
```

We scan through the WAREHOUSE relation, examining each record in turn for acceptability. For each WAREHOUSE record we may imagine that the system then examines the records specified by the inner SELECT-FROM-WHERE block. This group of EMPLOYEE records should not exist, that is, the set of records specified should be empty for the WAREHOUSE record being examined to be acceptable.

It is worth examining the inner SELECT-FROM-WHERE block more closely. It specifies those EMPLOYEE records whose child connection field matches the parent connection key for the WAREHOUSE record being examined, and whose SALARY field value is less than or equal to $21,000. In other words it is specifying the child EMPLOYEE records that have a SALARY field less than or equal to $21,000.

```
SELECT WH-AREA
FROM WAREHOUSE
WHERE (THERE ARE NO EMPLOYEE MEMBER RECORDS WHERE
(SALARY < = 21,000)
```

SECOND INTERPRETATION. What is the floor area of warehouses that each have one or more employees, all of whom earn more than $21,000?

```
SELECT WH-AREA
FROM WAREHOUSE
WHERE EXISTS  (SELECT
       FROM EMPLOYEE
       WHERE (EMPLOYEE.WHNUMB =
WAREHOUSE.WHNUMB)
AND NOT EXISTS (SELECT
       FROM EMPLOYEE
       WHERE (SALARY < = 21000)
       AND (EMPLOYEE.WHNUMB
       = WAREHOUSE.WHNUMB
```

with the data base the response is:

```
50,000
20,000
```

To see how the expression is constructed. We can scan through the WAREHOUSE relation, checking each record inturn for acceptability. For each WAREHOUSE record, we check to see if there are child EMPLOYEE records, as specified in the first inner SELECT-FROM-WHERE block. We also check to see that there is no EMPLOYEE child record with the SALARY field values less than or equal to $21,000. If these conditions are met, then the WH-AREA field is selected from the WAREHOUSE record begin examined.

Retrieval-11: Use of IS IN or EXISTS

What cities have a warehouse that is larger than 30,000 units in floor area and has at least one employee exactly $25,000?

```
SELECT CITY
FROM WAREHOUSE
WHERE (WH-AREA > 30,000)
AND WHNUMB IS IN (SELECT WHNUMB
                  FROM EMPLOYEE WHERE
(SALARY = 25000))
DALLAS
NEW YORK
```

We scan through the WAREHOUSE relation, selecting for examination those WAREHOUSE records that have a WH-AREA field value greater than $30,000. For each of these selected WAREHOUSE records, we check to see if the WHNUMB field value is to be found in the list of WHNUMB values for EMPLOYEE records with SALARY field value equal to $25,000. The CITY value is taken from WAREHOUSE records that pass this examination.

The structure of the above expression involves the use of logical-expression-1 and logical-expression-2 following WHERE. We recall that the general structure of the WHERE clause is:

WHERE logical-expression-1 AND/OR logical- expression-1 AND/Or...
AND logical-expression-2 AND/OR...

Logical-expression-2 involves a nested SELECT-FROM-WHERE block.

The quantifier EXISTS can always be used in lace of IS IN with a minor modification to the inner SELECT-FROM-WHERE block:

```
SELECT  CITY
FROM  WAREHOUSE
WHERE  (WH-AREA  >  30000)
AND  EXISTS      (SELECT
             FROM  EMPLOYEE
             WHERE  (SALARY  =  25,000)
             AND  (EMPLOYEE.WHNUMB                                =
WAREHOUSE.WHNUMB
```

Whenever we use EXISTS, we are in affect specifying the members of owner-coupled set occurrences. Thus for each WAREHOUSE record that has the required WH-AREA value, we check the child EMPLOYEE records to see if there is one that has a SALARY value exactly equal to $25,000.

Retrieval-12: Use of EXISTS and IS IN

What employees making more than $22,000 work in Dallas?

```
SELECT  EMPNUMB
FROM  EMPLOYEE
WHERE  (SALARY  >  22000)
AND  WHNUMB  IS  IN  (SELECT  WHNUMB
                      FROM  WAREHOUSE
                      WHERE  (CITY  =  'DALLAS')
```

The response would be:

```
E7
```

The expression has no new features as structure is concerned. However, we are seeking child EMPLOYEE records depending on a property of a parent WAREHOUSE record. IN previous examples we sought parent WAREHOUSE records depending on properties of child EMPLOYEE records. We could use EXISTS instead of IS IN:

```
SELECT EMPNUMB
FROM EMPLOYEE
WHERE (SALARY > 22,000)
AND EXISTS (SELECT
    FROM WAREHOUSE WHERE
    (CITY = 'DALLAS')
    AND (WHNUMB = EMPLOYEE.WHNUMB))
```

Elementary logic and SQL expressions

By now readers will certainly have concluded that the construction of SQL expressions requires a certain minimum proficiency in the use of logic. Fortunately, in the vast majority of expressions only elementary logic is required, but for the benefit of readers who are uncertain about what a logical expression is or about how such an expression can be evaluated, we now include a review of the subject. Readers who are comfortable with the type of logical expressions presented so far might well skip this section; however, they should note that it contains a brief discussion of logical expressions that contain elementary sets, which is what is specified in a SELECT-FROM-WHERE block and which is rarely included in discussions on elementary logic. Such expressions are of course central to SQL.

AND OR NOR, and the comparison operators

It is the comparison of two quantities that give rise to the simplest logical expressions. To symbolize the comparison operation, we use the comparison operators =, ¬=, <, > =, and < =. Thus we can have simple logical expressions where we know the logical value, for example:

(4 = 4)	value TRUE
(5 = 4)	value FALSE
(5 > 4)	value TRUE
(5 ¬= 4)	value TRUE

and also simple logical expressions where we do not know the logical value until we have evaluated the value of each variable involved:

(X = 4)	value TRUE or FALSE depending on value of X
(CITY = 'NEW YORK')	value TRUE or FALSE depending on value of city
(SALARY = 20,000)	value TRUE or FALSE depending on value of SALARY

Simple logical expressions may be combined using the logical operators AND, OR and NOT. Thus we may have the compound logical expressions.

```
(CITY = 'NEW YORK') AND (WH-AREA < 40,000)
(CITY = 'DALLAS') OR (WH-AREA = 30,000)
(SALARY = 20,000) AND NOT (WHNUMB = 'WH1')
```

with compound logical expressions involving three or more simple logical expressions, the parentheses affects the value of the expressions. Thus,

((3=2) AND (2 = 2)) or (9 > 6) is TRUE
(3=2) AND ((2 = 2) OR (9 > 6)) is FALSE

Truth tables are often useful for evaluating logical expressions. Thus, if L1 and L2 are logical expressions, then for the logical expressions and the following truth tables are valid:

Thus the rule for logical-AND is that both L1 and L2 must be TRUE for the compound expression to be true, while with logical-OR either L1 or L2 must be TRUE for the compound expression to be true.

To evaluate a complex logical expression involving three or more simple logical expressions, we first evaluate what is inside the parentheses and then treat the result as another logical expression. For example, suppose that L1 is FALSE, L2 is TRUE, and L3 is TRUE; then:

(L1 AND L2) OR L3 Evaluates FALSE OR L3, which is TRUE

However,

(L1 AND (L2 OR L3) Evaluates to L1 AND TRUE, which is FALSE

Imperatives and predicates

An SQL expression contains both an imperative and a predicate, as do all relational retrieval languages and many other languages as well. The imperative states what must be done to a potential list of objects, while the predicate gives conditions that place restrictions on the selection of the objects to which the command will be applied. We have this in everyday English. Thus the investment manager might issue the order:

Acquire 1000 shares of any company that has a price/earnings ratio less than 8 and has its headquarters in Frankfurt.

The imperative is clearly:

Acquire 1000 shares of any company

The object of the imperative is any company, while the predicate is:

(P/E < 8) AND (HQ = "FRANKFURT")

Predicates are always logical expressions, and in SQL the predicate follows the first instance of the word WHERE so that SQL really has the simple structure:

SELECT objects *WHERE* predicate

The predicate in SQL may be simple logical expression as in:

```
SELECT  EMPNUMB
FROM  EMPLOYEE
```

```
WHERE (SALARY = 25,000) .
```

or it may be a complex or compound logical expression:

```
SELECT EMPNUMB
FROM EMPLOYEE
WHERE (SALARY = 25,000) OR
(SALARY = 22,000))
AND (WHNUMB = 'WH1')
```

But regardless of how complex the predicate is, an EMPNUMB value will be selected only from EMPLOYEE tuples for which the predicate is TRUE.

But we have seen that we can have nested SELECT-FROM-WHERE blocks following WHERE, so that there nested blocks must be part of the predicate. Since we have also seen that the predicate is a logical expression constructed from simpler logic expressions, the question most students of the subject sooner or later get around to asking is: Is a SELECT-FROM-WHERE block itself a logical expression? The answer is most certainly not, and treating such blocks as logical expressions is a very common error among SQL beginners. Thus the expression:

```
SELECT CITY
FROM WAREHOUSE
WHERE (SELECT WHNUMB FROM EMPLOYEE
 WHERE (SALARY = 20000))
```

is complete nonsense, for what follows WHERE is not a logical expression. We mist therefore examine more closely what constitutes a simple logical expression when a SELECT-FROM-WHERE block is involved.

Some logical expressions and SELECT-FROM-WHERE blocks

We saw previously that the well-known comparison operators are common used to form simple logical expressions. However, there are other way of making up a simple logical expression. The most important of these are (1) membership in a group or set of elements, (2) existence of a certain quantity of elements, and comparison of two different groups or sets of elements. We take then in turn.

1. *Membership in a Set of Elements*. Suppose we have a set of elements such as persons:

```
'SMITH', 'BROWN,' 'GREEN,' 'BLACK', 'WHITE'
```

then

```
('BROWN' IS IN THE SET
('SMITH', 'BROWN', 'GREEN', 'BLACK',           'WHITE'))
```

is also a simple logical expression that in this case is TRUE. If we state:

```
(PERSON IS NOT IN
```

```
('SMITH', 'BROWN', 'GREEN', 'BLACK', 'WHITE'))
```

this is also a simple logical expression that is either TRUE or FALSE depending on the value in the variable PERSON. Also

(PERSON IS IN A)

is TRUE or FALSE depending on what is the value of the variable PERSON and the set of values in the set A. However, it is a set of values that is specified by a SELECT-FROM-WHERE block, so that the following is also a simple logical expression:

```
(WHNUMB IS IN (SELECT WHNUMB
              FROM EMPLOYEE
              WHERE (SALARY = 20000))
```

and is either TRUE or FALSE. In SQL, simple logical expressions of this type can be combined with conventional logical expressions to give compound expressions such as:

```
    (CITY = 'DALLAS') AND (WHNUMB IS IN    (SELECT  WHNUMB  FROM
EMPLOYEE WHERE (SALARY        = 20000)))
```

Any compound logical expression of this type can be used to form the predicate in the basic SQL expression:

SELECT object WHERE predicate

2. *Existence of Certain Quantities of Elements.* Suppose we have a set or group of persons elements as in above. Then

```
(THERE EXISTS AT LEAST ONE
('SMITH', 'BROWN', 'GREEN', 'BLACK',
'WHITE') ELEMENT)
```

is a logical expression, which in this case is clearly TRUE. If we state:

```
(THERE EXISTS AT LEAST ONE A ELEMENT)
```

or just for short, then this is clearly also a simple logical expression that will be TRUE or FALSE depending on whether A contains any elements. However, as we have seen, a SELECT-FROM-WHERE block is a specification of a set of elements, that is, a set of external records. Then

```
(EXISTS (SELECT
        FROM EMPLOYEE
        WHERE ((SALARY = 25,000)
        AND (WHNUMB = WAREHOUSE.WHNUMB)))
```

is another kind of simple logical expression and will have the value TRUE if the SELECT-FROM-WHERE block specifies or "retrieves" any records; otherwise it will have the value FALSE. As in the case if IS IN logical expression may be used in the construction of more involved logical expressions that can serve as SQL predicates.

3. *Comparison of Sets of Elements.* A simple logical expression can also be constructed by comparing the size and contents of two sets of elements. Suppose that we have the sets:

```
Set A:    ('SMITH',   'BROWN',   'GREEN')
Set B:    ('BROWN',   'GREEN',   'SMITH')
Set C:    ('SMITH',   'GREEN',   'JONES',          'BROWN')
Set D:    ('BROWN',   'GREEN')
```

Then the logical expression is TRUE, the logical expression D = B is TRUE is FALSE, is TRUE, is TRUE, is TRUE, and so on.

It will come as no surprises to the reader that SQL permits logical expressions of this type, where at least one of the sets of elements involved in a SELECT-FROM-WHERE block. Many of the simple logical expressions that are possible have the syntax:

(S-F-W-block = S-F-W-block)

(S-F-W-block ⌉= S-F-W- block)

(variable = S-F-W-block) That is, there is only on element in the S-F-W-block

(variable ⌉= S-F-W-block) Again, only one element in the S-F-W-block.

(S-F-W-block CONTAINS S-F-W-block)

(S-F-W-block DOES NOT CONTAIN S-F-W-block)

(set CONTAINS S-F-W-blocks)

(set DOES NOT CONTAIN S-F-W-block)

(S-F-W-block CONTAINS set)

(S-F-W-block DOES NOT CONTAIN set)

(set = S-F-W-block)

(set ⌉= S-F-W-block)

It turns that this type of simple logical expression is needed mainly in more complicated or perhaps even more subtle retrievals. We shall look at some retrievals involving them next.

SQL expressions involving comparison of set of elements

The retrieval examples presented here are slightly more difficult than those presented earlier, and readers interested in a more cursory treatment of SQL could conveniently skip these examples

Retrieval-13: Single-element-set comparison

Find the employees earning the same salary as employees 'E4'.

We could rephrase this as: Find each employee that has a salary equal to the salary of employee 'E4'.

```
SELECT EMPNUMB
FROM EMPLOYEE
WHERE SALARY = (SELECT SALARY
FROM EMPLOYEE WHERE EMPNUMB = 'E4')
```

With the data base the response would be:

```
E4
E7
```

For every EMPLOYEE record examined, the set specified in the inner S-F-W-block is always a set with one element. Thus the expression retrieves the employee numbers of each employee earning $25,000.

The difficulty with expressions of this type lies not so much in the understanding of them but rather in their formulation. The structure of the above expression is not difficult either. Following WHERE we have a simple logical expression, as explained earlier.

Retrieval-14: Use of CONTAINS

Find the warehouses at which salaries of $21,000 and $25,000 are paid to employees

```
SELECT WHNUMB
FROM WAREHOUSE
WHERE (SELECT SALARY
       FROM EMPLOYEE
       WHERE (WHNUMB = WAREHOUSE.WHNUMB))
CONTAINS
 (21000, 25000)
```

The response is:

```
WH7
```

When the WAREHOUSE record being investigated has key 'WH1", the set specified by the S-F-W-block is so that the WHNUMB value from this record can be selected. For all other WAREHOUSE records, the set of salary values specified by the S-F-W-block does not contain the specified set.

WE could use the IS IN type of logical expression for this retrieval. However, the following expression, which at first glance might seem reasonable, is incorrect:

```
SELECT WHNUMB
FROM WAREHOUSE
WHERE WHNUMB IS IN (SELECT WHNUMB
                    FROM EMPLOYEE
                    WHERE (SALARY = 21000)
                    OR (SALARY = 25000)
```

It would retrieve

```
WH1
WH2
```

Readers should attempt to construct a correct SQL expression that uses IS IN logical expressions.

Retrieval-15: Use of CONTAINS with Retrieval-9

We recall that this retrieval had two interpretations. We take only th first interpretation:

what is the floor area of warehouses whose employees all earn more than $21,000?

```
SELECT  WH-AREA
FROM  WAREHOUSE
WHERE  (SELECT EMPNUMB
     FROM EMPLOYEE
     WHERE  (SALARY  >  21000))
CONTAINS
     (SELECT  EMPNUMB
     FROM EMPLOYEE
     WHERE  (WHNUMB  =  WAREHOUSE.WHNUMB))
```

The response with the data base is:

```
50,000
20,000
13,000
```

To understand how this expression works, consider the second instead S-F-W-blocks. It in effect specifies the list of EMPNUMB values for the child EMPLOYEE records of the WAREHOUSE record being examined. These EMPNUMB values must be from EMPLOYEE records that all have a SALARY value greater than $21,000. Thus they must be a subset of, or be contained in, the EMPNUMB values from al EMPLOYEE records with the SALARY value greater than $21,000, and it is this set of EMPNUMB values that is specified by the first nested S-F-W-block. The set is always.

```
('E1',  'E4',  1E6',  'E7')
```

In order for the WAREHOUSE record with key 'WH2' to be retrieved, the above set must contain the EMPNUMB values from that WAREHOUSE record's child EMPLOYEE records, that is, it must contain the set. We see that it does, and so the record with key 'WH2' is retrieved and the WH-AREA value is extracted from it. Notice that the WH-AREA value from the record with key 'WH5' is also retrieved. As we might expect, the reason this time will again tell us a great deal about the fundamental nature of SQL.

When the WAREHOUSE a record being examined for possible retrieval has the key value 'WH5', that is a record with zero child EMPLOYEE records, the set specified by the first S-F-W-block is still

```
('E1', 'E4', 'E6', 'E7')
```

However, the set specified by the second S-F-W-block is now empty, since the WAREHOUSE record involved has no child records in EMPLOYEE. The logical expression.

```
('E1', 'E4', 1E6', 'E7') CONTAINS ( )
```

IS TRUE, since any set contains a null or empty set. Thus the WAREHOUSE record with key 'WH5' will be retrieved.

It seems unlikely that users would prefer the use of CONTAINS in retrievals of this type. Use of IS NOT IN appears to be more convenient.

Retrieval-16: Many-to-many relationships

What are the salaries of employees who have issued purchase orders to all suppliers?

For this data base we see that an employee deals with many suppliers while a supplier deals with many employees. The retrieval request is for those EMPLOYEE records for employees that deal with every supplier listed in the relation SUPPLIER. The SQL expression is:

```
SELECT SALARY
FROM EMPLOYEE
WHERE (SELECT SNUMB
      FROM PUR-ORDER
      WHERE (EMPNUMB = EMPLOYEE.ENPNUMB))
      =
      (SELECT SNUMB
      FROM SUPPLIER)
```

The response is:

```
21,000
```

The second nested S-F-W-block contains the set of all the suppliers in the SUPPLIER relation. The first nested S-F-W-block contains the SNUMB values from the child PUR-ORDER records of the EMPLOYEE record under consideration, that is, the set of supplier numbers of the suppliers of the employee under examination deals with. Suppose we are considering employee 'E3' for possible retrieval from the EMPLOYEE relation. From the child PUR-ORDER records we can determine that this employee deals with the suppliers ('S7', 'S4', 'S6', 'S3'). The complete list of supplier numbers taken from the SUPPLIER relation is ('S3', 'S4', 'S6', 'S7'). Thus the two sets are equal, so that employees 'E3' may be retrieved, giving $21,000 as the SALARY value.

WHNUMB	CITY	WH-AREA
WH1	DALLAS	37,000
WH2	NEW YORK	50,000

WH3	CHICAGO	20,000
WH5	DENVER	13,000

WAREHOUSE

WHNUMB	EMPNUMB	SALARY
WH2	E1	22,000
WH1	E3	21,000
WH2	E4	25,000
WH3	E6	23,000
WH1	E7	25,000

EMPLOYEE

SNUMB	SNAME	LOC
S3	TRONOTON	CALIFORNIA
S4	ROBOTEK	TEXAS
S6	MIKREL	ONTARIO
S7	RAYTEK	TEXAS

SUPPLIER

WHNUMB	SNUMB	ORDERNUMB	ISSUE-DATE
E3	S7	OR67	84/06/23
E1	S4	OR73	84/07/28
E7	S4	OR76	84/05/25
E6	S6	OR77	84/06/19
E3	S4	OR79	84/06/23
E1	S6	OR80	84/07/29
E3	S6	OR90	85/06/22
E3	S3	OR91	85/07/13

Fig.: Contents of the external data base

It is possible to construct this expression using the EXISTS type of logical expression. However, the expression is complex and requires the nesting of a S-F-W-block within nested S-F-W-block. It helps if we rewrite the request as:

Select the salary value for each employee for whom there is no supplier that he or she does not deal with.

```
SELECT SALARY
FROM EMPLOYEE
WHERE NOT EXISTS (SELECT
    FROM SUPPLIER
    WHERE NOT EXISTS (SELECT
        FROM PUR-ORDER
        WHERE (SNUMB=SUPPLIER.SNUMB)
        AND (EMPNUMB
          = EMPLOYEE.EMPNUMB)))
```

The expression is something of a brain-twister. Suppose we are checking an EMPLOYEE record for possible retrieval, and let us call this employee record X. Now let us attempt to specify or "retrieve" a SUPPLIER record for which no PUR-ORDER child record has the EMPNUMB value in X. Clearly, if there exists such a SUPPLIER record, then the employee described in X cannot possibly deal with all the suppliers described in the SUPPLIER relation.

Although this formulation is probably more difficult than the first time one, the two expressions have in common that two nested S-F-W-blocks are needed. The observant reader should by now also have noticed the expressive power of the English language. Quite involved retrieval can often be simply expressed in English in just one line or less, whereas corresponding expressions in SQL often require quite complex formulations. Retrieval-16 is almost a classic example of this, and similar retrievals with many-to-many relationships are frequently cited. A similar example with the data base:

Find the locations of suppliers who deal with all employees.

and the reader should try it as an exercise.

More complex SQL expressions

Our remaining retrievals will involve further requests that are apparently simple but which involve quite complex SQL expressions. They could well be skipped by all except those who wish to perfect their knowledge of SQL.

Retrieval-17: Four relations

In what cities have orders been issued to California suppliers?

What we in fact wish to retrieve is each WAREHOUSE record that has at least one dd EMPLOYEE record that has at least one child PUR-ORDER record that has a parent SUPPLIER record with LOC value equal to 'CALIFORNIA'. The SQL expression is:

```
SELECT CITY
FROM WAREHOUSE
WHERE WHNUMB IS IN (SELECT WHNUMB
 FROM EMPLOYEE
 WHERE EMPNUMB IS IN (SELECT EMPNUMB
       FROM PUR-ORDER
       WHERE SNUMB IS IN (SELECT
       SNUMB FROM SUPPLIER
 WHERE (LOC = 'CALIFORNIA'))))
```

For comparison purposes we give also the SQL/N expression

```
SELECT CITY
FROM WAREHOUSE
WHERE (THERE IS AT LEAST ONE CHILD
 EMPLOYEE RECORD
WHERE (FOR AT LEAST ONE CHILD PUR-ORDER            RECORD
 (THERE IS EXACTLY ONE PARENT SUPPLIER
 WHERE (LOC = 'CALIFORNIA'))))
```

The response would be:

```
DALLAS
```

Retrieval-18: Four relations

Give the names of Texas companies that have orders from Dallas warehouses.

What we are looking for here is each supplier that has at least one order from an employee from a warehouse in Dallas.

```
SELECT SNAME
FROM SUPPLIER
WHERE (LOC = 'TEXAS')
AND SNUMB IS IN (SELECT SNUMB FROM
 PUR-ORDER)
       WHERE EMPNUMB IS IN
       (SELECT EMPNUMB
       FROM EMPLOYEE
       WHERE WHNUMB IS IN (SELECT WHNUMB
            FROM WAREHOUSE
         WHERE (CITY = 'DALLAS'))))
```

The response is:

```
ROBOTEK
RAYTEX
```

Retrieval-19: Use of a label

Find the warehouses at which at least two different salaries are paid

```
SELECT UNIQUE WHNUMB
FROM EMPLOYEE X-EMPLOYEE
WHERE WHNUMB IS IN (SELECT WHNUMB
 FROM EMPLOYEE
 WHERE (SALARY ] = X-EMPLOYEE.SALARY)
```

The response is:

```
WH2
WH1
```

SQL expressions that require the use of a label are among the most complex, but they do give a deeper understanding of the nature of SQL. We are asking SQL to scan through the records of EMPLOYEE and check each one for acceptability. Let us suppose that the scan gas reached the first record, and that we are therefore interested in the check of the record:

```
WH2 E1 22,000
```

for acceptability. The requirements that this record must fulfill are specified in the predicate, but we have stated in the imperative part of the expression that we can refer to the record being checked as the X-EMPLOYEE record.

In the predicate records we are stating that 'WH2' must be among the list of

WHNUMB values taken from records that have a SALARY value different from the SALARY value in that record being checked, that is, the X-EMPLOYEE record, This list of WHNUMB values will be:

```
('WH1',  'WH2',  'WH3')
```

so that the predicate is TRUE and the first record of EMPLOYEE is acceptable, permitting its WHNUMB value 'WH2' to be extracted.

This whole procedure is repeated for the second record in EMPLOYEE, and so on. Note that there is a chance that duplicate WHNUMB values will be retrieved, so that a specification of UNIQUE is necessary.

Computational SQL retrievals

As mentioned earlier, SQL is relationally complete, that is, if the data is stored in the data base and can be specified as a relation, then it is possible to construct an SQL expression to get it out. It is important to understand that this definition of relational completeness does not include capability of retrieving.

1. Data that is not physically stored in the data base, but which can be calculated from data in the data base. An example would be the average salary of employees described in the EMPLOYEE relation.

2. Data for which a logical expression in the retrieval request predicate depends on data calculated from data in the data base. An example would be retrieval of the warehouse number of the warehouse with the best paid employee described in the EMPLOYEE relation; here the system would have to continue the maximum SALARY value before each EMPLOYEE record could be checked for compliance with the retrieval predicate.

3. Data that needs to be calculated from data in the data base as in (1) but which also depends on the result of other calculations as in. An example is retrieval of the average floor area of those warehouse whose employees all earn less than average.

Retrievals that require a computation in any of the ways described above are called *computational retrievals.* Where calculations are performed on the target of an SQL expression as in, the retrieval may be called *target computational retrieval.* Where the target of the SQL expression depends on comparisons with the results of computations on data in the data base as in, the retrieval may be called a *predicate computational retrieval.* A retrieval that is both a target computational retrieval and a predicate computational retrieval as in, is sometimes referred to as a *combined target and predicate computational retrieval.*

Computational retrievals are common and, as the use of the data retrieval languages such as SQL becomes more widespread among management personnel, may well become more common than noncomputational retrievals. It is probably also true that the subject takes us beyond the realm of data base management and into the realm of decision support systems. We can identify two distinct methods of dealing with such retrievals:

1. *Use of computational functions in the retrieval language.* This method allows for the use of common functions in languages such as SQL. We shall give examples of the use of such functions later. The main functions are:

COUNT (field)	Count the number of field values specified
SUM (field)	Sums the values of the fields specified
AVG (field)	Takes the average value of the fields specified
MAX (field)	Computes the maximum value in the fields specified
MIN (field)	Computes the minimum value in the fields specified

   It is clear that functions are quite simple and will be of little help if the computations involved are complex.

2. *Application of independent data manipulation systems.* In the simplest case this method requires the application of a statistical package such as SPSS to the relations containing the data on which sophisticated statistical computations are required. A variation involves first narrowing down the amount of data to be fed to the statistical package; this can be done by first applying SQL expressions to retrieve the data required for further processing.

   When special calculations are involved, then programs that carry out the special calculations must be written or acquired. A collection of such programs that can carry out calculations in a special area is referred to today as a decision support system, especially if the programs involved can be run interactively from a terminal. Examples of decision support systems are:

   (a) A market response system, for predicting product sales as a result of marketing errors such as advertising. The data base would contain data about customers, past sales, competing products, and so on.

   (b) The investment portfolio management system, for comparing portfolio performance with management goals and for predicting effects of portfolio changes.

Further analysis of the second method of dealing with computational retrievals is beyond the scope of this book. We now give some examples of the first method with SQL, beginning with target computational retrievals.

Retrieval-20: COUNT function

Find the number of supplier locations.

```
SELECT COUNT (UNIQUE LOC)
FROM SUPPLIER
```

If we neglect the COUNT function, the expression retrieves:

```
CALIFORNIA
TEXAS
ONTARIO
```

The COUNT function then counts the number of these, and the result would be 3. Note that we must use UNIQUE with COUNT in current System R SQL, except when counting records.

```
SELECT COUNT
FROM SUPPLIER
```

would count the number of records in SUPPLIER and thus give the number of suppliers.

Retrieval-21: SUM function

Find the total annual payroll.

```
SELECT SUM (SALARY)
FROM EMPLOYEE
```

This will cause all the SALARY values in the EMPLOYEE relation to be summed, whether duplicates or not. Not that in this case the expression

```
SELECT SUM (UNIQUE SALARY)
FROM EMPLOYEE
```

would be wrong, because duplicate salaries would not be included in the summation.

Retrieval-22: Sum function

Find the total annual payroll for Dallas and Chicago combined.

```
SELECT SUM (SALARY)
FROM EMPLOYEE
WHERE WHNUMB IS IN (SELECT WHNUMB
         FROM WAREHOUSE
         WHERE (CITY = 'DALLAS') OR
         (CITY = 'CHICAGO')
```

Again the SALARY values retrieved will contain duplicates, and these values are summed by the SUM function.

Retrieval-23: AVE function

Find the average floor area of warehouses whose employees all make more than \$21,000 annually (that is, none of whose employees make \$21,000 or less).

```
SELECT AVE (WH-AREA)
FROM WAREHOUSE
WHERE WHNUMB IS NOT IN (SELECT WHNUMB
```

```
        FROM  EMPLOYEE
        WHERE  (SALARY < =  21000))
```

The list of floor areas retrieved is:

```
50,000
20,000
```

and the average of this calculated. While it makes no difference with the data in WAREHOUSE, insertion of UNIQUE before WH-AREA would be wrong in general. If two different warehouse have the same floor area, we would still want to include two equal areas in the computation of the average.

Retrieval-24: MAX function

Who makes the most warehouse 'WH2'?

```
SELECT  MAX  (SALARY)
FROM  EMPLOYEE
WHERE  (WHNUMB  =  'WH2')
```

The expression retrieves the SALARY values:

```
22,000
25,000
```

and produces the maximum value. Use of MIN instead of MAX would give the minimum value. Notice that with MAX and MIN it makes no difference whether or not UNIQUE is used. The maximum values of a list of values will be the same whether or not duplicates are present.

Retrieval-25: Computations on child records for each parent

What is the total payroll at each warehouse?

```
SELECT  WHNUMB,  LARPAY
FROM  WAREHOUSE
WHERE  LARPAY  =  (SELECT  MAX  (SALARY)
        FROM  EMPLOYEE
        WHERE  (WHNUMB  =  WAREHOUSE. WHNUMB)
```

The expression has exactly the same structure as the previous one. This time, however, an auxiliary and imaginary WAREHOUSE field called LARPAY is assigned the maximum value of the SALARY field in a group of child EMPLOYEE records. This we retrieve:

```
WH1  25,000
WH2  25,000
WH3  23,000
```

Were a partitioned maximum function available, a much simpler expression would be possible.

```
SELECT  PMAX(WHNUMB,  SALARY)
FROM  EMPLOYEE
ORDER  BY  WHNUMB  ASC
```

Retrieval-26: Predicate computation with the AVE function

In what cities is there a warehouse whose employees have an average salary greater than $23,000?

```
SELECT  UNIQUE  CITY
FROM  WAREHOUSE
WHERE  23000  <  (SELECT  AVE  (SALARY)
        FROM  EMPLOYEE
        WHERE  (WHNUMB  =  WAREHOUSE.WHNUMB))
```

Here we perform no computations on the data retrieved, but a computation is specified in an inner S-F-W-block, which specifies or "retrieves" the average salary for the child EMPLOYEE records for the WAREHOUSE record being considered for retrieval. The response is:

```
WH2
```

Retrieval-27: Predicate computation with the SUM function

Find the warehouses with a floor area greater than 30,000 units that have a payroll exceeding $46,000.

```
SELECT  WHNUMB
FROM  WAREHOUSE
WHERE  (WH-AREA>3000)
 AND  46000  <  (SELECT  SUM  (SALARY)
        FROM  EMPLOYEE
        WHERE  (WHNUMB  =  WAREHOUSE.  WHNUMB)
```

The response is:

```
WH2
```

The structure of the expression is much the same as that of the previous expression.

Retrieval-28: Predicate computation with MAX function

Find the best paid employee or employees.

```
SELECT  EMPNUMB
FROM  EMPLOYEE
WHERE  SALARY  =  (SELECT  MAX  (SALARY)
FROM  EMPLOYEE)
```

The response is

```
E4
E7
```

Again this expression is not unlike the previous expressions, except that we are dealing only with one relation. It should also be clear that particularly this type of expression can be replaced by a sequence of retrievals:

1. Find the maximum salary:

```
SELECT MAX (SALARY)
FROM EMPLOYEE
```

   The response is:

```
25,000
```

2. Find the employee or employees earning $25,000.

```
SELECT EMPNUMB
FROM EMPLOYEE
WHERE (SALARY = 25000)
```

   The response is:

```
E4
E7
```

Retrieval-29: More complex predicate computation with MAX function

In what cities do the best paid employees work?

```
SELECT CITY
FROM WAREHOUSE
WHERE WHNUMB IS IN (SELECT WHNUMB
FROM EMPLOYEE
WHERE SALARY = (SELECT MAX(SALARY)
FROM EMPLOYEE))
```

The response is

```
NEW YORK
DALLAS
```

The first inner S-F-W-block together with the following nested S-F-W-block is a specification of the warehouse numbers with the best paid employees. With the data base in Figure this is the list:

```
WH2
WH1
```

The overall expression then specifies the retrieval of the CITY values from WAREHOUSE records whose WHNUMB values are in this list.

Updating the data base with SQL

Few users of a relational data base in a large organization can be expected to have permission to update the data base. There are three basic updating commands as we

Data manager's duties

1. Establish in conjunction with the customer's requirements and the program's functional requirements, a plan of operation, common understandings of requirements and applicable criteria, motivation for cooperation, coordination, good communities, and strive for performance excellence in conformity with the plan of operations.
2. Establish adequate banks of essential source data to support activities and data support development such as working agreement documents, project descriptions and plans, and administrative procedures. Assure proper ties between respositories within the outside the establishment facilities for mutual support.
3. Maintain compatibility and continuity between input source information and determine that their authority and credibility is acceptable.
4. Assure establishment of good correspondence administration.
5. Establish and maintain good forms management with understanding of desirable forms design, forms ordering/printing, and use control.
6. Coordinate with marketing, sales and customer services, and functions responsible for an establishment's development and support of hardware, computer software, facilities, personnel and related data in planning and integrating detail requirements.
7. Assist in pricing and assessing needs for proposed new support items of data and establish means for budgeting and controlling costs of data development when approved.
8. Assist to establish and maintain central accountability over data items in the process of development, procurement, and application. Assist to establish planning milestones that are both meaningful and measurable along with means of reporting actual status.
9. Input to and control the enterprise's visibility resources in a program control room or center.
10. Assist and support establishment and maintenance of control data to support a program action system.
11. Coordinate to assure timely transition of working data from active to semiactive and inactive retention files. Assist records retention schedules.
12. Assist to develop and maintain data requirements charts or trees, responsibility matrices, and optimized data flow patterns.

13. Establish and maintain data quality assurance requirements and controls. Sample and participate in key data assessment reviews and validations/ demonstrations to assure consistently high quality in performance of developing good data across the program.
14. Assist to plan and establish methods for effective data development, handling and processing storage and retrieval, and application with feedback to assess adequacy and assure corrective action when required. Coordinate authority for these methods in the development and maintenance of good policy and procedures.
15. Prepare inputs to and coordinate on all agreement paperwork, particularly data deliverables. Assist in maintaining excellence in clarity and completeness of agreement documents.
16. Maintain support acquisition or development of modern equipment and techniques for data management.
17. Review and assess opportunities for program improvements via application of innovations, automation, micrographics, and other devices which can reduce human error and improve performance effectiveness.
18. Participate in technical meetings where data packages play important roles to assure their adequacy and establish corrective action when required; assure proper action assignments and follow-up, with "get well" dates monitored/ reported appropriately.
19. Interface with customers and vendors to assure common understandings of data criteria. Periodically review and update requirement lists. Develop and coordinate for approval either modified or unique requirement descriptions for data items when standards do not meet requirements. Develop and process deviation paperwork for agreement clarification regarding potentially interpretable criteria when appropriate.
20. Develop guides, handbooks, announcements, bulletins, and other aids as deemed feasible for effective performance in data program processes.
21. Maintain continuous coordination to assure good data management relationships between organisation groups.
22. Assist to establish and maintain data addressee distribution lists. Assure to the maximum extent feasible that everyone with the "need to know" are either provided copies of data or advised when and where copies can be obtained in central files. Provide for culling of obsolete and superfluous listings.

data programs can usually find great savings in programs in which data management was not properly conceived or applied.

Privacy and protection of data rights and warranties

The Watergate episode exemplifies the need for security in assuring privacy and exclusive data rights. Safeguards against oral eavesdropping, which statistics indicate encompass about 80 percent (80%) of total data, is a growing concern. Wiretapping, bugging, and tape recording are common techniques that make it more and more difficult to secure private conversation. The criminal investigations of Watergate taught the public a great deal about the dangers of data rights invasion. Computer technology is similarly plagued by security problems with potential invasion via telephone terminals into data banks that are but one of many hazards. Sound proof rooms and shakedowns for gadgets may not be enough. And, good safes in secure buildings under both human and automatic guards, backed up by remote disaster files of records, are still subject to invasion if these safeguards should be bypassed by trickery.

Protection against the stealing of private information from authors/publishers may be protected in part by legal agreement documents and item markings that indicate their restricted usage. Similarly, protection can be given to the buyers and users of data that the information is adequate and accurate via warranties against deficiencies of a product. Protective clauses for data rights in legal documents such as copyright and contract are similar to those of patents that protect equipment/material/manufacturing inventors.

Neither patents, processes nor secrets are any longer assurance of success. The men responsible for the financing of industry have come to recognize that scientific methods have largely leveled down the advantages between one product and another. There are no longer any secrets in business—at least not in the most successful business.

Providing adequate security in enterprises for data might well not be worth the cost.

Unlimited rights to data

Agreement documents can grant rights to use, duplicate, or disclose data in whole, or in part, in any manner and for any purpose whatsoever, or to permit others to do so. Unless conditional provisions exist, the government claims unlimited rights to data developed at their expense.

Limited rights to data

When data are developed at private expense, retention of rights to the data may be claimed except for "limited rights" provisions of documented legal agreements. Clauses are placed in contract agreements that define the conditions of any limited rights to data. Their rights are stipulated in the interest of national security. Typically, government stipulations in agreement documents indicate that limited rights are the same unlimited except:

> data may not be released outside he government or used, duplicated, or disclosed in whole, or in part, for manufacture or procurement, except: (a) for use in national emergencies where it is not otherwise reasonable to restrict usage; and (b) for release to a foreign government in the interest of our own government as circumstances may require.

The provisions of either exception are still subject to the Basic limitations of law that preclude unfair competition to those originating data. Clauses in contracts also stipulate that data delivered under provisions of limited rights must be marked accordingly.

Private/proprietary data markings

With knowledge of the values at stake and the fundamentals of data rights protection in mind, the fine architecture of a data management system will provide for proprietary markings on items concerned.

Typical proprietary marking

> This material contains information that is trade secret *Proprietary* to and is not to be reproduced or trans-ferred to other documents or disclosed to others except (1) under agreed obligations of confidentially, and (2) with the written permission of Patent Council and, when so disclosed or delivered to others, not to be altered, adopted, or used for any purpose other than that for which furnished.

Marking are commonly provided as decals, gummed labels, stamps, and metal plates designed to be affixed on printed sheets, magnetic or punched tape rolls, card decks, film containers, and other unusual data forms.

Bound volume are marked on front, back, and title pages; loose sheets are marked *"Private-proprietary"* top and bottom. A more comprehensive limited rights legend is sometimes appropriate for inclusion in documentation being turned over to another organisation or a government customer.

Data rights for vendors

Rights for data items that are developed by vendors in contract with a prime contractor may also be protected. Vendors may, under data rights clauses of contracts submit data directly to the government rather than through a prime contractor.

Rights for information release for vendor developed items with repairable or replaceable parts should be negotiated in agreement documents. Provisions should be made to either furnish specification control drawings or design specifications, provided items are advertised or listed in the Federal Supply Catalog system. Listings must be available to the trade or public on an unrestricted basis at an established range of price. Specification or identification drawings should fully describe each interchangeable item that uses repair parts.

Rights to numerical (machine control) data

Easily reproduced, these data used to program automatic equipment that produce products are cause for particular concern; they deal with both complexities and interpretations of law. As mentioned before, such data can be regarded as physical hardware accessories, end products, or tools rather than data and deserve the same design disclosure protections. Total skill innovations of manufacturing and related specialties are often embodied in numerical control data; hence, competitive advantages for future sales are jeopardized if total rights to them are given. Thus, rights to these types of items, and the data that discloses how they are developed, should be given special consideration in negotiating new agreement documents.

Index